URBAN LIFE AND URBAN LANDSCAPE SERIES

BUILDING CHICAGO

SUBURBAN DEVELOPERS & THE CREATION
OF A DIVIDED METROPOLIS

ANN DURKIN KEATING

OHIO STATE UNIVERSITY PRESS

COLUMBUS

LIBRARY OF CONGRESS CATALOGING-IN-PUBLICATION DATA

Keating, Ann Durkin
  Building Chicago.

  (Urban life and urban landscape series)
  Bibliography: p.
  Includes index.
  1. Suburbs – Illinois – Chicago – History – 19th century.
2. Local government – Illinois — Chicago – History –
19th century. 3. Local government – Illinois – Cook
County – History – 19th century. I. Title. II. Series.

HT351.K42 1988   307.7'64'0977311   88–31457
ISBN 0–8142–0455–4

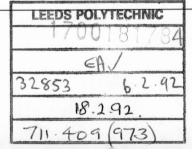

CONTENTS

TABLES

MAPS

Acknowledgments

This book could not have been completed without the help of many people. Henry D. Shapiro and Zane L. Miller have provided invaluable assistance as the editors of this series. Kathleen Neils Conzen guided my work through the dissertation stage and provided many suggestions for further improvements. Many others read and commented on all or parts of this work at various stages. Among them are: Louis P. Cain, Jerilyn Cascino, Michael P. Conzen, Daniel Durkin, John and Dorothy Durkin, Margaret E. Durkin, Michael H. Ebner, Jane D. Fruin, Barry Karl, Ronald Dale Karr, John J. Keating, Seymour Mandelbaum, Lamar Riley Murphy, Jon A. Peterson, Mark Rose, Christine Meisner Rosen, Howard Rosen, Patricia J. Tracy, and Marc A. Weiss. Elizabeth Brooks did the initial work on the maps. My heartfelt thanks for their time and effort. Howard Rosen and the Public Works Historical Society have graciously granted permission to use some materials previously published in their essay series. I would also like to thank Alex Holzman, Charlotte Dihoff, and the Ohio State University Press for their special help.

Introduction

Suburbs and Their Governments

Shopping malls, industrial parks, residential subdivisions, and automobiles are obvious parts of the contemporary American suburban landscape. Similarly familiar are the suburban governments that ring most U.S. urban centers. Indeed, for most of us, suburbs are so integral a part of modern American culture that a time when they did not exist seems almost inconceivable. Still, only one hundred and fifty years ago, suburban communities and their governments were either nonexistent or were largely indistinguishable from their rural neighbors. The purpose of this study is to explore the emergence and early evolution of suburbs and their governments, using the Chicago area as a specific case study.

Perhaps the hardest task for the late twentieth-century student is to see through the superficial view of the contempory suburban landscape. A fruitless search for fast-food franchises, Levittowns, or parking lots in the nineteenth century yields the impression that suburbs are purely a phenomenon of the years since 1945. Nothing could be further from the truth. Behind this facade lie characteristics that are found in other places, other times. Social scientists since the turn of the century have worked toward isolating a basic description of a suburb.

Building on their work, we can identify a number of core characteristics of the modern U.S. suburb.[1] First, suburbs are defined in relation to a city. Characterized by physical proximity to a city, they are distinguished from the urban center by their low population density. At the same time, many amenities provided in cities are available to suburban residents: both physical improvements like water and sewers, and services like schools and fire and police protection. Also, suburbs are more homogeneous than their city centers because they perform only some urban functions and contain only a portion of the city's population.

Both suburbs and outlying residential districts within city limits are organized internally by residents and hold some characteristics in common with a small town. Finally, although the specific forms vary among metropolitan areas, underlying the twentieth-century conception of a suburb is political autonomy.[2]

If we accept these characteristics, areas as diverse as Walnut Creek, developed largely since 1950 in the San Francisco Bay Area; Country Club Hills, built in the 1920s near Kansas City; and Riverside, founded outside Chicago in the 1870s, all are easily identified as suburbs. To apply this categorization simply to areas clearly suburban today, however, is to overlook those communities which nineteenth-century residents settled as suburbs but which have been both physically and politically engulfed by their central city. Vast stretches within cities like New York, Boston, and Chicago were originally built as suburbs but today are seen simply as urban neighborhoods. In order to study the early development of suburbs, we must include, then, not only those areas that are still clearly identifiable as suburbs, but the twentieth-century urban neighborhoods that began their existence as suburbs.[3]

By including areas that today are a part of the City of Chicago in this study of early suburbs, we are able to reach beyond the era when suburban government had become a requisite part of a suburb to an era when the governance of suburbs was just being worked out. Since government does not operate in a vacuum, other changes were most likely also affecting suburbs. Government here can serve, among other things, as a flag to indicate a time when the definition of a suburb outlined above did not yet apply.

For example, in the Chicago area until the Civil War, there were only two kinds of local government available to residents: the chartered urban form and the rural county/township organization. There was no "suburban" government. This situation reflected the absence of suburban communities as described above, which demand suburban governance.

This is not to say, however, that there was no outlying settlement. In antebellum Chicago, the word *suburb* sometimes described outlying communities that were essentially small agricultural towns or industrial sites.[4] More frequently, though, the term was used as an adjective—as in a suburban villa or a suburban home. J. Young Scammon, a leading Chicago banker and lawyer, built his retreat, Fernwood, on property to the south of the city in Hyde Park.[5] Contemporaries referred to it as a suburban villa, the second home of a wealthy Chicagoan whose family spent summers and holidays away from the congestion and disease of the city.[6] These isolated, outlying residents differed little from their rural neighbors as far as the demands they made on local government, and so the rural townships served both groups.

This early situation contrasts strikingly with the first years of the twentieth century. *Suburbs* by then referred to outlying communities, not isolated estates. In addition, the Chicago area was governed not only by a chartered city government and rural townships but by dozens of suburban incorporated villages, which catered to the commuter, and industrial communities, which by then ringed the city center. The object of this study is to explore this dramatic change and the choices that led to the now familiar city center surrounded by independent suburban communities. While the particulars are quite specific to Chicago, there are clear connections to similar developments in other cities in the same general time period.

The Shaping of the Modern Suburb

As the nineteenth century unfolded, a number of factors led to the dramatic changes highlighted above, both in suburbs and their governance, in Chicago and across the United States. Some were a part of the general process of modernization affecting the whole of American society. For instance, the increasing scale of business and industrial enterprises separated workplace from home, fostering the advent of strictly residential areas. Until the early nineteenth century, most people either lived and worked in the same place, or in close proximity. Transportational advances—the streetcar and the railroad in particular—made it possible for people to live farther away than walking distance from their place of work.

The impact of more advanced transportation on suburban development is evident in changing conceptions of suburbs in the Chicago area. With the first railroads in operation by the early 1850s, outlying settlement expanded rapidly. Towns tens of miles away from Chicago along the railroad line were identified as suburban.[7] Although it is unlikely that daily commuters would have lived as far away as Waukegan, near the Wisconsin border, or Wheaton, in the county west of Chicago, these towns were included as suburbs. Increasingly, the term *suburb* was used to designate the settlement surrounding a railroad station.[8]

By the 1870s the frequency and cost of trains to outlying areas were important factors in defining an area as suburban. Not simply the presence of railroad lines, but the availability of "relatively inexpensive" commuter tickets on those railroad lines were necessary for suburban development. An 1872 newspaper article attributed the availability of these commutation rates to "the growing importance and gigantic strides in wealth and population which the suburban towns within a radius of a few miles of Chicago have attained in late years."[9] Everett Chamberlin, a real-estate man who wrote one of the first descriptive accounts of Chicago's suburbs in 1874, also emphasized the availability of commutation tickets:

> Until the suburban movement was fairly begun in 1868, little else of note transpired relating to this particular estate. At that time, the rush of population to the city caused increased demands and consequently higher prices for rents, and the railway companies began making commutation rates to the suburbs, putting on extra trains, etc. which has had the effect of inducing a large number of our citizens to seek homes within their boundaries where they could enjoy the freedom of the country; its pure and healthful airs, romantic sites, and enticing woodlawns and streams, and at the same time pursue their active business life in the city.[10]

All of the sixty-four communities identified by Chamberlin in 1874 as suburbs of Chicago were located on railroad lines. This points to how local perceptions of a suburb had narrowed from the antebellum villa or outlying farming community. There was now a more specific conception of a suburb as an outlying town along a good transportation route, which at mid-century meant either a railroad or a streetcar spur. Chamberlin's description also highlights the shift toward considering a group of outlying homes, clustered in these cases along a railroad line, as a suburb. More and more often, a suburban villa conjured up the image, not of an isolated home, but of a part of a community filled with similar homes.

Curiously, major changes in city government also affected the development of suburban communities. Up until 1800 chartered city governments dealt primarily with issues of trade and transportation—wharves, markets, roads, and economic regulations. In the early nineteenth century, the extension of the franchise to all white men and the early phases of industrialization were among the factors that impelled urban governments to devote more time to improving, or at least maintaining, the urban environment through sewers, reservoirs, street lighting, and parks.[11]

By the 1850s, leaders in Philadelphia, Boston, New York, and Chicago had already confronted the problems of an inadequate supply of water by constructing elaborate aqueduct and reservoir systems. Attempts at systematic sewerage were just beginning.[12] Outside these cities, however, rural governments continued along a traditional path of serving agricultural areas by governments limited to collecting taxes, supervising elections, operating courts and schools, and maintaining roads and bridges.

The changes in urban government in Chicago and other cities affected home interiors and domestic life. Pipes for running water, sewer hookups for indoor plumbing, gas and electric fittings for lighting and appliances, as well as telephones for direct communication beyond the home revolutionized both domestic life and its connections to the outside world. Not only were the connections new, they were also a part of revolutionary integrated service systems. Homes became more intimately and physically attached to the communities around them largely through these new underground utility networks.[13] Fittings for indoor plumbing or illumination were of no use unless the building they were in was located adjacent to infrastructure systems to which it could connect. Initially, these systems were available only in the inner core of the nation's largest cities. Perhaps at no time before or after was the contrast between urban and rural living so dramatic.

Suburbanites entered the void between these contrasting worlds. Since many suburban dwellers, drawn outward along new transportation lines, came from city centers where new basic services were available, there emerged a demand for improvements in outlying districts. Among the first to recognize these demands were real-estate developers. They understood that they could use outlying residential subdivisions as a means of directing growth, cutting short the years of waiting for a natural accretion in land values. To attract settlement to their subdivisions, some speculators made use of the dramatic changes taking place within homes and provided the new kinds of service connections necessary to have running water, indoor lighting, and plumbing. Others simply laid out streets and built railroad depots. This range reflected both the amount of capital various speculators were willing to risk and the variety of conveniences that potential residents ideally wanted. While before 1880 only a few developers initially made major improvements—water, sewer, gas, or electric connections—by the turn of the century more and more improvements, including homes themselves, were offered by Chicago area developers.

It is important to remember here that metropolitan residents were not of one mind concerning the improvements they wanted in a suburban setting. Real-estate developers catered to this variety of demands, not by providing a variety within one subdivision, but by creating a range of internally homogeneous subdivisions across a metropolitan area. They physically brought together people with similar demands for improvements, essentially those able to afford the same amenities. Thus, developed subdivisions fostered class (and, to a more limited degree, ethnic and racial) segregation which, while crude in its early stages, is still found in a more refined state today.

Developments with a wide range of services radically changed public attitudes concerning the availability of services in outlying areas. Until the advent of such subdivisions, metropolitan residents could only receive public services within the city itself—and only recently there. Outlying residents had to build systems for themselves, employ a host of servants to do the work manually, or do without. Once real-estate developers had opened the possibility of these services being provided in outlying areas, the game changed dramatically. Outlying residents looked for urban services such as water, sewers, gas, and electricity and banded together to make these improvements themselves, or turned to local government with new demands. Areas that combined "urban conveniences" with "the special charms and substantial advantages of rural conditions of life" were more and more numerous in Cook County as the century came to a close.[14]

The rural county and township governments traditionally did not have the power to provide these services. Only those residents living within the confines of an urban chartered government could hope to have their demands met. By the 1870s this had changed for many suburban areas, where residents clamored for more government involvement in providing services. An 1874 newspaper account explained that suburban Hyde Park residents were ambitious to "engage in some enterprise worthy of a suburb of Chicago," like a more extensive sewer or waterworks.[15] While demands for expansion of outlying local government increased, they were not calls for the replication of urban forms in the suburbs. City government already had an unenviable reputation, as one 1869 newspaper editorial pointed out: "Municipal government in this country is a system of machinery to collect and consume taxes without returning anything like an adequate compensation. It has been refined, and expanded, and compounded to an extent that renders it next to unbearable."[16]

Outlying residents sought both to provide services and to avoid city government. They needed a new form of government that lay somewhere between those of urban and rural areas. Suburban government emerged as a new form by the end of the nineteenth century, providing many of the services and functions of chartered urban governments while also being shaped by existing rural governments. It developed over the course of the nineteenth century in response to the demands placed on it by suburban communities which themselves were only just emerging.

Previous Scholarship

Historians have begun to explore this transitional period, perhaps none more ambitiously than Kenneth T. Jackson in his overview of U.S. suburban history.[17] No one, however, has systematically examined the *evolution* of suburban government. The numerous studies that have examined suburban government accept the form as a given, rather than as an independent variable.[18] This study, for the first time, explores the dynamic development of suburban forms of government.

But this is not simply a narrow study of the evolution of governmental forms in one particular metropolitan area. Similar processes were taking place in metropolitan areas all across the country. In addition, it examines the origins and development of homogeneous subdivisions, which have evolved, especially since World War II, into acres and acres of tract housing. They are still a primary means by which class segregation is accomplished in metropolitan areas across the country. The origins of homogeneous subdivisions are not found in William Levitt and his contemporaries, but almost one hundred years before, when real-estate developers used service improvements, like water lines, sewer pipes, and gas connections, to attract a homogeneous clientele to their subdivisions on the outskirts of Chicago and other cities.

Too often historians have isolated the evolution of government from other city building processes.[19] Here I shall connect the origins of the homogeneous subdivision with suburban government, exhibiting the important interplay of public and private forces in the creation of the built environment. In more general terms, this study acknowledges that the evolution of local governmental forms and functions is intrinsic to the settlement patterns in a region and the timing of that settlement, especially with regard to technological advances. In other words, information about where and how people live—or want to live—is necessary background for understanding local government.

Also, residents' attitudes about and traditions in local government are critical elements in that government's formation. Implicit in this point are residents' notions of community and its relationship to local government. Finally, the overriding importance of the formative period of city building must not be underestimated. Once patterns have been established and local governments organized, the status quo generally has an advantage over any proposed changes. All of these factors influenced the forms and functions of local governments that emerged within metropolitan areas in nineteenth-century America and are crucial to understanding suburban government.

This kind of history, then, impinges very clearly on the present. The built environment and local government are areas in which the past remains an integral part of the contemporary scene. The suburban communities constructed in the nineteenth century are still a basic part of the housing stock and infrastructure of many metropolitan areas, both inside and outside the incorporated center-city limits. Likewise, suburban governments founded in the nineteenth century have not disappeared but remain a potent force in metropolitan areas like Chicago.

This case study examines the evolution of suburbs and their governments within the city building process in Cook County, which includes Chicago and its most immediate ring of suburbs. It argues that suburban governments emerged to meet the demands of residents and real-estate developers for services and amenities. There were a multitude of false starts and roads not taken. Both the triumphant suburban forms and those which were abandoned along the way are considered. An exploration of the choices available to nineteenth-century metropolitan residents provides a fuller explanation for the ultimate success of certain suburban forms.

The specific organization that follows explores in greater detail the argument I have outlined above. The first chapter traces the changes taking place in outlying settlements around Chicago across the nineteenth century. The second is devoted to outlining the changing functions of urban government in the nineteenth century and is followed by a chapter detailing the changes that took place within urban homes as a result of infrastructure improvements. The fourth chapter discusses the role of real-estate developers in providing urban services to outlying subdivisions. The fifth and sixth chapters explore the response of outlying local government to these changes, which ultimately resulted in suburban forms. The final chapter returns to consider some of the general issues raised by suburbs and their exclusive governments.

CHAPTER I

PATTERNS OF SETTLEMENT

   This chapter will provide an overview of the development of outlying settlement in the Chicago area in the nineteenth century, creating a base on which the real-estate and governmental history can be placed. Not simply commuter enclaves developed but also agricultural towns, resort communities, and industrial settlements. Again, it is essential for the reader to remember that areas which today are an integral part of the urban landscape in Chicago and other cities often began as outlying settlements only marginally tied to the city center. This means that it is important to look within the contemporary city, as well as outside its limits, to understand nineteenth-century metropolitan development. The functions of outlying settlements are not, nor have they been, static. Instead, as this chapter will evidence, they were responsive to changing conditions.

   Historians have begun the task of exploring nineteenth-century suburban growth. Most have identified improving transportation as the means by which outlying areas were brought into closer orbits with city centers, while tremendous population growth spurred further expansion. In cities as diverse as Boston, Cincinnati, and Los Angeles, such improved transportation drew outlying communities into suburban orbits. A progression from farming area to railroad commuter suburb to streetcar suburb to urban neighborhood was seen in nineteenth-century cities across the country. Of course, not all communities completed this progression, nor was transportation the *only* important factor in suburban development. Even before major transportation improvements, population growth and the rural ideal had triggered some suburban growth. Nevertheless, transportation improvements provide a useful organizing tool in reconstructing nineteenth-century suburban growth.[1]

This chapter will provide a closer look at the evolution of outlying Chicago settlements in the nineteenth century, primarily in response to population growth and changes in transportation.[2] It will examine the outlying communities in existence at different stages of transportation/ metropolitan advancement: the 1830s and 1840s, with the reliance on plank roads; the 1850s and 1860s, with the influence of early railroad development; and the expansion of the street railway and rapid transit network in the closing decades of the last century. We begin with a section on the early growth of the city center to provide the core around which outlying development took place.

Initial Settlement

Illinois's initial settlement centered in the southern half of the state, spreading north and west from the Ohio River. To the north, the land was inhabited by several Indian tribes through the early 1830s. One of the few U.S. settlements was Fort Dearborn, a frontier outpost on the southern edge of Lake Michigan at the mouth of the Chicago River. No more than a dozen families lived around the fort during the first three decades of the nineteenth century. Most were engaged in Indian trade, either as independent traders or agents for the American Fur Company. During the early days at Fort Dearborn there were few reminders of eastern civilization, but families like that of John Kinzie thrived on the frontier. Coming from Detroit after the completion of Fort Dearborn in 1804, Kinzie built up a lucrative trade with local Indians and soldiers at the fort. The Kinzie clan joined the rest of the settlement in pastimes such as wolf-hunting, horse racing, card sharking, shooting matches, and informal parties at the only hotel.[3]

This frontier life began to change with the opening of the Erie Canal in 1825. Western travel shifted northward to the Great Lakes, and settlers came more frequently from New England and New York. In 1830, this site was chosen as the endpoint for the proposed Illinois and Michigan Canal, to link the Great Lakes with the Mississippi River. The canal commissioners platted the town in that year, in the hope of raising funds for the project from the sale of lots in the platted area.[4] Significant settlement in the Chicago area began in 1834 with the defeat of Black Hawk and the remaining Indian tribes in northern Illinois. In that year, the federal government reached a land sale agreement with the surviving tribes, and farmers moved quickly into the area, buying much of the available land.[5] Farms soon dotted the surrounding countryside, and speculators, merchants, and artisans transformed Fort Dearborn into the booming town of Chicago.

Riding the crest of a national real-estate boom in the mid-1830s, the value of Chicago real estate skyrocketed. Many accumulated fortunes after only a few short years there. With a population of 4,170 in 1837 and at least 450 buildings, Chicago was indeed a boom town (table 2). The panic of 1837 grimly halted this progress. Within a few years, most Chicago businessmen "had been ruined or severely compromised."[6] After more than five years of depression, the infant city began to move forward again.

Chicago recovered slowly. Population continued to increase, and by 1850 more than 30,000 lived and worked in the area. Well-built homes and shanties were often juxtaposed on the same street, as the city strained to accommodate new residents. The visible contrasts were strong. One visitor in 1840, while admiring the new homes and hotels, could not help commenting that none of the streets had yet been paved.[7] The physical contrasts were accentuated by the fact that most Chicagoans lived in the same place as, or very near to, where they worked. This was due both to the poor traveling conditions within the town and the small scale of most industry and business.

As Chicago grew, patterns began to emerge from this jumble. While most people continued to live near their place of employment, the separation of residence and business was becoming more and more common. Residential areas, still within walking distance of the original town plat, developed in response to this movement. Exclusively residential areas began to appear. Wealthy residents constructed homes on south Michigan Avenue, while craftsmen, manufacturing laborers, and small shopkeepers were locating west of the original town.[8]

First Outlying Settlements

While most settlers outside Chicago were scattered on outlying farms, small market towns did emerge to supply the needs of the local population by 1850. Many of these settlements emerged near stopping points on the few roads in and out of Chicago, as commerce between the city and its hinterland expanded. Brighton, to the southwest of the settlement surrounding Fort Dearborn, began in the mid-1830s as an agricultural community. The threat of cholera and other diseases made these havens particularly attractive.[9] Besides farmers, some early Chicago residents bought acreage here on which to build second homes. John Wentworth, a colorful public figure who served as mayor, congressman, and editor of the *Chicago Democratic Press,* owned an "enormous farm retreat" near Brighton. Though Wentworth was known "for his love of the bustling life of the city," he nevertheless retained this property for decades.[10]

By 1850, Blue Island Road (Western Avenue today) and Archer Road, both near Brighton, had become two of the important livestock trails leading into the city from northeastern Illinois and northwestern Indiana. Drovers herded cattle past Brighton to stockyards like those northeast in Bridgeport. Several enterprising businessmen, among them an early resident and landowner, John McCaffrey, and John Evans (from whom Evanston derived its name) built stockyards and a hotel at Brighton Park to divert these cattle drives. In addition, they improved Blue Island Road, subdivided extensive lands, and constructed a racetrack.[11] A concentrated settlement began. By 1854, the *Chicago Democratic Press* predicted that the town of Brighton was "destined to become an important suburban village."[12]

By the Civil War, several other "suburban villages" punctuated the original farms and outlying retreats of wealthy Chicagoans. These settlements focused, not around commuter settlement, but around agricultural processing, local trade, taverns, and hotels. The early importance of cattle trails and plank roads into Chicago is often forgotten in light of the later preeminence of the railroad, but it was along these roads that the first outlying settlements in Cook County emerged.

The Arrival of Railroads

The introduction of the railroad in 1848 brought tremendous expansion in trade and manufacturing. Livestock and grain trading for the whole Midwest centered more and more in Chicago as it grew to be the rail center of the nation. Meat packing and related industries developed in response to the volume of agricultural products moving through the city. Chicago's population also expanded rapidly. Over 100,000 new residents had to be accommodated in the city between 1850 and 1860. The subdivided area of the city more than doubled between 1846 and

1857—to over twenty-four square miles. Settlement expanded as far north as Chicago Avenue, south to Roosevelt Road, and beyond Halsted to the west.[13]

The railroad also stimulated the growth of Chicago's agricultural hinterland. The population of rural Cook County nearly doubled between 1850 and 1860.[14] Farmers from eastern states, as well as from Europe, were attracted to this fertile region made more accessible by better transportation. The increasing urban population in Chicago itself provided a growing market for fresh farm produce. Other merchants and businessmen founded more new agricultural market towns, many along the new railroad lines. Barrington, Palatine, and Jefferson all trace their histories to the 1850s when they grew around railroad depots. Speculators platted these towns soon after they were founded, but their growth was slow and tied to the surrounding farms rather than to commuter settlement.[15]

The necessity of improved roads diminished dramatically with the advent of the railroad because they were no longer the fastest way in and out of Chicago. These changes brought some areas into a closer orbit of the city center while leaving others behind. Brighton's stockyards and racetrack were tied closely to the old roads and trails, not to the railroad. Soon other sites, on one or more railroad lines, were better located for stockyards than Brighton. The racetrack, too, lost ground to newer facilities along railroad lines farther from the city center but more accessible than the one at Brighton. The settlement was, by the Civil War, on the line of the Chicago and Great Eastern Railroad, which provided residents with transportation into Chicago; but it had already lost its original economic edge.[16]

The railroad influenced areas where well-to-do Chicagoans bought land on the outskirts of the city for private retreats. Initially, summer residents scattered their homes across accessible Cook County, at some distance from other settlements. One early Chicagoan, whose family built a summer home south of the city, remembered that they "lived in [this] isolation for years." She fondly recalled her days of solitude at "our summer resort, our blessed beloved home."[17]

The railroad changed this picture. It made areas farther afield accessible. Also, settlement began to congregate within an easy distance of the stations along the railroad lines. The 1856 construction of the Hyde Park House, south of the city along the lake, illustrates this movement. Paul Cornell, hoping to create a prominent resort area, bought three hundred acres of land along the lakeshore and reached an agreement with the

Illinois Central Railroad to stop near the hotel. He subdivided land around the hotel in large house lots in order to attract pioneering suburbanites along with resort goers.[18]

By the time of the Civil War, Hyde Park Center was known as a "resort" and a "retreat" from the congestion of the city, made easily accessible by the early erection of a railroad station connecting it to the city center.[19] However, it was a communal, not a private, retreat. In 1860, the *Chicago Press Tribune* commented that "no more delightful suburban haunt than where on our southern lake shore the Hyde Park Hotel rears its fine front and invitingly spreads its ample plazas. . . . It is just the place for a summer sojourn."[20]

The lots surrounding the hotel, and many larger ones farther afield, were soon bought by Chicagoans who valued both the country atmosphere and the congenial company fostered by Cornell's improvements. Near the hotel, men of means built suburban villas for themselves and their families, complete with extensive gardens.[21] Among those who built summer homes in this area were William Ackerman, an Illinois Central Railroad executive, Benjamin P. Hutchinson, a grain and livestock speculator, and Lyman Trumbull, one of the U.S. senators during these years.[22]

Beginnings of Commuter Settlement

Commuter settlement became increasingly common around Chicago after the Civil War. The emergence of yearly commutation tickets spurred suburban railroad developments. Newspaper articles by the end of the Civil War were describing areas over forty miles from downtown Chicago as "suburban" because of their railroad link to the city.[23]

Commutation tickets were usually sold at a yearly rate or per hundred rides. The price of these tickets varied considerably depending on the railroad company and the distance from downtown. Fares as low as $50 per year were available to Ravenswood, seven miles to the north of the city, and at Austin, six miles to the west in 1876. The final stops on these lines were over fifty miles from the center of Chicago, and yearly fares for 1876 were as much as $150.00.[24] Between were stops whose distances and fares were not nearly so extreme. The value of property in these suburbs was roughly in inverse proportion to commutation fares, leaving potential suburbanites with a range of options as to how to spend their housing dollars. This trend is clearly illustrated in the commuter line of the Illinois Central Railroad to the town of Hyde Park, immediately to the south of the city (table 3).

The cost of commutation tickets helped to determine the class of residents who could afford to live in an area. Numerous articles in the 1870s advocated cheap commutation rates to suburbs so that working men could afford suburban living.[25] Some suburban developments claimed that commuting to their settlements was no more costly than riding the horsecars and omnibuses in the city. Promoters of Maywood, to the west of the city, advertised that railroad fares to their community were "little above the cost of horsecars in the city."[26] To the south, on the Chicago and Rock Island Railroad, promoters of Englewood in 1869 reminded the public that commutation tickets costing $2 for twenty rides meant that fares were the same as the cost of a ride on the Wabash Avenue or Broadway omnibus.[27] The fact was, however, that a steady income and workplace was essential to suburban living.

The process by which a suburban station was opened and a commuter schedule established was not simply a matter decided by a railroad company. Often a commuter station was established along a rail line at the urging of local residents or property owners. The case of Paul Cornell in Hyde Park is illustrative. Other developers lobbied for the establishment of commuter stops as well as working in areas that already had railroad stations.

The development of Ravenswood, along the Northwestern Railroad, Milwaukee Route, came with the establishment of a flag stop and then a regular stop after the Civil War. The original decision to have a flag stop there was made by the railroad, and developers were soon attracted to the area. A number of Chicago businessmen formed the Ravenswood Land Company in 1868 and purchased property about eight miles north of Chicago from farmers in the area. The group platted over three hundred acres. It was hoped that Ravenswood would "be the first station of the continuous suburb that will extend before many years from Chicago to Waukegan."[28] The company also constructed the Sunnyside Hotel, indicating that while they hoped to make a profit in the sale of suburban lots, they were also opening the area to a resort orientation in case the area was still too far from the city for suburban settlement.

They had little to fear. While in 1869 only one passenger from the area went back and forth into Chicago regularly, by 1874 there were 75 regular commuters to the city. The trip into the city on the single-track railroad took twenty minutes, and there were fourteen daily trains in 1874.[29] Lots that sold for $4 to $8 a foot in 1869 were already worth between $20 and $30 a foot in 1874.[30] By 1874, one suburban watcher opined that most of the lots of the original subdivision were sold "long before it was anticipated."[31]

Glenview is an example of an established farming area that emerged as a commuter settlement by the turn of the century, due largely to a regular railroad stop.[32] Farmers first came to Glenview in 1834, after treaties had been signed with the local Indians. Among the earliest residents were the Appleyards, the Heslingtons, and the Dawes, all emigrants from England who came to Fort Dearborn and then traveled northward to Glenview. Another early resident was Dr. John Kennicott, a doctor, nurseryman, and naturalist, who brought his family to the area just north of Glenview in 1836. The early years were hard ones, as Kennicott describes:

> For some years thereafter we were all poor, having been drained by our land purchases, and more especially by the 50 percent per annum which we had to pay those who kindly loaned us a good share of the money. Few cared about planting trees until we could be tolerably certain we were planting upon our own land and this we had no evidence until after the surveys [1839] and no security until after the land sales [1841].[33]

During the 1850s and 1860s a number of new farmers came directly from Germany, completing the rural settlement of the region.[34]

This area was connected with the markets in Chicago during the 1830s and the 1840s by the Milwaukee Road, which stretched from Chicago to Wheeling. It was a planked toll road with a triweekly stage route that brought passengers, packages, and mail. Farmers in Glenview were connected to this toll road by an old Indian trail.[35] Early farmers brought their produce to Chicago for sale, even though the trip was a long and often muddy one.[36] Things changed little in 1850, when the Chicago and Northwestern Railroad ran a line through DesPlaines, because it was still miles west of Glenview. The Milwaukee Railroad built a single track through Glenview in 1872 to facilitate the transport of timber needed to rebuild Chicago after its disastrous 1871 fire. Area farmers were then able to trade more easily in Chicago.

It was not until 1892 that the Milwaukee Railroad laid a second track in anticipation of the crowds expected at the 1893 Columbian Exposition. It was at this point that regular daily trips to Chicago became possible, and commuters quickly came to the area, transforming its rural character.[37] In that year, the Swedenborg Society of Chicago subdivided land at Glenview for its members. Swedenborg Park soon formed the nucleus of commuter settlement in Glenview.[38] A neighboring farmer described the residents of Swedenborg Park, as "city people, thoroughly unused to country living." They stood apart from the English and German farmers who were their neighbors.[39] Businesses in Glenview in that year included several grocery stores, saloons, a plumber, carpenters, blacksmiths, a lumber company, and a warehouse, reflecting the needs of both commuters and farmers.[40]

The changing character of nearby Norwood Park also showed the impact of the railroad. Like Glenview, what would become Norwood Park began as a farming community in the 1830s. Farmers built their own homes, usually beginning with a small log cabin and adding onto the structure over the years. As one recent chronicler of Norwood Park history reminds her readers: "Neighbors rather than neighborhoods were often a mile apart. Settlements of several houses might be graced with a name, but taverns and inns were more likely to get onto a map."[41] Social gatherings before the Civil War were unusual, made more difficult by the split between German and English (or New England) farmers.

In 1864, the Northwestern Railroad built a train depot at Norwood Park, and change came quickly. A thirty-minute train ride brought Norwood Park residents into Chicago, and the first commuters began to settle in the area. A few years later, a group of 28 prominent Chicago businessmen incorporated the Norwood Park Land and Building Association and bought the six farms adjoining the railroad stop, totaling 726 acres. The Association platted the land into 94 blocks, and by 1873 only three of the original blocks remained unsold. As with other early developments along railroad lines, the association built a hotel to attract not only commuters but also summer residents, because it "was considered far out in the country, being hilly and well shaded by the branches of maple and cedar." In fact, the area was gradually settled as a commuter suburb, but never became a popular summer resort.[42]

Other summer retreats were affected by commuter trains.[43] For example, Charles T. Race bought acreage in Jefferson Township along the Northwestern Railroad in the late 1860s. He planned to build an expensive home and devote himself to gentleman farming. He built a home valued at more than $20,000 and began to improve the acreage with formal gardens and cultivated fields.[44] Race had been at his gentleman farming for only a few years when he was captured by the lure of suburban development and in 1869 subdivided some of his property for settlement. By 1873, advertisements for the area, now called Irving Park, boasted of homes built for sale. The advertisements reminded readers that Irving Park was the "only suburb near Chicago with a waterworks in complete operation," and that "sidewalks and water pipes [were] laid to every lot sold by us, without extra charge."[45]

Suburban Industry

Industry as well as residential development was attracted to outlying areas because of improved transportation and inexpensive land. Paul Cornell, so astutely aware of the value of the railroad for successful resort and commuter expansion, was also tuned to its importance for future industrial development. In 1855, at the same time that he was building the Hyde Park Hotel, Cornell purchased property to the southwest at the nexus of three railroad lines. His object was to establish a manufacturing town, called Grand Crossing, that would take advantage of the concentration of railroad connections. Due both to his work in Hyde Park Center and the intervention of the Civil War, it was not until 1871 that Cornell was able to devote much of his energy to Grand Crossing. An early resident of the area remembers Grand Crossing in the 1860s: "My folks were among the first settlers here, coming in 1864. At that time the place was a vast wilderness and around near what is today 79th and between South Chicago and Stoney Island Avenue was a young forest. . . . People had to forego luxuries and even comforts. Life was very lonely at that time."[46] There were not even many farmers in the region because it was so swampy. Another early resident recalled that Grand Crossing in its early years was "just a huge frog pond."[47]

During the 1870s, Cornell promoted the place as a manufacturing center. He filed a plat of his property in the region in 1871. By 1873, 150 trains passed through Grand Crossing daily, and all of them were required by law to stop because of the danger of the crossing. Two manufacturing establishments were located there, the Cornell Watch Company and the Hall Manufacturing Company.[48] In 1876, the watch company moved farther west, but a furniture manufacturing company, a sewing machine company, a rolling mill, and several other manufacturing concerns had established at Grand Crossing. A promotional pamphlet, touting the town's praises, claimed that "Now is a favorable time to launch in at Grand Crossing on the coming tide. Land is Cheap."[49] The settlement at Grand Crossing began to resemble Cornell's dream of a manufacturing town.

The expansion of industry in the hinterland greatly altered the agricultural rhythms of some areas. The far south Calumet region witnessed tremendous industrial development in the decades after the Civil War. The history of settlement at Roseland dates to the 1840s, when Dutch emigrants bought land in the vicinity for farming and stock raising. Roseland became a stopping point for farmers who lived even farther south on their way to the produce markets on South Water Street. In 1850, the Eleven Mile house was built as a refreshment stand and gathering place for Dutch farmers "who halted their teams there in the early morning on the way to the South Water Street [11 miles]."[50] By 1880, Roseland's population was around seven hundred, and most were engaged in general farming and stock raising. A school, a post office, and several churches had been established, and two railroads stopped at nearby Kensington.[51] One early resident described Roseland as "an idyllic village," where "all were friends and all shared each other's burdens."[52]

Over 1,500 dwelling units constructed during the 1880s and 1890s in Roseland quickly transformed the original farming community. Industrial workers, many of them immigrants, settled in the area to be near expanding employers. One longtime resident remarked: "Instead of the peaceful village we have, since 1900, the polyglot part of a great town."[53] Poles and Italians had established their churches alongside the older Dutch and German congregations by the turn of the century. During the first three decades of the twentieth century, close to ten thousand dwelling units were constructed to house immigrants and a growing number of black migrants attracted by the industrial expansion.

The area south of Roseland changed dramatically when George Pullman decided in 1881 to build his immense sleeping-car manufacturing works there. A retrospective newspaper account reads:

> The scene changed. Pullman built his shops and town eastward in the swamp along Lake Calumet. The Western Indiana and other railroads were built through the

region. A World's Fair was promised. As a result, a
building boom commenced. In Chicago, the elevated
railroad was built southward and from the city a street
railway was constructed further south across miles of
prairie to our village, now called Roseland.[54]

Homes "went up like mushrooms" to house workers at Pullman and
at a growing number of other industrial establishments. By the turn of
the century, at least five steel companies, three lumber yards, and a
variety of other concerns had located in Roseland.[55] One longtime resident remembered that many farmers were able to sell their land at a
"big price," and the pioneers of the 1840s became "rich overnight."
Some left agriculture, but others took their money and bought land
farther south in the Calumet Region or in western states.[56]

Not all attempts to build outlying industrial settlements were initially
so successful. Grand Crossing certainly took several decades before Cornell's dream of a manufacturing town began to emerge. To the west of the
city, Henry Austin, a prosperous salesman who invested his profits in
land, encountered numerous problems in trying to develop an industrial
center.[57] In 1864, Austin bought property along the turnpike to Galena
at the first stop of the railroad out from Chicago. Most area residents
were farmers. Within the year, he built his own home and subdivided
a 280-acre farm, calling it Austinville. With several other businessmen,
he sought to attract industry to the area because of its good transportation
and the availability of much open land. A clock company came in 1866
but failed. A series of manufacturing establishments tried to make a go
of it in the same building until it burned down in 1868.[58]

Rather than attracting more industry, Austin found his subdivided
property being sold to commuters who built homes there. According
to a contemporary writer, by 1874 "nearly all the heads of families . . . do
business in the city."[59] This situation changed somewhat in the following
decade, as residents also were drawn from the workers at the nearby
Northwestern Railroad Car Shops. Austin became a successful residential
suburb, in marked contrast to Pullman or Grand Crossing.[60]

Streetcars and Rapid Transit Lines

While the commuter railroad lines serviced outlying settlements, the growth of the street railway network served communities closer to the center of town. The history of street railways in Chicago dates back to 1856, when the city granted its first franchise to the Chicago City Railway Company. By 1861, three separate companies had franchises from the city to run streetcar lines in each of the divisions, and several omnibus lines continued to operate through the late 1870s. Lines also began to appear in the collar townships surrounding Chicago by the end of the Civil War and expanded rapidly in the closing decades of the century. Coupled with this expansion was the changeover to electric power, which essentially doubled the commuting range.[61]

These streetcars often were dubbed "the poor man's carriage."[62] As one 1873 newspaper account described:

> What streetcars have done towards developing the out-skirts of Chicago is hard to tell. One of the first things done by a young man who is beginning to make money in Chicago is to hunt up a corner lot in one of the outlying districts near to the streetcar which takes him to his business. He invests in a lot or two, if he had the money builds him a home, and settles down as a member of the class of the community which is the backbone of our city, whose business interests are in the city proper, but whose homes are away off, where on one side the prospect is roofs and steeples and on the other green or snow covered prairie.[63]

It was estimated that the annual cost of commuting via streetcars was not more than fifty dollars in the 1870s.[64] This meant that the most expensive streetcar commutes were comparable to less expensive railroad commuting.

The impact of streetcars and the elevated railroad on areas settled before their development was often striking. Hyde Park Center, Austin, Norwood Park, and Ravenswood, each initially oriented around a railroad stop, and set at a distance from Chicago, were by the turn of the century connected to the city center by both streetcars and elevated lines, which followed a path of continuous outward settlement. Widening accessibility brought greater variety to both their housing stock and their residents. The growing number of apartment buildings in these areas increased density, decreased homeownership, and led to more transience.

Hyde Park Center saw significant changes by the turn of the century. The 1893 Columbian Exposition in neighboring Jackson Park sparked a building boom in the area, further fostered by the completion of an elevated line that closely connected the area to downtown Chicago. In addition, the University of Chicago located in the area in 1892, providing an institutional center for the community. Gone was the era of Hyde Park as a remote summer retreat; now it was an inexpensive half-hour trip on the elevated from downtown. Apartment buildings filled in empty lots and blocks, and the area looked more and more like an urban neighborhood: "Whenever space was available, six-flats went up, squeezed in among the older housing." By 1899, there were nearly 4,000 dwelling units in the area, another 6,000 were constructed between 1900 and 1920, and 7,000 during the 1920s.[65] Excellent transportation drew many commuters to the area, while the economy of the community itself rested on providing goods and services to them, selling property, and building their homes. As one commentator has explained, the business of the area "was that of building itself." By 1889 there were forty food stores, as well as dry goods stores, tailors, dressmakers, and a local newspaper that catered to the needs of a growing residential population.[66]

The changes in the settlement at Ravenswood were also dramatic. A farming district in 1869, by the 1880s it was one of the most exclusive suburbs in the Chicago area: "Ravenswood in its time was considered one of the finest suburbs in the city. . . . Lawns were spacious and well landscaped, houses set far back from the road and trees lined the parkways." Most of the residents at the turn of the century in Ravenswood were professionals and businessmen who lived in Chicago. Among them were several wholesale grocers, the head of Brink's Express, numerous lawyers, doctors, and dentists, manufacturers and real-estate agents. There were also a growing number of residents who ran local stores and provided services within the community, including local grocers, shoe dealers, druggists, an undertaker, and a plumber.[67]

The early decades of the twentieth century brought the elevated railroad to the district, and its character was irrevocably changed: "factories and office buildings lined the area along the railroad tracks and apartment buildings have taken the place of the old frame houses."[68] Most of the dwelling units in the vicinity were constructed between 1900 and 1920, after the arrival of the elevated, and they increasingly were in apartment buildings.[69] But these changes did not come without a fight from many of the early residents. They wanted to retain Ravenswood's exclusive character. One resident explained: "every time anything which would spell advancement was started someone got up a petition to oppose it. . . . When the streetcar line was proposed, when there was agitation for a bus line, and when apartments were beginning to be built attempts were made by petition to prohibit them."[70] But these efforts proved futile, and by the 1920s Ravenswood, like Brighton and Hyde Park Center, was a part of the contiguous settlement from the city center and no longer a distinct outlying settlement.

Commuters comprised the backbone of Norwood Park's early settlement, journeying to the city on railroad. By 1893, there were approximately 160 homes in the area, and about 70 daily commuters on the trains running into Chicago. The extension of an electric streetcar line to Norwood Park along Milwaukee Avenue spurred the construction of another 400-odd homes in the area in the first two decades of the twentieth century. Three thousand dwelling units built during the 1920s transformed the area. Improved local streetcar connections, expanding industry around Norwood Park, and the growing importance of the automobile underlay this expansion. Railroad commuters became a smaller and smaller proportion of the area's settlement.[71]

Farmers, followed by early industrial workers, then railroad commuters, and finally streetcar and elevated commuters, settled in Austin in waves across the nineteenth century. Transportational innovations opened the Austin area to new settlers at each step: the first railroad in the decade before the Civil War; the establishment of a commuter schedule by the 1870s; and the extension of city streetcar and rapid transit lines by the turn of the century. The nearby railroad-car shops and the establishment of the massive Western Electric Plant in the early years of the twentieth century led to settlement by industrial workers in large numbers. The 3,000 dwelling units in the area by 1900 increased to 18,000 by 1920. That number more than doubled between 1920 and 1930. By 1930, the population of the region was over 100,000.[72] It was no longer an isolated settlement, but closely tied to urban settlement in the west division of Chicago.

Grand Crossing grew steadily in the closing decades of the nineteenth century, leading to a continuity absent in many of the other communities here considered: "For years, the identity of the original groups of settlers was maintained. Grand Crossing and neighboring districts were at one time regarded as a small village. Also there were elements of continuity embodied in the industrial and cultural groups. The employees of the hat rack factory, for instance, were said to have remained so nearly intact that they formed almost a family group."[73] While connected to the city center by several railroads, most residents worked at the local industrial operations through the nineteenth century and had little connection with Chicago.

The extensions of streetcars and cablecars to the vicinity after 1895 tightened the connections of Grand Crossing to neighboring communities. The growth of local industry in the early twentieth century attracted European immigrants and black migrants, who took unskilled jobs in these new establishments. Italians, Bohemians, and southern blacks joined the Germans and Swedes who had settled in the area after the Civil War. This expansion was reflected in the number of dwelling units in the district. About 3,500 units were constructed before 1899, with double that number added to the housing stock by 1920 and another 6,000 units constructed during the 1920s. By the 1920s, much of this construction was apartment buildings.[74] Due to similar development in adjoining communities, and to the expansion of contiguous settlement, by 1930 Grand Crossing was an integral part of the City of Chicago.

Turn-of-the-Century Suburbs

By the 1880s, even with an ever-increasing population in the Chicago area, there was still land which was neither farmed nor settled. Some of this property had been granted by the federal government to railroads in the area to help finance their construction, while other tracts were speculatively held for future use. One such area was in the far south of Chicago, where Harvey would ultimately appear. This land remained vacant until 1870, when several real-estate men tracked down its owners, including the Illinois Central Railroad, to create a 960-acre plot. The group platted the land on the south bank of the Calumet River with two railroads running through it, in the hope of attracting industry. Growth came slowly; its early settlement was largely in response to the establishment of a mower company, owned by Harvey L. Hopkins, which employed a hundred people. One 1884 commentator argued: "With the railroad facilities South Lawn affords, together with the reasonable price at which ground for manufacturing purposes can be obtained, it may doubtless become a desirable point for the location of that class of manufacturing whose interests do not necessarily compel them to remain within the city."[75] Despite a good location and active courting of industry, South Lawn did not enjoy spectacular growth.

In 1889, Turlington Harvey began to purchase land in the vicinity and by 1891 had acquired much of the land platted as South Lawn, as well as adjoining properties. Harvey invested funds, time, and energy in attracting both industry and a steady working population who could afford to buy residential plots.[76] He promoted the area as a temperance town in order to stress the reliability of its workers for potential manufacturers. Temperance covenants in the real-estate deeds strictly prohibited the sale of alcohol.

By 1892 the rechristened Harvey had five thousand inhabitants and ten manufacturing establishments. As a promotional pamphlet written about Harvey in that year reminded the potential purchaser: "nothing succeeds like success" and "to prosper yourself, cast your lot in a prosperous place." Many were attracted by advertisements placed in local newspapers across the country, touting the opportunities available in the Chicago temperance suburb of Harvey. Settlers from North Dakota, Missouri, southern Illinois, Michigan, and Ohio were all drawn by the "factories where men could earn good wages and where their children could grow up surrounded by the best influences."[77] Harvey's population increased from seven thousand in 1910 to over sixteen thousand in 1930. By the later year, it was identified as an independent city rather than a suburb, because of its varied economic base, which relied only a little on direct ties with Chicago.[78]

The vicinity in which Brookfield is located was until 1888 "composed wholly of farmers . . . who pursued their bucolic way undisturbed by real estate speculation."[79] Amid this tranquility, however, were some famous names. Much of the land in the area was owned by wealthy Chicago families who had outlying retreats to the west of the city, including the Swifts, Armours, and McCormicks. Also, John D. Rockefeller speculatively held large tracts in the area. In 1888, Samuel Eberly Gross entered this scene by purchasing several hundred acres in the vicinity. Unlike the Swifts or the Armours, Gross intended to subdivide the land and promote settlement. He reached an agreement with the Chicago, Burlington and Quincy Railroad to begin stopping at his new subdivision, Grossdale—later known as Brookfield. Using hard-sell tactics, Gross successfully sold the property in his original subdivision and two further ones, named East and West Grossdale by their developer. The area attracted railroad commuters, as well as those lured there by the promise of an extension of the streetcar system from the city.[80]

There were about fifty homes at Brookfield by 1893. By 1900, its population was over a thousand and had increased tenfold again by 1930. While some residents commuted to Chicago on the railroad, many more "were employed in nearby industries, particularly, in this area, Western Electric, Electro-Motive, Reynolds Aluminum and Corn Products— who desired a place to live that was free of smoke and noise."[81]

To the north of the city, another commuter settlement was developed before the turn of the century; but, unlike Samuel Gross, the developer of Kenilworth was intent not so much on profits (which did not come in his lifetime), but on creating the kind of community in which he wanted to live with his family. Joseph Sears moved to his subdivision and convinced many of his friends and old neighbors to do so as well. In 1889, Sears formed the Kenilworth Company and platted the property in 1890. An advertisement for the suburb later that year characterized it as the "Model Suburban Town," with many amenities and improvements. Joseph Sears personally directed much of this development, which attracted many of the wealthiest residents of Chicago.[82] Far from streetcar and elevated railroad extensions, Kenilworth grew up as an isolated retreat.

A Suburban Form Emerges

From these diverse backgrounds the modern suburb evolved. Single communities, oriented around commuter or industrial settlement, which catered to the specific demands of residents for services and amenities became increasingly common as the century drew to a close. Harvey, Brookfield, and Kenilworth, settled at the end of the century, clearly reflected this trend. Improving transportation was also drawing these communities into a tighter orbit of the city and, in fact, drawing some *into* the city. The communities founded earlier in the century responded both to changing transportation and to developing notions of outlying settlement.

To trace this evolution more closely, eighty communities within Cook County, located both within and outside Chicago at the turn of the century, were selected and information collected on their origins and development.[83] Four generations of settlement were identified, roughly corresponding to the national real-estate cycles: 1831–40, 1841–60, 1861–80, and 1881–1900. Information was aggregated for the communities founded in each of these cycles to provide information on changes over time. Specific community histories fleshed out this composite data.

By 1840, at least ten farming villages could be identified within Cook County, including Brighton, Thornton, Niles, Blue Island, and Gross Point. All had populations under five hundred (map 1 and tables 4 and 5). The villages served as the center for farm life, sometimes containing a church, a store, or a school that served as the focus for the community. Blue Island, to the south of the city, was an important stopping point for farmers hauling produce to market. Thornton, on the Calumet River, was settled in the 1830s and quickly became a local trading center.[84]

Forty years later, most of these communities were oriented toward agricultural processing and related industries. They also continued to serve as a basic market center for surrounding farms and homes. Blue Island had grown to be a significant industrial town by 1900, with a population of over six thousand. Brighton, closest to the city center, also grew rapidly with the extension of urban contiguous settlement close by. The others grew at a slower pace, continuing to serve local farms. Population accretion between 1900 and 1920, however, reflected an expansion in suburban settlement in these areas, as the automobile, interurban, and improved railroad connections combined with the city's continued outward expansion to adapt rural Cook County to suburban purposes.

Twenty-two new communities were founded in Cook County between 1841 and 1860 (map 2 and tables 6 and 7). By 1861 settlement in the Chicago area was well under way. Farmers populated much of the region, and Chicago itself had grown to be a city with over one hundred thousand inhabitants. Outlying settlements also dotted rural Cook County. Most of these were small market towns, serving their hinterland. Settlements with resort or industrial orientations also began to appear. The period had been marked by the influx of two distinct groups into Cook County: farmers came to the area to till the rich soil; boosters and speculators came to Chicago at the same time in search of fortunes in city building.

Until the Civil War, these two groups were geographically isolated, except for a few resort retreats built in rural Cook County for successful

Chicagoans. These communities exhibit an emerging distinction between commuter/resort/industrial settlements and agricultural market/service centers. All outlying settlements made in Cook County before 1840 were based on market and agricultural services. Between 1841 and 1860, nearly half of the new settlements were made for commuter or outlying industrial purposes. Commuter settlements during this period, however, did not represent areas where many residents made daily trips to the city. Instead they were resort areas, where families spent the summer months.

The railroad played an important role in settlement during these years. Only three of the communities founded during these decades were not railroad stops—Bowmanville, Niles Center, and Wright's Grove. The railroad consolidated outlying settlement around its stops, leading to larger towns. Eight of the communities had populations over a thousand by 1900, and in each of those communities commuter settlement, along with industrial or agricultural related services, were factors in its growth.

Between 1861 and 1880, thirty-seven new settlements were identified. An increasing number of them were planned as commuter settlements along the railroads coming into Chicago, although it was often not until the twentieth century that successful commuter settlement took place. By 1880, 43 percent of them were oriented toward commuter or industrial settlement. The economic base of over 46 percent of new settlements during these same years was either in agricultural processing or basic market functions (tables 8 and 9; map 3). Those in basic market functions reflected in large part an early inability to attract a large commuter population. Farmers demanded few new communities. Among the eleven communities in this generation whose economic base was in agricultural processing and industry, at least six were founded as industrial or commuter settlements, but were unable to attract that sort of development.

Eleven new communities were founded and incorporated in Cook County between 1881 and 1900 (tables 10 and 11; map 4). While only two of these settlements had a "commuter services" economic base, the orientation of settlement had definitely shifted from rural to suburban. Only one settlement, Riverview, relied on agricultural processing and related industry for its base.[85] More than half of these new communities—Chicago Heights, Grossdale, Harvey, Kenilworth, Riverview, and Edison Park—were founded by a developer planning on commuter or industrial settlement.

Chicago may have begun the century as a frontier fort settlement, but by the turn of the century, with the population within the city over one million, it had begun to take on the characteristics of a metropolitan area, including suburban development. By 1869, one commentator boasted:

> It is certain that there has been no public exhibit of facts
> that could afford such direct and conclusive evidence of
> the future greatness of Chicago. It is only when the
> tendency to seek suburban homes becomes general, as
> a result of the crowding of business upon the domain
> of urban homes, that the elements of a great metropolis
> assert themselves; and it is only after acquiring a famil-
> iarity with the number, the extent, the growth, the
> enterprise, and the character of these suburban settle-
> ments, that the vigor, the immensity, and the pos-
> sibilities of Chicago can be properly estimated. When
> a city has as many as forty towns that may be regarded
> as suburban . . . there is no longer any doubt of its
> metropolitan character.[86]

Such growth was used in claims for Chicago's greatness, but also present-ed monumental obstacles to providing a healthful, clean environment for metropolitan living.

Over time, many communities reoriented in response to changes in transportation, technology, and attitudes toward outlying settlements. Despite a short history, settlement in the Chicago area was indeed a complex maze by the turn of the century. Underlying this complexity was a progression away from farming communities and toward suburban residential and industrial settlement (table 12). Improving intracity trans-portation and the related physical expansion of contiguous settlement outward from Chicago brought outlying settlements into closer and closer connections with the city center. Farming and related commerce and industry did not disappear but became limited to areas farther from Chicago. After the initial decades of rural settlement in Cook County, outlying growth was decidedly suburban.

There were, of course, a variety of suburban communities: agricultural market towns transformed into commuter settlements; resort areas up-graded for commuters; settlements that emerged around outlying indus-trial sites and newly platted suburban areas oriented around railroad or streetcar commutation. While the role of older market towns remained an important one, the reasons for their origins are not tied to suburban growth. Therefore, I shall emphasize throughout the rest of this book those settlements whose origins were industrial or commuter-oriented. As outlined above, the majority of settlements founded in the decades after the Civil War in Cook County were oriented in this way.

While improvements in transportation play an important role in the settlement patterns observed, they do not completely explain the placement or relative success of various new communities. One important area that requires examination in this regard is the emergence of a battery of service improvements which transformed urban life, and then suburban life, over the course of the nineteenth century. The next chapter explores the infrastructure revolution in Chicago, setting the stage for that which followed in outlying areas.

CHAPTER 2

THE EXPANSION OF CITY GOVERNMENT

Historians have recently begun to rehabilitate the reputation of nineteenth-century city governments, once labeled "the conspicuous failure." In particular, Jon Teaford, in *The Unheralded Triumph*, argues that while corruption and inefficiency were a part of city government, they must be weighed against the stunning achievements in infrastructure improvements, parks, and other efforts to protect public health and safety.[1] This chapter will focus on the achievements of Chicago's city government during the nineteenth century, with special emphasis on the improvements that soon physically distinguished the city center from outlying settlements: water, sewerage and street work.[2]

The impetus for these improvements came from Chicagoans who staked their personal fortunes on the success of the city and strove to make it the great inland metropolis—and perhaps even the most important city in the United States. They worked to outdistance rivals like Cincinnati, St. Louis, New Orleans, and New York. To do so, they had to eliminate many of the natural difficulties facing Chicago, exploit every advantage, and create new opportunities through whatever means available.

Not all of the challenges to Chicago's success came from other cities. Some came from within Chicago itself. Built on a swamp, the city's growing population confronted dangerous water and drainage problems. By the late 1840s dense population, coupled with an inadequate water supply and sewerage system, created conditions ripe for disease. Cholera was a yearly visitor to the city between 1849 and 1855, along with dysentery and other infectious diseases. In 1855 alone, cholera claimed the lives of 1,549 residents. No amount of boosterism could overcome the simple fact that Chicago was not a healthy place to live or work.[3]

Not as life-threatening, but also menacing to Chicago's claims to being the great inland metropolis, was the sorry state of its streets and sidewalks. One Scottish visitor described an 1850s Chicago street scene: "There has been much rain and storm—which is not the kind of weather to see Chicago in. It is an immense place covering a vast area of level ground, only a few feet raised above the level of the lake. . . . In wet weather, all is mud, which the vehicles, rattling over loose planks, splash up on the passer-bys plentifully."[4] The mud and plank streets reminded visitors of Chicago's frontier status rather than its metropolitan aspirations. They also hindered movement and trade within the city and presented one more problem which would have to be solved if Chicago was to continue to grow.

These conditions could hardly have escaped the notice of Chicago's ambitious businessmen and promoters. Improvements within the city— to protect the health and safety of residents and visitors, and to create the proper backdrop for Chicago's rise to prominence—were as important as railroads, a board of trade, and the expansion of industry. Among the men who understood this best was William B. Ogden. An early convert to Chicago boosterism and the city's first mayor, Ogden time and again involved himself in Chicago improvement projects. He personally backed the infant city's credit through the 1837 panic, and he was one of the strongest supporters of the first railroad to Chicago in 1848.

Ogden was one of the first Chicagoans to fight for the creation of a water and sewer system that would alleviate the threat of disease and allow for the proper development of streets and sidewalks. In 1844, Ogden and John Wentworth, both of whom served as mayor of Chicago, attempted to improve drainage for their property in the south division by constructing a deep ditch emptying into the Chicago River. The project, familiarly known as the "Wentworth-Ogden Ditch," created more health problems than it solved, but it did demonstrate the interest and effort which Ogden and other businessmen took in such improvements. When the Board of Sewerage was organized in 1855, Ogden served as both a commissioner and the president of the board.[5]

Men like Ogden understood that a crisis had been reached by 1850. Without substantial public works projects, the city's inhabitants were likely to wallow in the mud from its streets and sidewalks or perish from infectious diseases. As they had done with outside threats to Chicago's growth, residents attacked their internal problems head on. They turned to local government to coordinate the large-scale projects necessary to improve the city's physical environment. They understood that effective improvements could not be made privately or haphazardly. Within a few short years, the needed infrastructure improvements were under way in a systematic and planned fashion. The promoters and boosters who had worked so hard to strengthen Chicago's national economic position had no intention of losing to local mud or invisible contagion.

Boosters and Urban Government

These promoters were the strongest supporters of local governments in early Chicago. Their interests centered around making improvements that would enhance the value of Chicago land and improve the quality of urban life.[6] The relaxation of voting requirements in the early decades of the nineteenth century meant that most male residents had become urban government constituents, and they served as an additional source of support for improving the urban environment. Businessmen sought to attract or sustain economic growth, while Chicago's residents supported many projects because they improved the quality of their own lives.

The move from consideration of markets, wharves, and livestock pounds to sewers, reservoirs, and parks reflected changing constituencies and expectations about local government, but did not reflect a basic reorientation. Urban government continued to respond to the economic demands of local promoters by fostering the image of a prosperous city that was a good place for investment and business. To do this by mid-century required the provision of certain services and amenities which impressed on investors the urbane character of an individual city. Similar realizations by businessmen and residents across the country were fueling urban improvements. In Springfield, Massachusetts, promoters following the Civil War explained: "We can't run Springfield like a small village, the increasing demands of a broadening, elevating, and embracing civilization impose unusual burdens. We must grow by being worthy of growth, and offering the facilities and temptations to the world around to join in their lot."[7]

Rapidly increasing populations and the threats to safety accompanying industrialization forced urban governments to intervene, if only to maintain previous levels of health and cleanliness.[8] In Philadelphia, Boston, and New York, leaders had already confronted the problems of an inadequate supply of water by constructing elaborate aqueduct/reservoir systems. Attempts at systematic sewerage were just beginning at mid-century. Chicago was among the very first cities in the United States to develop a sewerage system.[9]

Chicago's Early Government

These trends were evident in Chicago from its initial organization as a town in 1833. It had no more than two hundred people, but that was sufficient to incorporate under the Illinois general town law. The five elected trustees of the town were granted power:

> to abate nuisances, gambling, disorderly conduct; to prevent fast driving and enforce police regulations; to license shows, control markets, take charge of the streets and sidewalks and to provide the means for protecting the town against fire. The limits of the town were not to exceed one square mile within which limits the trustees were to have jurisdiction. They could call out any citizen to work on the public roads for three days a year. The tax levy was fixed at 50 on every $100 of assessed value.[10]

These limited functions of the trustees were essentially those traditionally granted to chartered governments oriented largely toward commercial interests.

The establishment of the U.S. Land Office in Chicago in 1835, the imminent completion of the Illinois and Michigan Canal, and the frantic speculative fever in Chicago land led many residents to call for an extension of corporate powers and privileges as the population of the town increased by a thousand between 1835 and 1836. Charter revision widened the city's responsibilities regarding fire protection and water supply. Not surprisingly, discussion concerning a city charter that would significantly expand corporate powers began in 1836. Representatives from the three divisions drafted a charter, which was later approved at a mass meeting of all residents. The document was sent to the State

Assembly, where it was passed in 1837 with only minor amendment.

The special city charter enlarged Chicago's ability to tax and borrow funds for much needed improvements. It also granted the city, for the first time, the right to supervise directly public works projects. However, perhaps as important for Chicago's promoters was the actual designation as a city. It was hoped that city status itself would attract business, investment, and settlement.

The charter called for the election of a council of aldermen, each member representing a specific geographic area of the city. The elected mayor had little real power, as the council was responsible for most municipal activities, but the post had considerable prestige attached to it from the start. The first mayoral election displayed the different factions already present in Chicago politics. The two candidates were John H. Kinzie, son of one of the earliest traders at Fort Dearborn, and William Ogden, a resident of the area for only two years. Ogden won handily, signaling the ever-increasing power of the new eastern arrivals who had tied their fortunes to Chicago.[11]

Local government expanded its functions to meet population and physical growth over the next several decades. Officials instituted a whole range of activities to protect residents and improve living conditions. They included provisions for fire and police protection, ferries and bridges, a scavenger service to collect garbage, and construction of sidewalks, streets, and sewers within the heavily settled areas. Sanitary regulations, a board of health, a pesthouse, and temporary hospitals during cholera epidemics further guarded the health of residents.

The city needed an increasing amount of revenue to finance these activities. In 1837, all revenues to the city amounted to just over $1,000. By 1843 this figure stood at $9,198, and by 1853 it had reached $398,865. Total revenues to the city in 1863 were over $1,000,000. While much of this money came from general property taxes, several other sources were important during these years. Licenses were required for a whole variety of occupations and activities, with a fee required for issuance. Other monies came from special assessments for public improvements, loans, and fees for certain services rendered by the city.[12]

The council's ability to respond to Chicago's growth was tempered by the limitations of the 1837 charter. The city was only able to provide those functions for which it had been granted express power by the state. The tension between the state legislature and local government during these years was not confined to Chicago. Expansion of municipal activities across the country required special legislation by state assemblies.[13] During the 1840s, Chicago requested a wide range of additional powers. Many concerned the construction of streets, sidewalks, and sewers, as well as their financing. The duties of the mayor also expanded during these years, as the administration of city government became more and more complex. After fourteen years of accumulating new powers from the legislature, in 1851 Chicagoans submitted a new charter that incorporated much of this special legislation for approval to the state assembly.[14] Further charter changes in 1863 and 1872 continued to reflect expansion of municipal activities in public works, education, police protection, and fire equipment. The city was responding quite seriously to the demands of businessmen, promoters, and residents regarding improvements.

Police and fire protection were among the early functions delegated to the city. The police department was under the direct control of the mayor, who acted as the police chief until 1861, when a separate police board was created to administer the sixty uniformed officers. By 1870, over half a million dollars was expended on the police force annually. Charges of corruption and inefficiency were frequent; they were blamed among other things, on the low pay of policemen and the fact that the force was simply too small to handle the increasingly complex urban scene.[15] At first, fire protection was in the hands of volunteers. A destructive fire in 1857, in which twenty-two people died, convinced the City Council that a paid fire department was necessary to protect the city adequately from the destruction of fires. The 1871 fire and threats of withdrawal by fire insurance underwriters led to a more active campaign to eliminate fire hazards in the city by the turn of the century.[16] Despite numerous innovations, the inadequate size of the department in comparison to the rapidly expanding population, low water pressure, and the uneven availability of water continued to cause problems.

Until the 1850s private academies educated most students, although public schools date from Chicago's beginning. During the decade before the Civil War, the city hired a superintendent of public schools and founded a high school to improve public education. By 1870, over forty thousand pupils were in attendance, and the closing decades of the century saw even greater expansion. Keeping pace with Chicago's rapidly expanding population, however, severely taxed both the administration and the facilities of the local schools.[17]

Water Provision

Water was among the first services the city tried to provide systematically. Private companies were the primary providers of water in the city's early years. Each summer between 1849 and 1855, cholera epidemics plagued Chicago. Contemporary medical research linked the disease with polluted drinking water. The support of leading businessmen, as well as residents, for a city-wide public water system grew in the face of these epidemic summers.

In 1851, upon the urging of Chicago politicians, the state chartered the Chicago City Hydraulic Company. It emerged as a public commission with three elected commissioners, receiving city funds and bond issues in order to build a water supply system, but not under city control.[18] The company hired William J. McAlpine, an eminent antebellum engineer, to come to Chicago and design the water supply system. McAlpine not only designed the system but gained increased support for it by stressing the improved public health and decreased fire risk that would result from its construction.[19] Because the community initiated the water system as protection against fire and disease, the commission initially laid pipe within a proscribed district in which the threat of disease was thought to be highest (map 5). Public hydrants were installed so that city residents could make use of the water supply even if they did not have a direct connection into their houses. By 1861, the commission had successfully laid water pipe over the originally designated territory, but the needs of the growing population demanded extensions for decades to come.

Although many residents supported the free use of water through public hydrants, they viewed a direct connection for running water into the home as a personal amenity and luxury. Thousands of residents took advantage of the opportunity to connect their homes directly to the water system during the 1850s, and by 1856 a majority had been connected (table 13). When individuals wished to connect their homes or businesses to the water system, the water commission charged a yearly fee based on the size of the building and the quantity of water consumed.[20]

Early on, the annual water rents and monies collected for water tap permits provided a significant and increasing income. Between 1854 and 1872, the water commission received over four million dollars from water rates, with over one million collected in 1873 alone. By 1878, the waterworks ended its fiscal year with a surplus, and the commissioners retired some of the bonds that had financed original construction.[21] The commission spent more money on extending the system than on retiring debts, though, through the turn of the century.

The tension between expansions for health and safety reasons and those made largely as amenities heightened over the century. Hydrants continued to be used by those not connected directly. Chicagoans who paid for direct connections through a yearly water fee began to resent those who used these public hydrants and did not pay for their water. Public hydrants were phased out of the water system by the end of the Civil War. Similarly, the commission at first had laid water pipe solely with regard to the health and safety of the community. By 1864, however, the commission simply did not extend water pipes into areas that would not yield a sufficient income in water rents, as evidenced in this passage from their annual report: "To avoid entailing a heavy, unproductive debt on the Water Works, the Board is compelled to limit the laying of the pipes to such places as are in most urgent need of the water and where, also, the buildings needing water are most numerous and will yield the greatest amount of water tax."[22]

While on occasion the pipe laid did not bring in this minimum revenue, it had been found that "laying of pipes is speedily followed by the erection of new buildings and such streets soon become self supporting."[23] Property holders willing to advance the money to cover the extension of water service pipes and mains into an area where not enough revenue could be generated from water rates could have the water system extended to their property. The general feeling was that, like extension of streetcar lines, the installation of water mains would attract both more settlement and higher prices from potential buyers. The water works was so successful at making a profit that an inevitable clamor, deftly ignored, arose demanding a general rate reduction.

So, Chicago began its water system for health and safety reasons but quickly reoriented to accommodate the demands of residents who wanted water as an amenity. This reorientation did not mean a complete reversal in policy as the most densely settled areas of the city, which posed the greatest threat of fire and disease, were also those most readily accommodated by the new approach. However, implicit in this policy was a strong interest in making a profit and providing water more as an amenity than as a public good. Throughout the nineteenth century, the water system expanded, although it was unable to keep up with demand through 1900 (map 6). The tension between the amenity and public health value of water extensions continued. While the system was financed initially by bonds, revenues from water rents kept debts lower and helped to finance expansion.

Sewerage System

With the introduction of a water supply system in Chicago came the cry for a companion sewerage system. Inadequate drainage, like an insufficient water supply, was a danger to public health. In addition, the availability of running water compounded the problems of sewage disposal as the amount of water used increased dramatically. The incorporation of a board of sewerage commissioners in 1855 signaled the start of the city's systematic involvement in drainage. This board was incorporated by the state and empowered to supervise drainage and sewage disposal, as well as to plan a coordinated system for the future.[24]

The construction of the sewerage system was rapid, but, like the water system, it could not match the growth of Chicago during the nineteenth century (map 7). Also like the water system, the city designated a sewerage district before the Civil War as the area in most immediate need of sewering. During the 1850s, however, the installation of water pipe far outstripped the installation of sewer pipe. By 1861, there were close to four thousand more buildings connected to the water system than to the sewerage system (table 16).

Chicagoans viewed sewerage, like water, primarily as a public good when systematic provision began in 1854. The city used both bond issues and funds from general taxes to build the initial sewer system. Using bonds implied that the whole community within the sewerage district would pay for services on the theory that it was ultimately a special tax. It also illustrated the fact that residents felt that they could share the burden of building this system with their future counterparts, who would also make use of it. This method remained popular because, as Mayor Carter H. Harrison explained in 1882, "the city was growing too fast for people of today to pay out of present taxation for that which would be needed fifty years hence. . . . The present generation should only pay their proportion."[25]

The promotion of the public good by improving sanitation did not come completely with the simple extension of sewers. It was not until after the Civil War that the city council passed ordinances to force owners to connect their homes and buildings to sewers. The aldermen began to realize that many buildings in densely settled areas, where the threat of disease was highest, were not connected to the sewerage system. Instead, most connections were made in newer, less densely settled areas. One examination in 1880 found that the wards with new sewers "immediately availed themselves of drainage," while the wards most fully provided with sewers had "the least ratio of private drainage."[26] Reasons for not connecting to the sewer system generally stemmed from an inability (or unwillingness) to pay either for the permit needed to connect private drains or for the installation of the indoor plumbing needed to take advantage of the hookup.[27] During hard times, property owners were "adverse to making avoidable expenditures," and sewer connections and indoor plumbing were often viewed as such. Owners of rented buildings were among those least eager to add these expenses.[28]

By 1864, the city council had passed ordinances that could force property owners to make private sewer connections when they were deemed to be for the public good. Tenement house inspectors, who worked under the health inspector, graphically illustrated the links between disease and inadequate sanitation. In the years following the Chicago Fire, the Board of Public Works and the Common Council made more efforts to enforce the law compelling persons to connect their dwellings with sewers; "much good was thereby done, and the sanitary condition of the city is much improved."[29] The promotion of the public good required more vigilance to derive general benefits, a marked contrast to the immediate and more easily derived benefits of the water system. By 1881, these inspectors issued a weekly report of conditions. Often published in the daily papers, these reports served as a reminder to Chicagoans of the dangers of poor sanitation and inadequate regulation.

Initially, there was little debate over the use of bond issues and general tax revenues for sewer construction. By 1872 the city had close to three million dollars in outstanding sewerage bonds, an amount which staggered the imagination of many residents, particularly because there was no apparent means of reducing the debt, as with the water system. As the debt from sewer construction increased, there was more and more discussion concerning alternative financing. Specifically, the issue of the amenity value of sewers for property immediately adjacent to sewers was raised. The 1866 Annual Report of the Board of Public Works advised:

> It seemed proper in providing for the ESTABLISHMENT of the system, to create a debt binding upon the whole city, but the system having been fairly set in operation, and its benefits extended to the business part of the city, and a greater part of the population, it would seem that the sewers afterwards laid might be dealt with as other special improvements, perhaps to be paid for in part by general tax upon the whole city, and in part by special tax on the property immediately benefitted.[30]

The introduction of indoor plumbing as an amenity required house-drain connections. A clear tension remained, however, between this perception of indoor plumbing as a personal amenity and its public value to the improved health of the city. Chicagoans debated whether to finance sewer construction by bonds, general revenues, or special assessments until 1890, when sewerage financing was finally modified to include special assessments. Until then, residents still awaiting the extension of sewers through general revenues successfully staved off the move toward special assessments.[31]

Street and Sidewalk Improvements

Sidewalks and streets also received systematic treatment by the turn of the century. City leaders knew that the muddy sewage that clogged Chicago streets contributed to disease. Good water and sewage were only a part of the solution: the streets themselves also had to be paved and cleaned. Chicagoans also perceived that unimproved streets were a major safety problem, which had a negative impact on trade and commerce and on the flow of information within the city.[32]

An early street paving project supervised by the city was the planking of business streets. Officials soon found planking to be an ill-advised choice for wet and heavily used streets and quickly abandoned its use. In 1863, Chicago had 363.5 miles of streets within its boundaries: 1.8 miles were paved with wooden blocks, 1 mile with block stone, 2.5 miles with cobblestone, and 22 miles were macadamized. Despite agreement on the value of paved streets, most remained unpaved through the 1871 fire, due largely to the tremendous expansion of settlement. The city financed pavement projects with special assessments on abutting property instead of through bond issues. The city's involvement extended only to planning and authorizing street improvements, which were still valued mainly for the benefits derived by adjacent property. An 1859 newspaper account reflected this sentiment: "If people will have their streets raised to the grade, and paved or graveled, they must make up their minds to pay for the improvement. They can't eat their cake and have it at the same time."[33]

During the 1850s, a board of three street commissioners, one from each division, was organized to expedite street improvements. These commissioners, operating within the street department of the city government, determined where improvements were most needed and made recommendations to the city council. The commissioners also supervised the actual work done on streets within their respective divisions. The city council, meanwhile, passed an ordinance for every street improvement, whether it was financed privately or through special assessment.

This layered administration meant that there were several alternative routes to the creation and passage of these ordinances. Property owners desiring improvements could petition their street commissioner, the council committees on streets and alleys, their alderman, or even apply directly to the full council. Also, petitions for improvements could come from the street commissioners or the council itself. The corporation newspaper generally published requests for bids. The street commissioners either granted the contract to one of the bidders, or the work was done directly under the supervision of the division street commissioner. The property benefited by the improvement was assessed a portion of the cost, with intersections paid for by general street funds designated for each division. Until property owners paid the whole of the assessment, work did not begin.

One newspaper account estimated that it was "two years after a portion of the property owners have paid before the work will be done, then the men who pay will be at the mercy of tax-fighters."[34] Tax-fighters were property owners who filed court suits to halt improvements already in the assessment stage, or who simply refused to pay their portion of the assessment. The city held a lien on both the property and the building on any site under special assessment, and tax-fighters who were not officially protesting in court ran the risk of having their property sold to pay the assessment at public auction.

Among the more prominent and imaginative street assessment dodgers was J. Young Scammon, previously introduced as the owner of an outlying estate at Hyde Park. The *Chicago Tribune,* no friend of Mr.

Scammon's, published a tale of his involvement in an assessment on Dearborn Street, where he owned frontage. According to that newspaper, just before the 1871 fire, Scammon divested himself of all but a small piece of frontage to avoid paying a substantial assessment, estimated at more than $40,000. Then he delayed payment on the smaller assessment, around $10,000, until abutting property owners put up half of that amount as an incentive to Scammon to complete his payment. As soon as the assessment was under way, Scammon regained ownership of the frontage on improved Dearborn Street, and then sold the whole piece at a profit.[35]

Rebuilding after the 1871 fire began quickly and strained the special assessment system. Residents wanted things to return to normal promptly, and the slow pace of special assessment procedures was even more irksome than it had been before the fire. Compounding the problems was the destruction of virtually all the records of the Board of Public Works, including assessment maps lost in the fire.[36] In addition, an 1872 Supreme Court decision ruled illegal most of the special assessments then in effect. For nearly ten years the courts debated the issue of assessments, and in the interim the construction of streets and sidewalks fell more and more to private contracts made by abutting property owners.[37]

By 1880, the courts finally upheld the constitutionality of special assessment laws. This did not, however, end the city's problems with the assessment process. For instance, a single property owner, or the street commissioners themselves, sometimes initiated the improvement process without the general approval of property owners to be assessed. Affected and unwilling property owners objected either to the improvements or the assessment. Some property owners petitioned to make the improvements themselves. Others objected after finding a lower bid for the work than that of the city-appointed contractor.[38] The appeals of these property owners for the repeal of specific improvement ordinances filled the council minutes. Often they were successful in blocking much needed improvements. Occasionally property owners took their objections to the circuit court. They sought court injunctions to be served on the street commissioners, which prohibited "the corporation from proceeding with the work."[39]

Problems also arose because of the wide variation of improvements across the city. The street commissioners and local aldermen controlled what general funds there were for street improvements. Fraud was endemic. Sometimes this involved granting a contract to someone other than the lowest bidder. At other times, city officials took money from city coffers or from contractors.[40] Still, the city made miles and miles of improvements by 1889 (table 14). Given the enormity of the task accomplished and the changing technologies, fashions, and demands, the achievement was impressive.

The construction of sidewalks within the city followed a similar pattern. Like street improvements, a number of court cases during the 1850s established that the city was liable for injuries due to sidewalks in poor repair.[41] The city acquired the power to collect special assessments for sidewalks from abutting property owners in its very first charter. It did not, however, have the right to build or repair sidewalks until charter revision in 1863. Instead it had the power to make special assessments for these improvements. Since these assessments were less costly than those for street paving, there were fewer objections, resulting in several times more paved sidewalks than streets (see table 14).

Creation of a Public Works Board

At the same time that Chicago worked to pull itself out of the mud, it was laying heavy demands on the original commissions set up to supervise public works. Distinct commissions carefully planned and executed the water and sewer systems, but there was little coordination between them, or with city departments. The city graded and paved streets, only to have them dug up months or years later to install sewers or water pipes.[42] Responding to this disorganization, the city council organized a Board of Public Works in 1861 to consolidate the administration of all public works in Chicago. The board took over the tasks previously performed by the water commissioners, the sewerage board, the street commissioners, the city superintendent, and the special commissioners for making improvements. This board supervised all contracts for municipal improvements, and all building construction, public and private, within the city was subject to its approval. The coordinated administration of public works also came in response to the tremendous expansion in expenditures. Between 1863 and 1873 total city expenditures increased from around two to eleven million dollars.[43] This increase was only partially offset by the growing population (table 15).

The differential methods of financing each kind of improvement continued even after administrative coordination. The use of general funds, bonds, and special assessments in varying combinations reflected the divided motivations for sponsoring the improvements. These funding decisions also reveal which groups were viewed as the prime benefactors of specific improvements. The use of general funds implied that taxpayers saw the work as being primarily for the public good. Issuing bonds placed at least a part of the burden of payment on future taxpayers, indicating that current taxpayers felt that the improvements would benefit future residents as well as themselves. The city resorted to special assessment when benefits fell largely on the individuals fronting an improvement. Different combinations for financing each improvement considered here point to the lack of consensus about whether improvements were for the public good or personal amenities. Not one of the improvements was considered for long as *only* an amenity or a public good.

These funding combinations also indicate changing attitudes. For instance, the city council originally made street improvements only by special assessment, but over time they used more general funds for crossings on all streets, upkeep, and the paving of streets deemed essential for public transit. The sewer system was originally financed through general funds and bonds, but after 1890 special assessments were also added to the equation. This change reflected the evolution of the attitude toward sewer extensions from being exclusively for the public good to being primarily amenities for the abutting property owners. The transition of funding for sewer extensions also points up the influence of debts on funding decisions. As the city fell further and further into debt because of its sewer system, residents became more and more willing to turn to special assessments. The level of debt, then, must be considered alongside other factors when analyzing improvement funding.

Politics and Varied Demand for Services

Another crucial determining factor in infrastructure patterns was the role of politics and corruption. A traditional view, first proposed by early twentieth-century reformers, purported that infrastructure maps in cities like Chicago could be read strictly as the embodiment of the politically powerful over time. From this perspective, payoffs and graft were the keys to the creation of municipal infrastructures.[44] While this issue is quite important to any discussion of city services, it is *not* the only influence that determined improvements during these years. Financing methods, the amenity value of improvements, and other factors must also be weighed in order to understand public works fully. However, when demand exceeded supply for infrastructure extensions, politics could not be ignored. Decisions made by the council or the public works board were crucial to whether an area would receive services the next day, the next year, or the next decade.

The confused state of water, sewerage, street, and sidewalk improvements in Chicago left ample opportunity for corruption and graft. Corruption within the Chicago City Council was widely acknowledged during these years, much of it associated with the undue influence of aldermen concerning improvements in their wards.[45] One 1884 newspaper account related: "Every section is clamouring for additional and improved sewerage, but only those districts from which Aldermen may have been selected stand any show for improvements. The great fourteenth ward, for instance, which has about 59,000 in it, is obliged to depend on two Aldermen who think only of prospective votes."[46] Service extensions were provided by politicians in return for political support, providing an anchor for boss politics. Savvy politicians could also garner further support by influencing contract decisions for infrastructure construction.

After the 1871 fire, cries concerning corruption in public works led to the creation of the Citizens Association. Among a myriad of other activities, the group sought to loose the control of politicians over public works extensions. They were most successful in areas where the public health and safety were clearly endangered by politics, such as fire hazards or threats of contagious disease.[47] With the urging of the Citizens Association, the Department of Public Works took a more active part in the decisions concerning infrastructure extensions. While the Department of Public Works exercised greater control, the council retained the final word, as they controlled appropriations.[48]

The many ways in which the service infrastructures were extended reflected not only distinctions between the public good and private amenities, improvement finance decisions and political power, but also the wide variation in both the demand and the ability to pay for these services of residents. Ubiquitous demand cannot simply be assumed across all classes and residential areas at any time in nineteenth-century Chicago. An 1885 newspaper article gives some insight into the situation:

The mud streets and those large tracts of the city where no efforts have been made to raise the grade, have a poverty stricken look, though it is only from the contrast with the handsome and finished thoroughfares. . . . A very large proportion of these people own their own homes. Should they be called upon suddenly for special assessments for street improvements it could create great distress. To find the very poor you will not look in the little frame houses on unpaved streets, but in the tenement houses which by law and inspection are provided with sewer connections and sanitary provisions.[49]

This diversity will be explored more fully in a later chapter, but it is important to set it alongside other factors that determined the timing and extension of service extensions in nineteenth-century Chicago.

City Government Success

Ultimately, the accomplishments of the city government in meeting the variable demands of its constituents for infrastructure improvements remain the striking achievement of the period. The most important parameters operating in Chicago during the final decades of the nineteenth century with regard to service improvements were: the tremendous expansion of the city's population and housing stock, which exerted a constant pressure for infrastructure extensions; health and safety issues; the perceived amenity value of the improvements; ward politics and corruption; and the ability and desire of residents to pay for these improvements.

Despite obvious problems, by the late nineteenth century Chicago's businessmen and promoters were rightly proud of their achievements, and many rested on fortunes made on the city's growth. Business and industry flourished, as Chicago's population passed one million by the turn of the century. The city government had met the challenge of protecting the health and safety of residents, and a proper setting for the inland metropolis was beginning to take shape. Although not always administered in a straightforward fashion, the Department of Public Works accomplished a tremendous amount during these years. In addition, changing attitudes and technologies dramatically reshaped the role of service improvements in urban life, as well as expectations concerning local government.

In no other settlement were aspirations or pretentions so high. The provision of municipal services by Chicago's city government went hand-in-hand with the development of economic and cultural institutions befitting a modern metropolis. These systematic improvements dramatically distinguished the city from surrounding rural areas. The municipal services developed in Chicago not only supported boosters' claims to Chicago's metropolitan stature but set the city apart from the rest of Cook County. No other community in the county provided such a range of services and improvements. Chicago was not simply the largest settlement in the county, it was also the only settlement in the middle of the last century with municipal institutions and infrastructure.

This situation, however, did not last long. While the municipal services highlighted in this chapter were initially developed for health and safety reasons, within a matter of a few decades they had become essential amenities in many urban houses. It was not long before outlying residents, too, sought these kinds of connections. The following chapter explores the transformation in urban, and then suburban, homes that made these service connections increasingly attractive.

CHAPTER 3

TECHNOLOGICAL CHANGE AND CHICAGO HOMES

This chapter will begin to explore the connection between technological changes inside homes in the nineteenth century and the settlement patterns found in metropolitan areas like Chicago. As outlined in chapter 1, advances in transportation are critical to understanding settlement patterns in nineteenth-century metropolitan areas. However, service provisioning also played an important role in settlement decisions in the nineteenth century. These decisions began inside homes but quickly shifted beyond them, because homeowners required connections to larger infrastructure networks.[1]

Homebuilding underwent radical changes in the closing decades of the nineteenth century. When Potter Palmer built more than fifty large homes on Chicago's near north side between 1889 and 1891, he hired an army of specialized workers to install the most up-to-date conveniences. They included plumbing and gas fittings, bells and speaking tubes, copper work, sewerage and cold-air ducts, steam warming and ventilating apparatus, interior woodwork, furnaces, hot-air pipes, sidewalks, and electric work. Palmer even contracted for clothes dryers in several of the houses.[2] Though most Chicago homes did not have these elaborate installations, dramatic changes were still taking place. Water pipes for running water, sewer hookups for indoor plumbing, gas and electric fittings for lighting and appliances, and telephones for direct communication beyond the home revolutionized both domestic life and its connection to the outside world.

These changes were not confined to Chicago homes. At the turn of the eighteenth century, water for urban residents in both Europe and America was being drawn from rivers, lakes, wells, or being purchased from peddlers. In the space of only a few decades, cities across Europe and the United States developed water distribution systems. Once available, running water revolutionized cooking, cleaning, and bathing through stationary baths, kitchen sinks, laundry tubs, and other innovations. As domestic labor-saving devices they simplified life but greatly added to the building cost of the home.[3] By the 1880s, urbanites viewed water connections within the home as essential for healthful living:

> In the attempt to secure the highest sanitary results in a household, the use of water is of the most essential character. . . . Water in plenty, in profusion, should be supplied in every city, and its plentiful use—not its waste—should be encouraged. Cleanliness is next to godliness, and he is a good Christian who spares no pains to make his own residence a healthful and beautiful home, and in doing this not only sets an example to his neighbor, but assists in preventing the origin or the spread of unhealthful agencies.[4]

Intensive development of sewerage followed water extensions. It was possible, once water pipe was laid, to install indoor plumbing, with water closets to replace backyard privies. Water threatened to drown cities as it poured freely from taps and hydrants. Without adequate drainage, cesspools flourished, breeding disease. Sewerage systems responded to this crisis. Over time, they helped eliminate both backyard privies and cesspool drainage. By the 1870s urban dwellers across the country were installing plumbing in their homes.[5]

Lighting also changed dramatically with the introduction of gas and electricity. In the decades leading up to the Civil War, gas provided a steady power source for streetlights, which were needed for public safety as cities grew. They made traversing unfamiliar streets at night easier and aided the night watch, which guarded a population increasingly uncomfortable with its growing heterogeneity. Following the use of gas for streetlights, domestic and business establishments made connections for indoor lighting. In contrast to water and sewer connections, private companies constructed and operated gas lines, although the companies needed government-granted franchises.[6]

Electricity competed with gas as a source of both outdoor and indoor lighting after the introduction of the incandescent lamp in the 1880s.

Like gas, franchised private companies provided service. The superiority of electricity over gas was touted in an 1890 *Scribner's Magazine* piece:

> Among the greatest gifts that electricity has bestowed on domestic life, is the incandescent electric light. . . . It neither consumes nor pollutes the air in which it shines, whereas the ordinary sixteen candle power gas burner vitiates the atmosphere with its products of combustion. . . . As the gas jet develops some fifteen times as much heat as the electric lamp of equivalent power, the latter adds greatly to the comfort of a house in warm weather. In the nursery it is particularly welcome, for it requires no matches, cannot set fire to anything, even if deliberately broken when lit, and effectually checks the youthful tendency to experiment with fire.[7]

The all electric kitchen at the 1893 World's Fair was quite a sensation but viewed as something from the future. Electricity, unlike gas which was widely used in Chicago by the turn of the century, was still a novelty.[8] By World War I, however, a range of home appliances, including vacuum cleaners, sewing machines, electric heat and irons, were available to those who had electricity, providing added incentive for its installation.

Americans connected their homes to the outside world for other services by the turn of the century. Telephones made instantaneous communication outside the home possible and by the 1920s were a familiar domestic fixture. Other service connections, unfamiliar in homes today, were not as successful. Entrepreneurs attempted to market, among other things, piped-in refrigeration, heating from a central power source, and pneumonic tubes for mail and small packages in urban areas across the country.[9]

Home Economists and New Services

Contemporary sources chronicle these changes in numerous ways. Increasing interest in domestic services such as water, sewers, and gas is evident from an examination of manuals of home economics. By the late 1870s, home guides and manuals spent pages discussing both the problems and advantages of the various improvements being installed. One 1878 manual discussed water, drainage, heating, lighting, and ventilation in separate chapters.[10] Home economists assumed the existence of indoor plumbing, heating systems, and gas lighting in the homes of their students. The turn-of-the-century lectures of home economist lecturer Helen Campbell focused on the dangers of various systems, teaching the homemaker about these new and probably mysterious improvements. Campbell explained that "sanitary engineering is a new profession, and sanitary engineers are by no means sufficient in number . . . the time is coming when [they] will be as much an essential in planning the houses as is the architect, but even with such expert service, it is still women who must listen and learn."[11]

Another home economist, Ellen Richards, estimated in 1905 that a house costing five thousand dollars in 1850 cost as much as twenty thousand by 1900 due to the "increased sanitary requirement" and "the finish and fitting" demanded in good homes.[12] The changes that had taken place within the home led her to conclude that "our houses in America are mere extensions of clothes; they are not built for the next generation. Our needs change so rapidly that it is not desirable."[13] Richards was not decrying the decline in building standards as much as commenting on the tremendous changes inside homes—particularly through service improvements which rendered homes obsolete in the space of a generation.

Plumbers and the Installation of Improvements

From the perspective of the homebuilding industry, the construction process became increasingly complex and many-faceted as the century came to a close. The pattern books which carpenters and builders used to design homes testified to the introduction of service improvements to urban and suburban homes. By the mid-nineteenth century, indoor plumbing had become a standard feature in urban house plans, although it was not always found in suburban and rural home plans.[14] By the 1870s indoor plumbing was a more frequent fixture in outlying house plans, and by the turn of the century it was an integral part of ideal house plans in all areas.[15]

Plumbers, sanitary engineers, electric and gas fitters, sewer and water-main builders, and street graders and pavers found their work new or radically changed by improvements within homes. The changes for plumbers were tremendous. At the beginning of the nineteenth century, plumbing was barely an occupation. Metal-working craftsmen created any specialized pipe or metal items needed in homes or business. As the nineteenth century unfolded, plumbers emerged from the ranks of more general craftsmen to cater to the specialized needs of water, sewer, and gas systems. At first, they made their own fittings, as well as installing them. By 1900, though, plumbers seldom manufactured their own materials, working almost exclusively with fittings.[16] To keep up with changes, a master plumbers' association was organized nationwide in 1880, with a strong Chicago chapter from the start. The association regulated apprenticeships and through regular newsletters and meetings kept its members abreast of the latest changes in plumbing technology and engineering. Chicago and several suburban governments began to license plumbers in order to regulate the installation of sewer, water, and gas pipes within the city. This served as a further acknowledgment of the complexity of the work of plumbers and its growing importance to public health.[17]

Many plumbers began to specialize exclusively in gas and electric improvements. Gas fitters were a distinct group in Chicago by 1869, when at least twenty firms specialized in this work. The expansion of electric service took place largely after the 1881 introduction of the Edison electric light. By 1891 there were at least forty companies dealing in electric power, fixtures, and fittings for industrial, commercial, and residential purposes.[18]

Debates concerning the "best" construction methods, designs, and fixtures for water, sewer, gas, and electric improvements made the work of plumbers challenging. The plumber in many cases was called on to advise home builders. One Chicago master plumber in 1880 explained that a plumber "should stand in the same relation to his customer as the family doctor does to his patient—that is as an advisor."[19] The heated debate concerning the existence and the avoidance of "sewer gas" was typical. Several theories were presented concerning ways to avoid disease. Underlying each was the need for careful planning of these improvements. By the turn of the century, many homeowners were convinced that "the plumbing is the most important work that is put into a building."[20]

Architects and Physicians

Chicagoans invested more and more money in plumbing and other service fittings for their homes. A contemporary estimated that of the $112,000,000 spent in construction of new buildings in Chicago in 1885, $2,500,000 was spent on plumbing alone.[21] Plumbers were an increasingly important part of new home construction. Often, they bid on the package of water, sewer, and gas fittings. The growing interdependence of architects and plumbers came as a result of these elaborate service installations.

Their relationship was not initially a smooth one. Plumbers complained of oversights in specifications, irregularities in bidding, and the ignorance of architects concerning their work. Architects complained of roughly the same things, and both sides had ample proof.[22] It was years before architects and plumbers developed mutually satisfactory working relations, as their specific roles became more routinized.

The *Inland Architect and News Record* and *American Architect and Builder* both devoted numerous articles to the changing demands placed on architects by their domestic clients. In one article, the Chicago architect William L. B. Jenney stressed that plans for dwellings should include arrangements for "proper sanitary conditions, the satisfying of every need of the members of the family, pleasing prospects from the rooms most in use during the day and cool exposure for summer sleeping rooms."[23] Architects pondered the various debates in drainage during the closing decades of the nineteenth century. Architects and their clients considered both design strategies and health concerns their province. This had long been the case, but dramatic changes in service provision involved architects not only in scientific debates but in dealing with a variety of new craftsmen. Some articles in professional journals set out the latest theories and trends.[24] Others devoted themselves more generally to the changes in sanitation, water, and lighting taking place in cities around the world to keep architects abreast of changes.[25] By 1926, an architecture text concerned with domestic design considered: electric and gas plants, water supply, hot water supply, vacuum cleaners, refrigerator plants, house telephones, laundry devices, water supply, drainage, sewers, septic tanks, and plumbing fixtures. The architect's job truly had become a complicated one.[26]

The plumber and the architect were joined by the doctor as the individuals most responsible for the health of residents in urban areas:

The family physician has a part to play in this drama

of household life. It is he who, more than all others, can reach the comprehension of the heads of the family. He can point out the danger and insist on the remedy; and when he, in the language of the learned sanitary engineer and plumber, James Allison, of Cincinnati, shall take his place in the happy trinity of Doctor, Architect, and Plumber, then will the sanitary millennium have made its appearance.[27]

Although the introduction of service improvements to new homes was a complicated project, demands also mounted for their installation in previously constructed homes. Homeowners confronted an added set of problems here. Running pipes and lines into the home, converting spaces for indoor plumbing, and installing fixtures in existing homes took great ingenuity and skill. Gas fitters frequently installed gas lines in already occupied buildings:

In every city and suburban district there are many of the better class of dwelling that are without gas, and in which lighting does not meet the requirements of tenants or owners. This state of affairs causes constant changing, extending and fitting of gas pipes in houses already built. To fit a finished house with gas, some ability and aptitude is required on the fitter's part other than that necessary for ordinary fitting. He may have to remove the furniture, take up and replace the carpets and floors, as neatly as a carpenter and carpetlayer could, in order to give satisfaction.[28]

The inconvenience of this whole process, not to mention the cost, was considerable. One attractive alternative was simply to move to a house which already had these improvements.

Growing Connections Outside the Home

Of course, the existence of fittings for indoor plumbing and gas or electric light was of no use unless the building was located adjacent to infrastructure systems to which they could connect. Not only were the connections new, they were also a part of revolutionary integrated service systems. Homes became more intimately and physically attached to the community around them, largely through these new underground utility networks. The home had changed irrevocably from an independent unit to a part of numerous service systems connecting it with the outside world. Comfort and health at home relied not only on the abilities of its occupants but also on the availability of service connections in a particular area.[29]

In order for homes to receive these services, local governments had to extend basic infrastructure improvements over their settled areas. Confined largely to the core settlement at Chicago before the Civil War, urban residents had originally made these improvements to protect their health and safety. Once in place, however, their value as amenities essential to many domestic innovations became clear. Systematic improvements connected an increasing number of Chicago homes during the decades of the mid-century (table 16). While the need to keep pace with population growth accounted for many of the water taps and private drains that were connected during these years, these services reached a larger and larger percentage of Chicago's population. For instance, in 1862 there were 18.5 residents per water tap. By 1876, the number of residents per tap had been reduced to 7.1.[30]

Homes located within the city's original water, sewer, or gas lamp districts quickly made these connections. City residents outside these areas were not so lucky. One solution was simply to move to a serviced area—sometimes even moving house as well as belongings to an area where hookups could be made. Many of the wealthiest residents of Chicago moved several times in the closing decades of the nineteenth century in response, not only to the changing typology of preferred residence areas within the city, but also to the ease with which the most modern services could be acquired. The elite migration from the near west side to the Prairie Avenue district to the near north and North Shore suburbs spanned the second half of the nineteenth and early twentieth centuries. To some degree, this movement can be matched first with the introduction of running water and indoor plumbing, and later with amenities like electricity. The areas abandoned by the wealthy were inherited by less well-to-do Chicagoans, who received the services originally built for the city's elite.

The moves which Bertha Honore, who subsequently married real-estate magnate Potter Palmer, made over the course of her lifetime illustrate the elite migrations in the Chicago area. In 1858, her father, Henry

Honore, built a "stately home" near Union Park on the west side. Within a decade the elder Honore moved "his family to more fashionable precincts at the southwest corner of Michigan Avenue and Adams Street." The near west side was losing its favor with the wealthy during these years due to encroaching industry and the introduction of streetcar lines, which brought the area into a much closer orbit of the city center. Following the marriage of Bertha Honore to Potter Palmer, she moved to a large mansion on the newly posh Prairie Avenue about a mile south of her father's home. They remained there for just under a decade, moving to their still famous near north "castle" some years ahead of their elite friends. In each case, changing neighborhoods, but also greatly improved services, fixtures, and fittings motivated their moves.[31]

Others sought to bring infrastructure systems to their homes. Neighbors banded together to make improvements by themselves or to call their demands to the attention of local government. The Chicago City Council meeting minutes in the final three decades of the nineteenth century abound with petitions for improvements from neighborhood groups.[32]

Often these improvement associations were founded on a street or block level. This was a natural size for such a group, as assessments for water, street, and sidewalk improvements were levied on a block-by-block basis. Of necessity, agreements among homeowners had to be reached concerning improvements on this level. The Central Boulevard Association was organized in 1876 by west side residents living near the boulevard. The association hoped to "influence the Board of Public Works to allow this section its proper share of the appropriation for building streets, culverts, and school houses." Their motivation came not only from a desire for services but from the realization "that they own property that can be made worth twice its present price, as it ought to be, by little personal effort."[33] Similar meetings and demands came across the city from residents with the means to pay assessments and the understanding to demand all that they could from its general funds.[34]

Groups organized on the ward level in order to pressure aldermen for help in gaining improvements. Residents of the 13th Ward met in May of 1873 to discuss the lack of improvements in their ward, particularly sewers. Although the alderman was present, the group concluded that "not a single individual at the time had undertaken to press the claims of the ward, and it so turned out that the thirteenth ward got none of the sewers."[35] Many demanded that the alderman present the needs of the ward to the council. In other wards, citizens also pressed their aldermen for more improvements.[36]

Organization of whole divisions within the Chicago area to demand service improvements also took place. Prominent property holders in the west division organized in 1873, claiming that "the west division paid all the taxes and received none of the benefits."[37] The city countered this claim by detailing the proportion of services and funds allocated for the west division, which was over and above its due share. North division residents joined with the citizens of the Town of Lake View when they created the North Side Improvement Company in 1870. These property owners were intent on making their property as attractive as any other in the metropolitan area.[38]

Affected aldermen translated these demands into ordinances for improvements within their ward, which they presented to the City Council.[39] The result of this multitude of petitions was a yearly appropriation bill for the Department of Public Works composed mainly of an unsystematic collection of ordinances. By 1877, the *Chicago Tribune* reported: "Almost every Alderman has made some request for a sewer in his ward, and the orders have been for some time collecting in the hands of the Council. As the time approaches for the passage of the appropriation bill, the Aldermen have been particularly active in piling up 'imperative demands' for sewerage."[40] Despite such complaints, this system enabled those who most insistently demanded services and mobilized support to obtain them.

Shifting Municipal Power Base

These informal improvement associations heralded a shift in political organization and power in the city. As long as municipal government was concerned primarily with business and commercial matters, politics organized itself in response to those interests. But as a greater and greater share of municipal budgets was earmarked for infrastructure improvements, the demands of property owners increasingly preoccupied local government. In turn, the block and the neighborhood, translated politically into precincts and wards, increasingly became the basic units for political organization. Politicians worked to provide services demanded by local improvement associations, and in return they expected the support (translated as votes) of an already mobilized political group within a ward or precinct. This, coupled with the patronage involved in granting improvement contracts and hiring labor for massive public works projects, laid the basis for boss politics by the turn of the century.

While many groups and individuals battled to receive service extensions during these years, there were those who could not afford them. Chicagoans who had just barely scraped together the money to buy a home had no additional funds for perceived luxuries like sewer and gas hookups. These residents fought service extensions, successfully and unsuccessfully, across the metropolitan area throughout the nineteenth century. Their insistence on keeping taxes and assessments to a minimum heightened the contrast between serviced and unserviced areas in the city.

Outside Chicago

Of course, not all residences in the Chicago area fit neatly within the boundaries of Chicago where attaining service improvements through the city government was possible. As previously outlined, residential growth in the Chicago area was composed of many outlying settlements governed primarily by rural township governments. These rural governments did not move forward quickly to provide basic services, primarily because there was little reason for them on the bases of health and safety. They also did not lie within their regular powers.

This was just fine with some settlers, who had left the city for outlying subdivisions beyond the reaches of Chicago's special assessments and taxes for improvements. Services came decades after the initial settlement, when residents were better able to pay for them. One Swedish immigrant, who in the early 1880s moved outside the then city limits, explained that he and his friends came there because lots were cheap: "When I came out here I did not expect to have city improvements; when they did come, after annexation, they came slowly and were considered a matter of course."[41]

Many residents sought outlying residences to avoid paying for improvements they could not afford. For instance, the early settlers at Grand Crossing "had to forego luxuries and even comforts." They moved to the area, not to farm, but to work in the local industries and were willing to live in an area with few prospects for service provision in order to get jobs.[42] Similarly, the early residents of Austin found "a vast prairie," with little to distinguish it from the surrounding countryside. By 1898, however, former city residents in both areas demanded service improvements and were provided through township governments whose functions had been expanded by the state legislature.[43]

Similarly, early suburban residents, such as those of Norwood Park, did not expect urban services. It was not until the 1890s, after many commuters had settled in the area, that service improvements were begun. Nor did early settlers in Glenview expect much from local government. This changed as "city people" moved into the area after the second railroad track to Chicago was laid in 1892. These new residents, according to one of their established neighbors, demanded that telephones, sidewalks, and electricity be brought to the area.[44]

Increasingly as the nineteenth century came to a close, urban-oriented settlers in outlying regions sought service improvements. The Citizen's Association of Irving Park tackled the problem of water supply and fire protection in their area of Jefferson Township in 1887 in a manner not unlike improvement associations within the city. The local association arranged for the sale of an artesian well to the town to assure the area of a public source of water.[45] In Ravenswood the problems associated with getting the services required by a well-to-do population were solved again through a local improvement association. The residents of Ravenswood made most of their improvements through private subscriptions, as the township government of Lake View was unwilling to meet their needs. The rest of the township was composed of residents who opposed the creation of service systems.[46]

To the south of the city, Hyde Park Township was providing services to its residents by the 1880s. Like Chicago, however, it could not keep up with requests, and local groups organized to demand services. Typical was the Hegewisch Improvement Association, organized in 1886 to petition the Village of Hyde Park for improvements for the suburban subdivision of the same name. With a membership of five hundred that must have included most of the residents and property interests in the subdivision, the club petitioned the village board for its fair share of improvements:

> It asks for protection against fire, police protection, street improvements and a water supply. Artisans in the employ of the U.S. Rolling Stock Company are afraid to build homes for fear of fire. . . . The place is badly in need of a public highway connecting its streets with those of South Chicago, where lumber, provisions and

supplies are principally purchased.[47]

By the early decades of the twentieth century, outlying areas exhibited a wide range of service improvements available to residents, provided through both public and private channels.

Service Options

Growing quickly during a period of changing attitudes and technologies regarding service improvements, Cook County made available a wide range of options to its residents during the closing decades of the nineteenth century. There were options both in the kinds of services available and the means of procuring them. Some of this latitude was the result of the tremendous physical and population expansion that characterized these years, but it also reflected resident demands for a variety of improvement combinations.[48]

The area resident had not only a large number of service combinations to choose from, but a variety of public and private routes to achieving them. Also important to understanding these patterns was the lack of consensus concerning which services people wanted or could afford. Not everyone wanted water, sewer, gas and electric hookups or paved streets and sidewalks. Some did not value the improvements enough or pay the special assessments for their installation. Others simply could not afford the cost.

This possible range of basic improvements is quite foreign to our late twentieth-century mentality. Today basic infrastructure improvements cover our metropolitan areas, and new residential areas usually provide for their installation before settlement. Running water, indoor plumbing, gas and electric power are all taken for granted and assumed to be ubiquitous across a metropolitan area. This ubiquity is not the result of a consensus regarding improvements or the proper method of making or financing them. Rather, it is the result of the filling in of an improvement map which in the early twentieth century was still widely varied.

Service improvements, as well as extensions of transportation, affected the ways in which settlement took place in nineteenth-century Cook County.[49] Residents were drawn to areas that provided service packages both affordable and attractive to them. The following chapter will examine the ways in which real-estate developers used improvements to direct settlement patterns.

CHAPTER 4

THE BEST OF BOTH WORLDS

It is vital to remember that the residential land development process in fact consists of at least *two* distinct procedures. Today, an initial developer transforms an improved tract of land into manufactured lots, which have service and infrastructure improvements required by local government and custom. Then either that same developer or another constructs homes by contract or on a speculative basis. The number of lots involved may range from just a few to hundreds.[1]

This system evolved over the course of the last two centuries. The emergence of developers who construct homes as well as develop land is largely a phenomenon of this century. Only rarely in the nineteenth century did a builder construct more than a few homes at a time. This fact is central to Sam Bass Warner's analysis of Boston's streetcar suburbs in the late nineteenth century, where he showed that the "building process rested in the hands of thousands of small agents."[2]

By focusing on the building process, one can argue that nineteenth-century residential growth was the result of "the weave of small patterns."[3] Only in the twentieth century would developers exert much influence on suburban growth. This interpretation, however, does not adequately consider the first half of the residential development process: the creation of manufactured lots to be purchased by individual or small-scale homebuilders. As the authors of *Shaky Palaces* have recently emphasized: "the building of homes is not the only phase of the building of suburbs. Providing transport access and utilities, and subdividing the farms and woods for small-scale builders to purchase, are also part of the suburbanization process."[4]

This chapter traces the emergence of this initial phase of suburb building in the nineteenth century. As has been shown in the previous chapters, it was during the mid-nineteenth century that service improvements revolutionized homes and their connections to the outside world. In twentieth-century terms, it was at this point that manufactured lots— those with a variety of service connections and improvements—became a possibility.

Chicago Developers

Real-estate developers and speculators, careful observers of Chicago's growth, soon saw a connection between changes taking place in outlying settlement and in the basic services being adopted within the home. Suburban settlement brought an increasing demand for urban services and amenities in formerly agricultural precincts. Rural governments were often slow to respond to these changes; but real-estate developers were not. They developed residential subdivisions that provided a wide array of services and amenities to potential residents. In doing so, most hoped not only to attract purchasers but to increase the value of their property.

Although the development of improved residential subdivisions was new, Chicago speculators had for years banked on creating fortunes in land based on the city's growth. The city's early promoters invested heavily in transportation, industry, and commerce, but they also purchased some—and sometimes a great deal of—Cook County real estate in the expectation that the city's growth in other areas would be reflected in rising real-estate values. They were not disappointed. The value of Chicago-area land, while rising and falling over real-estate cycles, was on an upward spiral. Downtown property values rose ten times between the boom year of 1836 and the depression year of 1879 (table 17). It is little wonder that real estate was the lifeblood of Chicago's development, and claimed the center of attention even down to its "small talk."[5]

Some property holders were content to hold large tracts, watching their value increase naturally with the city's growth. This method was popular with nonresidents who had invested in outlying Cook County property. Many remembered the spectacular increases in land values in Manhattan in the first half of the nineteenth century[6] and saw the possibility of a similar boom in Chicago. Charles Butler and his New York neighbor Arthur Bronson, for example, invested heavily in Chicago property through their agent, William B. Ogden. Ogden himself became an excellent example of a traditional speculative property holder. He did not expect rapid and spectacular gains over a year or two but a healthy increase over a number of decades. His work as a Chicago booster and entrepreneur helped to assure the continued rise in property prices.[7]

A healthy fortune was needed to pursue this form of real-estate speculation, for one could not expect an immediate return. This style has been characterized as the one "followed by the Astors in New York," who bought property on the outer edges and held it indefinitely, counting on urban growth to increase values.[8] Other real-estate speculators were less patient in waiting for urban growth to raise property values. These men saw the possibility of acting as catalysts for metropolitan growth that would increase their real-estate values quickly and more directly. They well understood that certain institutions, business establishments, transportation advantages, and improvements would attract growth to an area more quickly than if the property had none of these advantages.

Potter Palmer, a leading dry goods merchant, hotel owner, and real-estate speculator, was one of the first Chicagoans to act on this principle on a grand scale. In 1869 the main retail street was Lake Street, running east to west just south of the main branch of the Chicago River. Palmer owned a considerable chunk of land on State Street, which was more a stream than a street running north and south several blocks west of Lake Michigan. He anticipated that the congestion on Lake Street would sooner or later force business to move elsewhere. Predicting it would be sooner, he privately made street and sidewalk improvements on State Street, built his elegant hotel there, and convinced Marshall Field to move his department store to a magnificent new building a few doors away. The 1871 fire destroyed Palmer's work, but he rebuilt State Street, as did other retailers, who saw the street as their future. Palmer, of course, cashed in on the remarkable increase in State Street property values and made himself another tidy fortune.[9]

The key to this "new" method of real-estate speculation was active participation in the decisions shaping future urban growth.[10] The development of improved residential subdivisions was one particular form this speculation took. By directing growth, real-estate speculators were trying to cut short the years of waiting that the older, "Astor" method of speculation had required. Fortunes were to be made handily by channeling settlement in one direction rather than another. Of course, the time, money, and effort expended on improvements and promotion increased the investment and the risk if the speculator judged poorly. It was attractive, however, to speculators who hoped to make their fortune, not just buttress it, in urban land.

Speculative Residential Developments

The popularity of this method of real-estate speculation is exhibited through the growing number of new residential subdivisions made in Chicago. Real-estate developers scattered small subdivisions over the region, as streetcars and railroads linked more and more of these areas to the central city. An 1870 real-estate journal explained that these speculators knew that: "Within a desirable distance of the city there will never be another foot of land than there is at the present time but there will be many times as great a population, who must have homes, and many of whom must live in the suburbs."[11]

Many subdivisions were opened by syndicates, land companies, and improvement associations. They allowed a group of men to bear the risk of speculation and were particularly attractive to individuals active in other businesses, who sought quick profits without much work. The syndicate generally had one member who actually directed the development, or they hired an outside developer to negotiate the day-to-day operations. Among the companies formed were the Ravenswood Land Company, the Maywood Company, the Irving Park Land Company, the Rogers Park Land Company, the Calumet and Chicago Canal and Dock Company, the Norwood Park Land and Building Company, the West Chicago Land Company, the Blue Island Land and Building Company, the Riverside Improvement Company, and the Melrose Company. Each was granted a special charter in the late 1860s by the Illinois State Legislature. The purpose outlined in the 1869 Riverside Improvement Company charter is typical of those granted before the state adopted a general incorporation act: "Laying out the same [property] into lawns and residence lots, with the necessary avenues, roads and walks and with the purpose of improving, beautifying, and developing the same so as to render said property attractive, that he may be able to sell the same for first class suburban residence purposes."[12]

The work of these speculators and improvement associations contrasts strongly with the patterns of settlement that had been set in the early decades of growth in Cook County. Then, urban settlement around Chicago had been compact, and outside the city settlement was almost exclusively rural. Advances in commuter railroad travel and the extension of street railways led to the development of truly suburban communities: areas of housing beyond the contiguous settlement of the city whose residents were employed in the city itself, or outlying industries whose locations were dependent on proximity to the city. Between 1861 and 1900, nearly half of all settlements made in Cook County were oriented toward commuter or industrial settlement (see table 12). Development companies played a critical role in the growth of new settlements aimed at commuters. They founded over half the settlements between 1861 and 1880 (tables 18 and 19; map 8).[13]

Through these improvement companies, speculators sought to direct urban growth out into the hinterland. Improvements to attract settlement to particular subdivisions fell into two basic categories: those made outside the subdivision itself; and those made directly in it. Among the improvements outside a subdivision which heightened its marketability were extensions of street railway and commuter railroad lines, the creation of connecting highways, and the development of neighboring parks and boulevards. Within subdivisions, commuter railroad stations, industries or businesses, home construction, and infrastructure improvements were among the ways speculators attracted urban residents outward.

Parks and Transportation Developments

In the Chicago area, parks and boulevards directed much outlying development in the decades after the Civil War (map 9). This led to the subdivision and development of land surrounding the parks, both within and outside the city limits. Land values rose rapidly near the parks. Wealthy Chicagoans sought them as prime locations for expensive homes and mansions. Early transportation along the paved boulevards facilitated this growth, along with proximity to the parks themselves. Park commissioners improved the land along the parks and boulevards by installing water pipes, sewers, and gas mains. These services provided an added incentive for growth, as few other outlying areas could hope for these public improvements for years to come.[14]

Not everyone appreciated park development. Special assessments for park purposes were an added burden for property owners during these years.[15] Many potential homeowners could not afford the heavy assessments and so sought other residential areas. Critics of these improvements included *The Nation,* which condemned parks across the country as "artificial but seductive stimulants to a gigantic real estate speculation."[16] But even the critics acknowledged that these improvements had the power to direct settlement.

Real-estate developers influenced both the original location of the parks and boulevards and the subsequent development around them. Paul Cornell, Jonathan Y. Scammon, George M. Kimbark, and other large landholders in South Chicago and Hyde Park worked for years toward the development of the South Parks system after its 1869 organization. They had much to gain by this improvement, as land values in and immediately surrounding the parks increased as much as 90 percent between 1868 and 1870.[17]

Because of the attractiveness of the parks and boulevards, developers laid out subdivisions near them. The subdivisions of the Humboldt Park Residence Association, along the city's northern border, were typical. Under the leadership of Henry Greenebaum, "the leading German banker of Chicago," the association purchased forty acres fronting Humboldt Park and sold lots to its members. Only a few years later, it was predicted that the area would "take rank among our leading suburbs."[18] It is well to point out that Greenebaum was one of the commissioners of the West Park Board when it chose the original parklands. He was also the owner of considerable property in the area in and around the parks.[19]

Improving transportation with railroads and streetcars clearly influenced the growth of residential areas in the late nineteenth and early twentieth centuries. Sometimes the link with real-estate speculation was very strong, as in cases where men involved in the extension of street railways were also involved in such speculation and development along the projected routes. Charles Walker, Superintendent of the Chicago City Railway Company, laid out a residential subdivision along his company's State Street route extension in 1866.[20] Charles Tyson Yerkes, who consolidated the streetcar companies in Chicago during the 1880s, is another example of someone with inside knowledge doing subdivision work, particularly on the northwest side.[21]

Speculators influenced the direction of residential growth through these metropolitan-wide improvements. Many had an inside track on shaping park and boulevard improvements and transportation extensions. Others, however, worked to attract settlement through improvements within subdivisions. Speculators used home construction, various infrastructure improvements, and other amenities to increase the marketability of their property.

Speculative Homes

The most obvious method of directing residential growth was to construct homes for sale or rent in outlying areas within and outside the city limits. It was also the most expensive and therefore the riskiest. Unlike today, developers did not build homes as a matter of course. It was the rare speculator who constructed more than a few homes as a draw to his property. Most homes were constructed by the prospective occupants or as one of a few homes built speculatively by a builder or property holder. There were, of course, a few large-scale operators, and their numbers increased over the course of the late nineteenth and early twentieth centuries. One such project undertaken by Levi, Wing and Company in 1875, consisted of thirty westside homes for men "with moderate means and small families, who covet a home of their own, but have hitherto been compelled to rent on account of difficulty in building such houses as they want and within their means."[22]

Most speculators in the late nineteenth century were in the business of selling land, not houses. However, once homes were built and occupied, the value of adjoining property rose with the realization that this was not simply a paper development. The construction of a few homes helped to convince potential buyers in unsettled areas that the subdivision was soon to be settled, but it was not seen as good business sense to invest capital in homes instead of land.[23] Sometimes promoters offered lots at a discount to those who would build and occupy immediately.[24]

In other subdivisions, speculators built homes and offered them for sale along with lots. The Blue Island Land and Building Company was one of the first to offer this option in Cook County.[25] In 1869 the company platted two subdivisions south of the city: Morgan Park and Washington Heights. The company only installed sidewalks and graded streets before sale, but offered to build "houses upon them [the lots], thus enabling people of moderate means to secure a home."[26] Some developers simply offered house plans to lot purchasers in the hopes of directing building. As well, the size of lots platted also served to shape development. Smaller lots could accommodate only small to moderate size homes, while larger lots afforded space for larger homes.[27]

Samuel E. Gross was perhaps the most famous Chicago developer in the late nineteenth century to build a substantial number of homes. He built homes in almost all of the twenty-odd subdivisions he made in the closing decades of the nineteenth century, beginning with his first subdivision in Jefferson Township, Gross Park. By the time he developed Brookfield more than a decade later, Gross had a standard technique for selling homes in order to make his subdivisions more attractive. His way of operating was to sell on installment terms, one-tenth down and the rest in monthly payments, which went as low as ten dollars. This included both a lot and a house. The initial investment for Gross was large, while profits returned slowly. He devised promotional techniques that helped to insure the success of his subdivisions. Extensive advertisements in all the local newspapers offered free lunches and excursions, band concerts, and fireworks to prospective purchasers.[28]

Service Improvements and Speculation

Real-estate developers like Gross also understood the appeal of moving to an area with all desired improvements already in place—an appeal that could be translated into an advantage for a developer's property in the metropolitan real-estate market. Many developers foresaw the host of problems residents in incorporated areas would have to face when trying to get service extensions: organizing their neighbors, petitioning local government, confronting possible political corruption and graft, wading through the special assessment process, and then making the improvements within their own homes in order to utilize the infrastructure extensions. They also understood that in many instances public improvements could not "keep pace with private enterprise," which left many area residents without the improvements they desired.[29] Developers offered to negotiate these steps for the potential residents of their subdivisions, offering a package of infrastructure extensions useful to them. In return, they hoped to direct residential growth to their property and spur rising real-estate values.

The means by which developers improved subdivisions varied across the metropolitan area. Improvements ranged from a full complement of services to simply grading streets and building a railroad depot. This range reflected both the amount of capital that various speculators were willing to risk and the variety of improvement combinations that area residents ideally wanted. The interaction of developers and local government concerning the provisions of services also varied depending both on the kind of government and on the attitude of the developer.

In the decades after the Civil War, more and more new outlying subdivisions contained improvements. An examination of settlements made by developers between 1861 and 1880 shows that in a majority some improvements had been made by 1880 (see tables 18 and 19). More specifically, seventeen of the twenty-one developers made limited improvements such as grading and paving streets, sidewalks, railroad depots, and tree plantings. Only four developers made any major improvements—water, sewers, gas or electric connections—within their subdivisions. More extensive improvements awaited the arrival of suburban government. Despite growing demands for urban service improvements in outlying subdivisions, most speculators provided only those amenities deemed necessary for land sale. The task of providing most services was left to later residents and local government.

Limited improvements were made in subdivisions closest to the line of settlement growth. Such was the experience of the Ravenswood Improvement Company. Organized in 1868 to develop land along the Northwestern Railroad in Lake View Township, the company built a hotel, a railroad depot, and a schoolhouse, graded streets, and planted trees. The effort was quite successful with these few improvements and was sold out in only a few years. Everett Chamberlin, writing about Chicago suburbs in 1874, felt that the lack of improvements at Ravenswood was owing to its success. If more lots had remained unsold, the company would have been more inclined to make improvements in order to increase the desirability of their property.[30]

Sometimes a lack of services was by design. Few improvements were made in subdivisions aimed at those who could barely afford the cost of the land. Urban improvements simply added to the original cost of the land and further delayed the building of a home under this system. For instance, Gustavus Anderson, himself a Swedish immigrant, subdivided and sold land on north Clark Street in the 1880s in an area that came to be known as Andersonville. As he remembered years later: "We didn't do much improving of our subdivisions. We didn't have the money and people paid so slowly that we couldn't afford to. All we did was survey the land and mark the lots and streets and put in plank sidewalks."[31] Further improvements came to Andersonville only after the annexation of the area to Chicago in 1889. These conditions were also found in subdivisions developed by workers with funds saved through building and loan associations. The Humboldt Park Residence Association is one such example. Although subdivisions within the city and some suburban jurisdictions offered many more urban services, the costs of providing them were too high for many working-class families intent on owning their own homes.

Four of the subdivisions examined in Chapter 1 were made with limited improvements before sale: Norwood Park, Austin, Grand Crossing, and Roseland. Norwood Park, like Ravenswood, was aimed at commuters but was not nearly as successful. Improvements and real population growth came only after local government provided the necessary services. Austin, initially subdivided for worker housing surrounding outlying factories, at first provided no services. By the closing decades of the nineteenth century, commuters settled in the area, and, like the residents of Norwood Park, they turned to local government with their service demands. Grand Crossing and Roseland were settled primarily by workers employed in neighboring industries. The original subdividers provided few improvements, and again residents had to wait for local government to meet their demands for improvements.

More improvements were found in areas trying to attract industry as well as workers. The subdivision made by the Calumet and Chicago Canal and Dock Company at South Chicago around 1870 exemplifies those which catered to industrial development. An 1874 promotional pamphlet describes the numerous benefits afforded to industry locating there, including railroad and paved road connections to Chicago, harbor improvements, and water from the Hyde Park Water Works. The various manufacturing establishments, employing more than two thousand people, were also described as further inducements for potential industrial settlers. Residents in these industrial suburbs were more likely to have services because developers and industries bore much of the cost.[32]

Some improvement companies provided a full range of urban services to prospective buyers in subdivisions aimed at business and professional people. The Riverside Improvement Company was considered among the most innovative and comprehensive. In 1868, a group of eastern businessmen formed a company to develop property west of the city on the DesPlaines River. The company was strongly influenced by the romantic tradition. They hired Olmsted, Vaux and Company to design a suburb that would "unite at once the beauties and healthy properties of a park with the conveniences and improvements of the city."[33]

Among the improvements made were water and sewer mains, individual gas hookups, paved roads, street lamps, sidewalks, parks, and a railroad depot. In addition, deed restrictions on lots sold in Riverside included building-line guidelines, community parkland adjoining lots, minimum home prices, and the outlawing of fences. A hotel on the DesPlaines River built in 1870 served to familiarize people with the area as a potential suburban residence site. The hotel was filled to capacity in October 1871 with wealthy refugees from the Chicago Fire. In spite of all this, the venture was not an immediate success. While the Chicago Fire drove refugees to the Riverside Hotel, it directed homebuilders to Ravenswood. Riverside was still viewed as too far from the downtown area to permit daily commuting. It was not until the 1880s that many homes were built.[34]

Still, the planning and improvements at Riverside were employed in more and more new subdivisions as the nineteenth century drew to a close. To receive a full range of improvements within Chicago required long years of special assessments and waiting, to say nothing of the discomfort of living with streets perpetually ripped up. In Riverside, these improvements were in place before lot sale. A contemporary account reminded potential residents that "parties buying at Riverside will have the satisfaction of avoiding the demand upon their resources for taxation in the way of improvements, so constant in all towns."[35]

Kenilworth, along the shore of Lake Michigan in New Trier Township, is an example of a community that early acquired a wide array of improvements and amenities. The man behind this development was Joseph Sears, a wealthy Chicago businessman. In 1889 Sears bought the land for the suburb and formed the Kenilworth Company. The village was platted in 1890, and an advertisement for the suburb late that year characterized it as the "Model Suburban Town" with the following improvements and amenities: a complete sewerage system, pure filtered lake water, one half mile of lake frontage, railroad commuter service, illuminating and fuel gas, broad macadamized avenues, shaded parkways, a 36-foot elevation, magnificent timber, and attractive homes. Local government was organized in 1896, in the wake of these improvements.[36] In this process the role of Joseph Sears as the organizing force working in place of local government in the village's early years was crucial. In addition, the path was considerably eased by the wealth of both Sears and early residents. Because residents could easily afford improvements, as evidenced by the expensive homes they constructed, few objections were raised concerning projects because of cost.[37]

Improvement work was also important in other suburbs carefully developed during these years under the guiding light of one individual. South of Kenilworth, along the lakeshore in Lake View Township,

J. Lewis Cochran pursued his dream in the closing decades of the nineteenth century. In 1885 Cochran bought 380 acres, subdivided them into city lots, and named the subdivision Edgewater. He worked only a small portion of the acreage at a time but made a large number of improvements. An employee of Cochran's remembered later that they had installed sewers, streetlights, sidewalks, water pipes, and macadam streets in the subdivision. Cochran also founded the Edgewater Light Company, which provided electric light in his subdivision. It was unusual for electricity to be available outside the city before the turn of the century, and Cochran mentioned this amenity prominently in any advertisement for Edgewater.[38]

The subdivision called Harvey, to the far south of Cook County, was something of an instant town or, more aptly, an "instant city." In 1890 "no such town could be found on any map." By 1892 it had five thousand inhabitants, ten manufacturing establishments, seventy-three miles of streets, a complete sewerage system and water works, 850 buildings, two systems of electric lighting, seventy passenger trains daily, twenty thousand shade trees, and other amenities such as churches, schools, newspapers, building and loan associations, a masonic hall, parks, and boulevards.[39]

The man behind much of this early development was Turlington Harvey. He made substantial land purchases in the area in 1890 and organized the Harvey Land Association to direct the development of the property. A Chicago lumber merchant and "capitalist," Harvey foresaw an impressive future for the subdivision:

> Under the guiding hand and ambitions of Turlington W. Harvey frame and masonry houses ejected themselves from the soil as mushrooms. Ribbons of cement sidewalks replaced the dirt paths, a business area belched forth as paved streets replaced wagon tracks. Water and sewer lines were laid forming the foundation of what eventually became the modern, efficient facilities of today.[40]

A Variety of Service Improvement Packages

Some developers appealed to these various constituencies by building subdivisions with different improvement combinations across the metropolitan area. In late nineteenth-century Chicago no one tried harder than Samuel E. Gross. Beginning in 1881, Gross platted, subdivided, improved, and sold a chain of more than twenty suburbs. As mentioned previously, he was also one of the few Chicago speculators to build housing in some of his subdivisions. This work earned him the title the "Napoleon of home builders."[41] The range of improvements Gross provided varied among subdivisions and corresponded closely to the value of the homes he constructed. Improvements at his first subdivision, Gross Park, on the near northwest side, were limited to grading streets, planting trees, and building homes. This subdivision was aimed specifically at workingmen, particularly those employed at the nearby factory that manufactured implements or at the local brickyards. Later Gross developed more expensive subdivisions, among them Brookfield. Improvements there included a system of walks, sewers, gas, water, parks, trees, and paved streets.[42] His work illustrates the discrete pools of potential purchasers who could be attracted through different improvement combinations.

Over the course of the late nineteenth and early twentieth centuries, the role of real-estate speculators evolved and became more systematic, as developers learned which techniques and improvements made their land more marketable and valuable. Beginning with limited improvements made to subdivisions in the mid–nineteenth century, developers responded to increasing demands for services in residential areas. In addition, more and more developers built homes in their subdivisions in order to attract buyers and increase the value of their investment.

By the late nineteenth century, subdivisions with "attractive improvements" were made, along with ones that continued to provide the barest minimum of development before sale. It was increasingly clear, however, that "while the lots of the improved subdivision must be sold at a sharp advance over the unimproved, experience shows that buyers are more readily secured for the higher priced lots with all improvements included."[43] Real-estate developers by 1888 recognized that the advantages of making improvements were "obvious, for at once a high character is established for the property, and the buyer while paying for the cost of such improvements in the price of the lot, pays less than the same improvement would cost for the individual lot if done by himself."[44] By 1892, those developers who did not provide a full range of services were chastised by their fellow workers in the *Real Estate and Building*

Journal: "There ought to be a law against the upbuilding of a town or village where there are no sewers and no hope of getting any. The narrow, stingy, miserly plan in view among many land owners and subdividers will not do when the public health is looked after. Their plan is to stave off these needed improvements until the newcomers and home seekers get possession of their lots."[45]

In the final decades of the nineteenth century and early ones of the twentieth, homes became an increasingly important part of the package of improvements provided by real-estate developers. By 1930, most subdividers delivered "a completed product to the purchaser . . . in the shape of a house and lot ready for use."[46] By then, the real-estate developer was seen as an important force in the creation of an adequate housing supply, which was crucial to continued growth and health. Some went so far as to label the subdivider as "the unsung and unromantic hero of modern civilization. It is he who makes a real home possible for the cliff dweller. . . . He is the magician who changes, overnight, the village into a town, the town to a city, and the city to a metropolis."[47]

Speculators and developers who chose to follow "modern" real-estate methods sought ways to make their property and subdivisions more attractive to potential residents and buyers than other areas within Cook County. Whether it was park or boulevard frontage, proximity to local transportation, deed restrictions, a location inside or outside of the fire limits, a ready-built home, or basic infrastructure improvements, speculators were intent on making their property more marketable. Because of this, suburban subdivisions and improvements were grounded in differences rather than similarities.

It would be misleading, however, to imply that nineteenth-century developers achieved the homogeneity found in present-day subdivisions. Several factors worked against this and should be kept in mind. Because developers did not usually build housing, they could not directly control the cost of housing—except through deed restrictions and lot size. Zoning restrictions did not exist, so only in subdivisions with a large number of deed restrictions was dramatic homogeneity achieved; in fact, it was not achieved in most of these subdivisions.[48] Rather, the point of this chapter is to show that the process of sorting *began* during these years.

Another factor important to bear in mind at this juncture is that there was no absolute connection between high-income residents and a high level of services or low-income residents and a low level of service provision during the nineteenth century. The previous chapter highlighted the fact that individuals had varying demands with regard to services—demands tied only partially to the issue of class. That is, some people who could afford improvements saw little need for them or forwent them in order to spend their money on other purchases. Initial purchasers at Ravenswood and the Swedish clients of Gustavus Anderson provide two examples of this sort. At the other end of the spectrum, Harvey provided a wide range of services aimed at workers, while Kenilworth also provided many improvements aimed at wealthy commuters. The size of lots, the locale, and other amenities drew different classes of people to the two subdivisions. It was not until the twentieth century that the ubiquitous demand for "basic" services emerged.[49] By then, other amenities such as schools and parks, as well as homes themselves, became important determinants in creating homogeneous subdivisions.

The fact that provision of services within subdivisions was ubiquitous, in the face of widely varying services across the metropolitan area, *did* foster a growing neighborhood homogeneity. Suburban improvements also confronted metropolitan residents with the example of outlying areas receiving urban services, a fact that would have a significant effect on attempts to govern the metropolitan area.

CHAPTER 5

LOCAL GOVERNMENT RESPONDS TO SUBURBANIZATION

Until the mid-nineteenth century, there was no such thing as "suburban government": there were only urban or rural governments. Suburban government evolved from these older forms as a hybrid. The previous chapters have outlined the development of suburban settlement in the Chicago area. This chapter will show the response of local government to the demands of new suburban residents. Essential to understanding the evolution of suburban government are three points: the important distinction between the colloquial and legal usage of the terms *town* and *village*; and the facts that each state has a distinctive local-government history and that in Illinois there were two systems of local government, one imposed by the state and one generated (with the approval of the state legislature) by individual communities.

The distinctions between the colloquial and legal usages of descriptions of communities and their governments complicates any discussion of local government. Settlements are often called cities, villages, or towns at the whim of writers or commentators. State legislators, however, used these same terms to designate very particular forms of local government. That is, in Illinois an incorporated city or village, and a town or township, designate different kinds of local governmental forms.

The second point is one often overlooked: every state developed its own designations and categories of local government. For instance, the forms and functions of a township vary considerably across the country.[1] Of course, some states served as models, particularly for quickly settling western territories. By mid-century, Illinois legislators and jurists modeled their system primarily on that of New York, but in the years immediately following the state's 1818 ratification, Virginia had been its model. The switch reflected the shift in incoming settlers from the middle south to the northeastern states.

This shift included the kind of local government imposed by the state legislature. Before 1850, the basic jurisdiction was the Virginia county. That is, legislators designated every square inch of territory in Illinois to the jurisdiction of a county. After 1850, the state legislature added townships, which were more familiar to recent northeastern settlers. So for most of the period under discussion, the whole Chicago area was governed by counties and townships. These bodies performed the basic functions of taxation, law enforcement, building roads, running schools, and holding elections. They were, in essence, rural governments. In Illinois, they were *not* considered incorporated governments but arms of the state.[2] This fact would have important implications for urban and suburban governments.

Incorporated governments became the exclusive domain of urban, and then suburban, governments in Illinois. The first incorporation in Cook County was Chicago's, in 1833. In contrast to counties and townships, local communities petitioned the state legislature for charters for incorporated government. These incorporated governments, then, were initiated within the community, not imposed by the state legislature. If the state legislature granted the petition, and this generally appears to have been the case, the community became an incorporated town, village, or city. The area remained under the jurisdiction of counties and townships for some purposes, while new functions and representation were afforded by the incorporated government. Among the functions possible only with incorporation were: increased taxing powers, higher debt limits, and the ability to provide many urban infrastructure improvements. The distinctions between village and city were standardized after the 1870 constitutional convention, which created general incorporation laws for Illinois. Differences included: larger population requirements for cities; at-large representation in villages; ward representation in cities; and higher debt ceilings in cities.

One further form of incorporated government found in nineteenth-century Cook County was the incorporated township, which took the imposed rural township designation and grafted incorporated government upon it. Unlike an incorporated village or city, which could consist of only a piece of one or several townships, the incorporated township encompassed the whole of the designated rural township. Once a township was incorporated, no sub-area of it could incorporate separately as a village or city.

Suburban government emerged from this set of imposed/community-generated and incorporated/unincorporated governments. This chapter will build on these available forms to show how residents of outlying Cook County took the options available to them and created the first suburban governments in Illinois. To do this, the story must return to outlying settlers and their demands.

Suburban Growth

The discreteness of urban and rural settlement in Cook County eroded following the Civil War (table 20). Commuter railroad stations, streetcar lines, parks and boulevards, institutions, and industries drew settlement outward from the city in an irregular fashion, resulting for a time in geographically isolated suburban communities surrounded by farmland and empty tracts. The development of suburban areas in Cook County was the result of both a transition of older settlements, made for resort or agricultural purposes, and new subdivisions aimed specifically at prospective suburban dwellers. In 1869 a pamphlet published as a prospectus for these developments commented that:

> It is probable that comparatively few even of the oldest
> residents of Chicago are aware that there are forty towns,
> more or less populous, that are strictly suburban to
> Chicago, where gentlemen doing business and having
> all of their interests in Chicago live with their families.
> These towns . . . are increasing in size very rapidly, and
> there are few of them where the advantages of improve-
> ments are not now recognized.[3]

Outlying residents looked for urban services such as water, sewers, gas, and electricity. Former residence in the serviced city shaped these expectations.

Local governments did not initially make improvements in these outlying districts, for they were far beyond the scope designated to traditional rural governments. Instead, real-estate developers, who understood that "at the root of all urban growth is the land development process—the conversion of rural or vacant land to some sort of urban use," initiated improvements.[4] Speculators provided these services to outlying areas as a means of drawing purchasers to their properties. Historians have begun to explore the significant role private developers worldwide between 1860 and 1914 played in urban improvements. C. M. Platt, in a 1983 article, commented:

> At best, municipalities themselves made only a modest contribution to total expenditure. . . . Private entrepreneurs, contractors and companies paid for the public utilities. Private proprietors contributed to the improvement of paving, street widths and alignments, storm drains and sewers. . . . The interested proprietor, assisted by the increment in land values and operating with little help from the city administration, was the basis for financing of expansion and modernization of western cities before 1914.[5]

These developers acted as brokers for the varied demands of residents concerning residential growth in much the same way as urban government did. In contrast to local government, however, the developers were directors rather than reactors in the city building process. Of course, developers did not operate in a governmentless vacuum. Nor did they make all of their improvements independently of government. On the contrary, many successfully manipulated the functions and power of local government to their own advantage. Within the city, this could mean making political donations to key aldermen who made locational decisions for services or simply working through regular channels of government.

For instance, some real-estate developers in Chicago worked quite closely with the Department of Public Works when arranging improvements for their outlying tracts. Ogden, Sheldon, & Co., which had substantial holdings on the west and north sides of the city, developed its property near Wicker Park on the northwest side in the mid-1870s. This area was inside the city's boundaries but was only lightly settled and lacked urban services. The firm paid to extend the city water system to the tract rather than create an independent water supply. The cost to the company was nearly seven thousand dollars, but the city agreed to refund that "as soon as the extension would pay 15% interest on the investment." This was the point at which the city normally would extend water mains. The move was so successful that within the year the firm had its money refunded and the city was working directly with other property owners in the area about extending water service even farther.[6]

Outlying Government and Service Demands

Outside of the city boundaries, the story was a bit different. Although Chicago was first incorporated in 1833, it was decades before other areas in Cook County followed suit. The rural population outside Chicago made few demands on local government, in contrast to city residents. Before the Civil War, only Chicago's chartered government had the power to provide municipal services and collect taxes or special assessments for them. It was the only settlement where local government was actively involved in the provision of water and sewerage. Settlements outside of the city either did without these services or provided them privately. The county served as the only government for these outlying areas, collecting taxes, supervising elections, operating courts and schools, and maintaining roads and bridges (table 21). After 1850, the twenty-seven townships took over many of the county's functions by serving a growing rural population (map 10 and table 22).[7]

Although these new townships improved representation for outlying communities, their basic functions remained rural. In contrast, their populations became more and more urban-oriented as the century came to a close. Both the number of people living in outlying areas and the population densities on the city's outskirts increased dramatically in the closing decades of the nineteenth century (see table 20). The location of this outward expansion of population was influenced by a variety of factors, foremost among them innovations in transportation. These changes affected the settlement of the county by making time rather than distance to the city center a decisive factor. The introduction of new railroad lines, the continued expansion of horsecar and cable car routes, and, after 1890, electric streetcar routes, as well as the creation of the area's first elevated railroads in the late 1890s, dramatically changed the relation of many outlying areas to the city center, bringing them into much closer orbit.

Of course, this outward expansion did not simply encompass undeveloped tracts of prairie awaiting the growth of Chicago. Subdivisions like Ravenswood, Austin, and Hyde Park Center had originally been developed under older transportation and economic constraints and were

forced to adapt to changing conditions. Although a relatively new population center, Cook County by the 1880s was engaged, not only in a
settlement process along its fringes, but a filling-in process, as new
technologies and conditions made different lands attractive for settlement
and development. A straightforward method of dealing with increasing
densities was simply to increase the number of townships in heavily
settled areas. Six new townships emerged by 1880 (map 11). They provided better representation and a smaller area to negotiate but did not
expand on the rural functions designated township government by the
state.

Cicero was organized as a new township directly west of the city in
1857; Hyde Park, to the south of the city in 1861; and Calumet, from
Hyde Park in 1867. In response to the petition of local residents, an
election concerning township organization was held in each area. Some
areas within these collar townships were closely linked to Chicago by
rail or streetcar, while others had only infrequent contact with the city.
For instance, in Hyde Park by 1880, industrial concentrations at Oakdale,
Grand Crossing, and South Chicago contrasted with commuter suburbs
like Kenwood and Hyde Park Center and agricultural settlements like
Rosedale. In Lake the industrial development of the stockyards region
was set against commuter settlement in Englewood and Normalville to
the south (table 23).

The other three townships organized during the nineteenth century
resulted in more homogeneous local units: Evanston, Norwood Park,
and Riverside. The town of Evanston had been platted in 1854, around
the infant Northwestern University. The area was a part of Ridgeville
Township until 1857, when residents petitioned to be separated from
the southern half of the town. Similarly, Norwood Park Township was
organized in 1872 because residents felt little kinship with the rest of
Jefferson. Area inhabitants rather dramatically concluded that "taxation
without improvements [is] . . . equally intolerable to the citizens of Norwood Park as was taxation without representation to certain other patriots
one hundred years before."[8] Riverside separated from Proviso Township
for similar reasons in 1870.[9]

Neither the county nor the townships had the power to provide the
sorts of services available through the incorporated urban government
at Chicago. Because of this, many developers, especially the early ones,
made whatever improvements they considered useful for the marketability of the land without the help of local government. Some developers

provided more substantial service improvements, including water and sewer connections. A few continued to provide these services without the aid of local government. A local improvement association, organized by Joseph Sears, made major improvements in Kenilworth without any initial help from local government. At Pullman:

> The car company assumed many of the functions usually held by a city corporation. It furnished the residences with water, gas and electric light. The streets of the town had never been dedicated to the public, and no plat of the town has ever been filed for record with the county authorities. To all intents and purposes, the town of Pullman is still an acre tract.[10]

Most developers, however, did not have the resources available to Pullman and Sears to provide a full range of services outside of government. They turned to local government for aid in providing services that would make their subdivisions attractive as suburban settlements. The immediate problem with petitioning local governments outside of the city for these services, however, was that they did not possess the powers to provide them either. And even if the townships could have supplied the services, their many rural residents were opposed to tax increases to offer better services to suburban communities within their midst.

Incorporated Villages

One answer to this quandary was to adapt urban government to suburban needs—that is, to create incorporated villages in outlying areas which would have much the same powers as incorporated urban government, but on a much smaller scale. This was a new concept in incorporated government, which up until the mid-nineteenth century remained primarily the province of cities. By the mid-nineteenth century, state legislatures across the country, especially those strongly influenced by precedents in New York, granted village charters to virtually any community that requested them, encouraging this new application of what had once been a rarely granted privilege. Tremendous geographic and population expansion left western legislatures with little time to consider each case carefully. At first, boosters in western towns used incorporations to further their civic pretentions. Would-be metropolises, not suburbs, first took advantage of legislatures' loosened grip on charters. Suburbs followed their lead.[11]

The first six outlying settlements in Cook County that incorporated did so between 1865 and 1870: Evanston, Barrington, Palatine, Des-Plaines, Glencoe, and Winnetka. Evanston and DesPlaines were incorporated under the general town incorporation act as revised in the 1849 state constitution.[12] The other four were granted special charters which originated within the local community through a petition movement for incorporation (see table 8). Each, located miles from downtown but adjacent to a railroad depot, accommodated hundreds of new residents in the years around the Civil War. Residents sought incorporation as a means of responding to this growth. When settlement remained largely rural, as in Barrington, Palatine, and DesPlaines, incorporation helped residents to improve roads and regulate animals and nascent agricultural industry. In contrast, the settlers of Evanston, Glencoe, and Winnetka used their new powers to initiate improvements like those being made in Chicago.

A general incorporation law, adopted in Illinois in 1872 to alleviate some of the work before the state legislature, made the acquisition of a charter even easier. Chicago and most of the other specially chartered communities reincorporated under this general law. In addition, sixteen new communities incorporated as villages between 1870 and 1880. New suburbs, founded after the Civil War, were numerous among this group of newly incorporated communities. In 1873, the *Real Estate and Building Journal* characterized this development: "All suburban towns out of Chicago are growing so rapidly, and becoming so popular that one after another steps into a village charter and organizes as a village under the general law of 1872."[13] Among the group of suburbs incorporated were several that owed their origins to development companies and real-estate speculators. Washington Heights, South Evanston, Rogers Park, Wilmette, Riverside, and Norwood Park were all part of this group.

The incorporated village form became even more popular as the decades progressed. Eleven new communities were founded and incorporated in Cook County between 1881 and 1900 (see table 10). While only two of these settlements were based in "commuter services," the orientation of settlement had definitely shifted from rural to suburban. Over half—Chicago Heights, Grossdale, Harvey, Kenilworth, Riverview, and

Edison Park—were founded by a developer planning on commuter or industrial settlement. Three of these—Grossdale, Harvey, and Kenilworth—had improvements made before or soon after being founded. The incorporation of many of these communities came in response to the demands of property owners for urban services such as water, street improvement, gas lights, and sewers. Residents expressed these demands through public meetings, newspaper articles, and other more informal channels. Considerable discussion concerning incorporation generally accompanied these proposals, and residents held numerous meetings to debate the move.

The powers granted to local areas under both the special incorporations and the general incorporations after 1870 were similar. They included: actions protecting the health of the communities, police and fire protection, the establishment of hospitals, the construction and maintenance of streets, sidewalks, sewers, bridges, streetlights, and parks. Perhaps most important, the incorporated city or village had the power to make special assessments to pay for these improvements. This was a power never granted in Illinois to the rural-based county or township, so that "if part of a township or county wanted a special service, and this part was not within the jurisdiction of a governmental form that had the power of special assessment, the service could not be provided."[14]

Turlington Harvey and Samuel Gross were among the most successful real-estate men to foster the incorporation of an outlying subdivision to aid them in its development. They saw incorporation as a means of legitimizing claims about their subdivisions, in a way not unlike the boosters of Chicago who had backed its original incorporation. As in Chicago, public works and improvements ultimately convinced investors and future residents that potential growth was legitimate.

Improvement work at Harvey early made the transition from private to public supervision. The Harvey Land Association only supervised the first year of improvements. In 1891, Harvey incorporated as a village, and in 1895 it reincorporated as a city. The Harvey Land Association strongly supported both moves. Sewer construction was typical of the close relationship between the village government and the developers. In 1890 the association hired a civil engineer to plan a sewer system and paid for the earliest sewer work. After the incorporation as a village, however, local government assumed responsibility. Of course, the association paid for most of the work in the early years because it owned much of the property within the village.[15]

Some Harvey residents were quite critical of this early move to public responsibility for improvements. In 1893, some local residents raised a cry concerning the special assessments and taxes. These residents felt that they were paying for improvements that would largely benefit Turlington Harvey by increasing the value of his still large real-estate holdings. *The Real Estate and Building Journal* contested this view: "Any person acquainted with Harvey affairs knows that since the incorporation of the village, the question of new improvements is handled exclusively by the village board elected by the citizens in the regular way, Mr. Harvey personally having nothing to do with it."[16] Still, Turlington Harvey had the most to gain financially from the success of the community in the early years after its incorporation. Early residents were not so far from the truth.

Early residents at Grossdale also confronted an influential developer. They organized Grossdale as a village in 1888 to facilitate improvements, much like early residents of Harvey. Also, residents used incorporation to assert the independence of the subdivision from neighboring communities that were threatening to annex Grossdale. At first, the relationship between Gross and the community was a close one. Gross's brother lived in the community and served as its mayor five times between 1888 and 1902. Within two years of incorporation, paved streets, sewers, a waterworks and streetlights were among the services completed. Improvements helped Gross sell lots; but he shouldered most of the financial burden for these improvements through taxes and assessments.

Relations between Gross and Grossdale residents became increasingly strained by the turn of the century, due largely to two matters: Gross's tardiness in paying assessments on the considerable property he owned in the village and debate over street openings. In 1905, in a symbolic move, residents voted to change the name of their community to Brookfield. Developers, like Gross and Harvey, who worked early with incorporated government received help in financing improvements for their subdivisions, but their interests were quickly subsumed by resident demands.[17]

Of course, outlying areas did not incorporate simply at the instigation of developers. For instance, in communities where the original developers provided few services, later residents organized local government to do so. Rogers Park is an example of a settlement that incorporated after much of its land had been sold by the Rogers Park Land Company. The Land Company, organized in 1872, opened and graded streets, sold lots, and "induced the purchasers to build on them." The company did not attempt major improvements, nor did it actively seek incorporation as was the case in Grossdale and Harvey. By 1874, at least fifty homes had been constructed costing between twelve hundred and eighteen thousand dollars. This was clearly *not* a settlement with a homogeneity of homes. The fact that the Land Company initially made few improvements left open the possibility for settlement by a wide range of economic classes. Still, within a matter of years, these residents were able to reach agreement on the need for further improvements. Many of the residents were commuters, traveling on the Northwestern Railroad to downtown Chicago on one of five daily trains.[18] In 1878, they decided to incorporate as a village "in order to improve the streets, take care of storm water, install sanitary sewerage, and consider means of getting a supply of water for household use."[19]

In this case, the dearth of improvements made by the original improve-ment company caused residents to band together early in their history to form a village government that could administer the public works projects. As one later source explained, "the people felt that they must organize to secure these improvements."[20] Incorporation was one clear way of making improvements demanded by commuters but not origi-nally provided by development companies.

As discussed previously, while real-estate speculators developed more and more of the new outlying communities, the evolution of older, agricultural communities into suburban enclaves was also a part of nineteenth-century Cook County growth. Agricultural communities along railroad stations experienced yearly increases in commuter popu-lation. Glenview is one example. Commuters settled after the railroad laid a double track in 1892, and were soon clamoring for a local govern-ment that could provide urban services. In 1899, these new commuters, as well as older rural settlers, approved the incorporation of the area as Glenview. Early officers of the town were a combination of farmers and commuters, and they argued often about the kinds of services demanded and how they would be financed. Still, by World War I the village had successfully paved streets, created a water supply system, laid sewers, and provided night lighting for most streets.[21]

Older agricultural settlements, even those without a heavy influx of commuters, also incorporated by 1900. The motivation for these incorporations lay less with urban services than with the temperance issue. The growing strength of the temperance movement in the 1880s and 1890s led to the incorporation of many rural settlements. The state granted incorporated cities and villages the power to prohibit and regulate the sale of liquor in their own communities.[22] Residents wished to legislate for or against the sale of liquor and the existence of saloons there.

For instance, Arlington Heights, one of the larger country towns that incorporated in the final two decades of the nineteenth century, had a population of 1,200 in 1884, increasing to 1,380 by 1900. In 1884 there was only one identifiable commuter, a doctor who traveled the twenty-two miles to Chicago on the Northwestern Railroad. Most residents were farmers or were employed in the local stores, hotels, schools, or small factories. Incorporation in 1887 came in response to the temperance issue. Most residents favored making Arlington Heights a dry town. The early work of the village was confined to erecting a number of oil street lamps, grading the main streets, and building sidewalks on the same. As more commuters arrived by the first decades of the twentieth century, the village government began to install more substantial improvements, like water and sewer systems.[23]

By 1880, the incorporated village was an established fixture in the Cook County governmental landscape. Born of the demands of outlying residents and real-estate developers for government provision of services previously only available in urban areas, the incorporated village serviced a growing suburban population. It was used by developers intent on servicing their outlying subdivisions, by residents who demanded services not originally provided by developers, and by residents intent not so much on obtaining services as exerting local prerogatives on issues like temperance.

Suburban subdivisions were clearly set apart from adjoining rural areas and served as centers for many newly incorporated villages. The subdivisions and improvements made by original development companies determined the nucleus of the community and the base from which future work would be done. The early work of developers fostered homogeneity. Of course, it was not a strict homogeneity such as that found since World War II in suburbs like Levittown. It was just that roughly equal land prices and improvements attracted similar residents. This homogeneity was crucial to the governments that emerged after incorporation.

Incorporated Townships

The incorporated village was not the only governmental response to suburbanization. Many of the older rural townships, once consisting only of farms and small market towns, experienced suburban settlement after the Civil War. While some of these settlements incorporated as distinct villages, others directed their demands toward their township governments. As mentioned previously, townships possessed only limited powers, but methods evolved after the Civil War to augment them. In particular, settlements just outside the city limits often turned to their township for improvements. Residents in the "collar" townships demanded water, streetlights, paved streets and sidewalks, and sewers. Township governments had not traditionally provided these urban services, and they did not have the proper powers of assessment and taxation to do so. The only governments which did have the scope to furnish these services were incorporated towns, villages, or cities.[24] So suburbanites pushed for the incorporation of their townships in order to meet these demands.

Residents demanded urban services not simply for reasons of comfort. Their health and safety demanded it. As population in these areas increased, problems that had hitherto existed only in Chicago began to crop up more and more frequently. Threats of disease due to inadequate water supplies and nonexistent sewer systems, and safety problems caused by impassable streets and sidewalks, soon plagued these outlying areas. The situation reached a crisis level first in Hyde Park and Lake, where populations increased from under two thousand in 1860 to over fifteen thousand in both towns by 1880. Most of this growth took place during the 1870s, with increases of over ten thousand residents in each town. This growth was not evenly spread across the towns but was concentrated in settlements within each town.

Each of the townships contiguous to the city, along with several others, incorporated in the 1860s under special charters passed by the state legislature. As with the city charters granted Chicago, they came only in response to the petitions of area residents. Special charters extended the functional scope of townships to include paving and repair of streets, alleys, and sidewalks, constructing drains as needed, and making improvements in parks or on public lands. In addition, these townships were granted the power to assess property holders for these improvements. A part-time board of trustees oversaw the work of the town. The number of full-time employees was small, with much of the work in the town completed under contract by private firms.

Variations did occur among the collar townships. Hyde Park—home to industrial settlements such as South Chicago, worker's suburbs such as Cummings and Roseland, and elite suburban communities such as Kenwood and Hyde Park Center—seriously tackled water, sewer, and utility provision by the late 1870s. The incorporation of Hyde Park Township in 1867 inexorably joined the fates of the disparate communities within the township. Once incorporated, settlements within this township could not incorporate individually unless they were first designated as new townships by the state legislature.[25]

The Hyde Park town trustees levied special assessments for most improvements there. The only bond issue made for public improvements in Hyde Park was for the construction of its waterworks. The trustees provided other services on demand:

> Next in order, after a supply of water, the ordinary resident requires an improved street which includes sewer, sidewalk and roadway. Such improvements, under our plan of work are paid for by special assessments on the property adjoining or benefitted and are usually made at the time and in the manner desired by the owners of a majority of the property.[26]

This contrasts with the City of Chicago, which financed both sewers and waterworks primarily through bond issues and general funds.

By 1882, the Hyde Park trustees made over $500,000 annually in special assessments for these improvements. There were 95 miles of paved streets, 51 miles of sewers, 106 miles of water pipe, 1,023 water hydrants, 190 miles of sidewalks, 1,238 oil lamps, 933 gasoline lamps, and 85 miles of lighted streets in the township by 1889. Despite so many miles of services, they did not cover the town. Rather, Hyde Park was a hodgepodge of settlements with a wide range of services. Through the use of special assessments, only those who wanted *and* could afford improvements received them.

Hyde Park and Lake attempted a combined waterworks in 1871, which was soon inadequate for their needs.[27] Hyde Park residents received most of the water, even though Lake residents had paid half the cost of the system. The problem was resolved in 1881 when the Town of Lake bought out Hyde Park's share in the combined water system. Hyde Park then built a new waterworks.[28]

Other demands from Lake residents eventually led to the provision of a variety of basic services in that township. In 1884, over $500,000 was collected in special assessments for improvements, including water pipe extension, sewers, street lamps, and street improvements. Little distinguished it from the government of Hyde Park, except perhaps its politics. The town administration appears to have been particularly plagued by a "ring rule." Specific complaints in 1883 centered around the following: "Improvements were ordered to be made by special assessment and taxes were levied and collected and then used for other purposes than for that particular improvement and were sometimes put into the general fund and so disbursed."[29] Lake residents were familiar with corruption in politics generally associated with urban, not suburban, governments.

Lake View, to the north of Chicago, began to grow rapidly in the 1880s. With the population under 2,000 in 1870, it had grown to 6,600 in 1880, and to a phenomenal 45,000 in 1887. Lake View's quick growth in the early 1880s placed severe strain on its existing water, sewer, and street improvements. As in Hyde Park and Lake, after years of debate concerning improvements, the town was suddenly confronted with a crisis level of demand and need. The response was rapid. The number of miles of water mains went from none in 1878 to seventy-three in 1888. In 1887 alone, over twenty miles of sewers, eight miles of street paving, seven miles of water pipe, five miles of private drains, and six miles of water service pipes were constructed within the town of Lake View.[30]

Again, residents paid for most of these improvements by special assessments. By 1887, Lake View was working annually with $500,000 in special assessments. The township's work was done, as in Lake and Hyde Park, by just a few salaried officers, under the supervision of a part-time board of trustees.[31]

One of the most prominent members of the Lake View government during these years was Edgar Sanders, who served as supervisor and treasurer of Lake View while it was still a village, and as commissioner of public works after it reincorporated as a city in 1886. Sanders was a florist by trade, and some of his earliest encounters with local government came from contracts for flowers and trees that he filled for the West Park Board in the 1870s. He handled special assessments, dealt with the Lincoln Park commissioners concerning payment of improvements, presented materials to the Chicago City Council concerning shared water conduits, and granted the contracts on special assessment work. Sanders performed these tasks as a part-time employee of the township.[32]

J. Lewis Cochran, the real-estate speculator who developed the northern subdivision of Edgewater, provides an example of a developer working within the incorporated township of Lake View. In contrast to incorporated suburbs such as Harvey or Grossdale, Edgewater was never a self-contained community governed by an incorporated government that matched the boundaries of the subdivision. Instead, Edgewater was a part of a larger governing body which had to mediate the interests and demands of residents across all of Lake View. Cochran built all of his improvements under the ordinances of the City of Lake View, and the subdivision was connected with the Lake View waterworks and sewer works, largely at Cochran's expense.[33]

The final two townships to complete the ring around Chicago were Jefferson and Cicero. Smaller in population through the turn of the century, their suburban communities were nestled in largely rural regions. Several settlements interrupted Jefferson's rural landscape in 1880, bringing some railroad commuters. Like the more populous collar townships, those areas of Jefferson which wanted services paid for them largely through special assessments. The suburban settlement nearest the Chicago city limits, named for nearby Humboldt Park, was the first to demand urban services like water. Receiving no help from the township government, in 1884 its residents petitioned to connect with Chicago for water service. The petition, similar to one made by the Town of Lake just a few years earlier, was tabled by the Chicago City Council. One alderman explained the council's inaction: "if one town was supplied others could not be refused and the council should go slow until first assured of a sufficient supply for our own citizens."[34] At the same time, without a large bond issue, the construction of a comprehensive water system by the township was out of the question. Instead, like Cicero and parts of Lake township, suburbanites relied on smaller systems supplied by artesian wells. Irving Park, for instance, developed its water supply by purchasing and donating an artesian well to the Town of Jefferson for this purpose.[35]

James W. Scoville almost singlehandedly organized the public water supply in Cicero during the 1880s. Scoville was one of the most prominent residents of the western township and a leading landowner. He had a financial and political stake in the continued growth and success of the entire town. Taking this stake quite seriously, Scoville bought and developed a spring-fed pond whose water he offered free to suburban developments across the town if property owners would construct their own water pipes. In addition, Scoville constructed a water tower to provide pressure for fire needs. Scoville "had no doubt this would be sufficient to supply 14,000 people with all the water they would need, this later figure being his estimated limit to the future population."[36]

Interested in sewerage as well, Scoville played an active role in the town board's discussions about installing sewers in Oak Park, one of the suburban communities in the township. While numerous suggestions were put forth, Scoville recommended that a wooden box sewer be constructed. His suggestion was accepted when he offered to pay five thousand dollars beyond his regular assessment toward its construction. Clearly the democratic process was nudged along with the offer of financial assistance from someone whose landholdings would increase in value. But like Hyde Park, Lake, Lake View, and Jefferson, the bulk of these improvements were made through special assessments.[37]

Scoville's interest in Oak Park caused problems for other settlements in the township, especially for Austin. The town hall was located at Austin, but much of the power in the town resided with Scoville, to the west of Austin in Oak Park. Austinites had trouble gaining the services they wanted because of the scheming of other settlements within Cicero to thwart its efforts at improvement. In particular, Austin and Oak Park disagreed in almost any discussion of township improvements.[38]

The case of Cicero again illustrates the close connection between real-estate interests and local politics and government. It was not unusual for supervisors or trustees of incorporated townships to be involved in real-estate operations.[39] The situation in the incorporated towns was similar in a general way to that found in outlying incorporated villages. In both areas, developers pressed their demands on local government. In incorporated villages, though, developers had fewer competitors for the ears of local officials. In contrast, within each incorporated township were numerous settlements, backed by different developers. They were, however, home to ten of the twenty-one new settlements made by developers between 1861 and 1880 (table 18). All but three were a part of the incorporated collar townships surrounding Chicago.[40]

The incorporated township was an entity in which compromise was essential. The debates over appropriations and the political maneuvering were not unlike those taking place in Chicago. Some residents, as an

1873 newspaper account explained, demanded that "city privileges reach them."[41] For these residents, services were deemed crucial to successful growth. Other residents were not interested in promoting growth in their settlements and were intent only on keeping the costs of government and improvements below those of the city.[42] In none of the incorporated townships considered here did improvements reach all corners of their area. Rather, only those sections where the services were crucially needed or strongly demanded were apt to have them.

By 1880, Cook County residents had developed three types of incorporated governments, which expanded the scope of the basic local governments imposed by the state (table 24). Residents in Chicago opted for the city form that supervised major public works projects undertaken to insure its continued expansion and success. Residents in the rural townships ringing the city expanded their powers through incorporation and mediated the demands of widely varying populations (table 25). They were forced by the 1880s to provide services to protect the health and safety of residents, much as Chicago had before the Civil War. Outlying suburban settlements did not turn to their townships, which remained largely rural. Instead, they incorporated as distinct villages, borrowing from the chartered urban form, which could service their growing demands for community improvements.

These governmental forms were closely tied, of course, to the growth of outlying suburban settlement. Underlying that suburban growth were changing demands for urban services, transportation advantages, and the work of real-estate developers. These factors radically changed the rules regarding government in areas outside core urban settlements. For the first time, outlying residents were demanding services and improvements previously only found in cities. Because of these new demands of suburban residents, older urban and rural forms changed. Truly suburban forms did not emerge overnight. They evolved slowly from older ones until the best match was achieved.

A similar process took place in other metropolitan areas as suburban communities emerged. Of course, differences in forms and functions of local governments, and the receptivity of state legislatures to changes, led to different kinds of suburban governments. Perhaps the best-studied metropolitan area with regard to the emergence of suburban government is Boston. Because the state courts in Massachusetts ruled that the imposed townships *were* incorporated forms of government—in contrast to Illinois, where townships were *not* considered corporate governments without the addition of a charter—suburban governments necessarily developed from this form. Incorporated villages were simply not a part of the repertoire in Massachusetts. Suburban government had to emerge from rural townships, or new townships could be created from portions of older townships.

Suburban residents in nineteenth-century Boston utilized both alternatives. For instance, by the Civil War, Cambridge evolved from a rural township oriented toward fringe functions to a suburban township providing a wide range of services and improvements. This did not necessitate the creation of a new form of government, but simply the addition of functions and the expansion of representation within the older forms.[43] In constituency, location, and form, Cambridge resembled the incorporated townships contiguous to Chicago.

Also, suburban communities often chose to break away from otherwise rural townships and form new towns whose bases were largely suburban. Suburbanites created over twenty new townships in the Boston metropolitan area during the nineteenth century. Belmont is one such residential suburban community; in 1859 it formed a separate township whose government was suburban from the start. The suburban governments formed in this way resembled the incorporated villages that emerged in Cook County during the same period to serve suburban settlements.[44] Because the incorporated village was not an alternative in Massachusetts, the creation of small townships was popular.

There are clear similarities to the cases outlined for Chicago. Some suburban communities tussled with fringe neighbors for years within the constraints of a township, and suburban forms emerged slowly. Other suburban communities separated themselves from fringe settlements, hastening the creation of suburban government.

Once formulated, the paths of many of these suburban governments were not easy. Problems with service provision and representation threatened these new forms. Too, city government confronted rivals, albeit small ones, for the first time within the metropolitan area. The next chapter will consider these challenges to nascent suburban governments.

CHAPTER 6

SUBURBAN GOVERNMENT AND ANNEXATION

One of the most puzzling questions for historians of metropolitan areas is why, since the early part of this century, so little territory has been annexed to established cities in the Northeast and Middle West. Recent research identifies several factors as important in explaining the halt to annexations around the turn of the century. Metropolitan areas were increasingly divided by issues of race, ethnicity, and class.[1] Coupled with these divisions was the fact that by the end of the nineteenth century incorporation as a suburban municipality was an easy process. These suburban municipalities, as well as special districts, dramatically improved the services available outside the city and eliminated what had been the strongest drawing card of annexation to the center city—better and less expensive services.[2]

These factors go a long way toward explaining annexation patterns. I would like to add another dimension to this discussion, grounded in the maturation of suburban government forms. In particular, annexation as a normative process ended when the central city had absorbed both contiguous unincorporated suburban territory and many problematic suburban government forms. In the case of Chicago, the period of major annexations ended when the incorporated township form of suburban government disappeared from the landscape, leaving the incorporated village as the basic form of suburban governance.

The following pages will explore annexation primarily from the perspective of the communities that composed much of the area annexed to Chicago—the incorporated townships.[3] These were governments which faced tremendous problems before their annexation to Chicago in 1889. The incorporated townships surrounding Chicago grew at an extraordinary pace after the Civil War. The populations of these townships, while not approaching that of Chicago, were as much as ten times greater than the largest outlying incorporated suburb (table 26).

This growth strained existing infrastructure and fostered a crisis in both the forms and functions of local government. No longer were running water and good sewerage luxuries to be provided as amenities. Instead, they had become necessities to protect the health and safety of many township residents. Compounding the townships' problems was the differential need for these services in their distinct settlements, ranging from agricultural communities to wealthy commuter enclaves. The crisis which arose in the 1880s came because services were inadequate, representation was poor and often nonexistent, and the townships were of such a size and population that their problems called for bold, and usually expensive, solutions.

Residents of the collar townships drew from their rural background and the example of Chicago in their attempts to improve local governments and service provision. Neither cities nor small rural areas, the collar townships tried combined public works projects, legal separations, increased powers, and annexation by 1890. Some of the attempts focused on better service provision, while others aimed to improve the administration and representation of the government.

Combined Projects and Special Districts

One very appealing method of raising service provision was for these townships to band together on a specific project. Several partnerships were formed to construct sewer or water systems, which were expensive and required large-scale planning. Only a very few ever left the drawing board. One attempt already discussed was the combined waterworks of the towns of Lake and Hyde Park, constructed in 1873.[4] However, the economies gained by building a combined waterworks were offset by the more than fourfold increase in population. The partnership dissolved in 1880 and the two towns spent years expanding their waterworks and fielding continuing complaints about inadequate water supplies.[5]

To the northwest of Chicago in the town of Jefferson, water supply was also a problem. The population of Jefferson was only 4,876 in 1880, and the cost of a waterworks borne solely by the residents of Jefferson seemed prohibitive. So, like its southern counterparts, Jefferson began casting about for partners. Township trustees first turned to their southwest neighbor, Cicero, about building a combined waterworks. Although discussed at various times, especially as an alternative to annexation to Chicago, this idea had one very serious drawback—both towns were landlocked. The proposed schemes necessarily relied on well water, which was unsatisfactory, both because of its poor quality and its limited quantity.[6]

Jefferson officials eliminated these drawbacks by turning eastward to Lake View Township. Lake View not only fronted on Lake Michigan but also had a waterworks in place by 1881. Jefferson trustees made numerous proposals for extension of this system through the township in the following years. Residents of the eastern portion of Jefferson went so far as to suggest annexation to Lake View.[7] The problem was that Lake View itself was suffering water shortages during these years. Lake View ignored these proposals until it realized that its sewerage system had to cross Jefferson. With this leverage, negotiations between the two towns began seriously. Still, by 1889 their trustees had not found a mutually agreeable plan to combine water and sewerage systems. More than a decade of talk had resulted in little, while the towns' problems were heightened by continued population growth.[8]

Along the same lines as these combined projects, special districts appeared in the Chicago area to provide specific services to areas which encompassed multiple incorporated governments. In contrast to projects such as the combined Hyde Park/Lake waterworks, these special districts were governmental units in their own right. Cooperation, so vital to informally combined public works ventures, was unnecessary here because the special districts did not rely on their component incorporated governments for support. These districts helped outlying governments by solving large-scale problems extraneously.[9] Special districts also increased the taxing powers and debt ceilings of local areas.[10]

Upon the petition of area residents, a referendum vote was taken in the area that would comprise the special district. If the vote approved the creation of a special district, state enabling legislation was still needed. In Illinois in the closing decades of the last century, the legislature approved most special districts placed before it. By 1889, four special districts operating in Cook County had jurisdiction in the collar townships: the Lincoln Park Board, the West Park Commission, the South Parks Board, and the Metropolitan Sanitary District. In each case, the special district performed functions across incorporated government boundaries and had special taxing powers. The Metropolitan Sanitary

District was the largest and most comprehensive of these. Organized in 1889 to confront large-scale sewerage and drainage problems, the district included Chicago and much of the settlement contiguous to it. It came too late, though, to have much affect on the collar townships.

The park boards were another matter, all three having been organized before 1870. Each board consisted of one division of the city and the adjoining collar township(s). For instance, the South Park Board consisted of the city's south division and the townships of Lake and Hyde Park. Because of the large expanses of free land needed for these ambitious park systems, park commissioners purchased property on the outskirts of settlement, beyond the reach of Chicago's service systems (see map 9). These boards initiated many improvements for recreational and ornamental reasons rather than to protect the health and safety of residents. The gardens and lawns needed an abundant and inexpensive supply of water in the parks and along the connecting boulevards. Likewise, the commissioners installed sewerage to properly drain the parkland for various recreational uses. Sidewalks, streetlights, and drives allowed easy access both to and within parklands.

While much of the park boards' work proceeded without complication, these special districts did not completely eliminate tension among local areas. Complaints about preferential treatment to some areas continued. Illustrative was an 1880 meeting of the South Park Board:

> A delegation from the town of Lake who were in attendance stated that . . . the board had plenty of money now and should do something for the park and boulevard improvements demanded outside of the town of Hyde Park. . . . The property owners who had patiently borne and paid the large park taxation for ten years past, felt the board should do something now for those property owners in Lake Town, who had done so much for the park system and yet for whom the system had done so little.[11]

Improving Representation in the Collar Townships

Though the park boards provided improvements that would probably have been impossible for individual townships to duplicate, the complaints about inadequate and differential representation were ever-present. Inadequate representation, as well as inadequate service provision, underscored the crisis in the collar townships. Problems here led some to advocate splitting these growing town governments into more manageable units.[12] The large geographic size of many of these townships, and the existence of dozens of discrete communities with disparate interests and demands for local government, fueled separation talk.

One of the least complicated proposals came from the town of Lake in 1880.[13] The rural areas in the western part of the township unsuccessfully sought separation from the industrial and commuter settlements to their east. These farmers wanted to annex to adjoining Proviso Township, where rural interests still predominated. The proposal failed for lack of support from the dominant industrial and commuter interests.

Residents of Hyde Park also considered separation. The area of Hyde Park was forty-eight square miles, a third more than that of all of Chicago. The communities within the township were quite diverse, with a concentration of suburban residences in the north and industrial establishments to the south. An 1883 proposal to split Hyde Park called for three new townships: Hyde Park, made up of the northern suburban areas; South Chicago, composed of southern manufacturing interests; and Pullman, which encompassed the manufacturing establishments and residential areas surrounding the sleeping-car company.[14]

Enabling legislation was needed from the state legislature, a majority of all resident voters had to approve the division, and the equitable distribution of public debt had to be determined. In Hyde Park the debt distribution proved the ultimate stumbling block to separation. Since the distribution of improvements was uneven across the township, there was considerable discussion about how to divide the debt. The southern sections were quick to point out that "this debt represents largely the improvements which have been made in the northern portions."[15]

Although residents in several townships seriously discussed separation in the 1880s, none followed through on proposals. Two decades later, however, the town of Cicero finally approved a separation proposal. In 1901, the imminent opening of the monumental Hawthorne Works Plant of Western Electric in Cicero and the extension of the elevated railroad line into the township sharpened the distinctions between settlements in the township, as well as fostering a sharp rise in the population. Separation was made easier because the town had a limited debt and few public improvements to divide. Residents in the township voted to separate into three distinct townships: Cicero, Berwyn, and Oak Park.[16]

City Incorporation to Improve Services and Representation

Another alternative to inadequate service provision and representation was to reincorporate as a city. Considered most seriously in Lake View and Hyde Park, the city form would bring ward- rather than village-wide representation and would also increase borrowing power. As early as 1881, when Hyde Parkers were contemplating massive water and sewerage projects, they considered city incorporation. Lake View residents also found their village form of government inadequate and considered city incorporation. In both towns, the moves failed at first. A Lake View club that opposed the move explained:

> The main reason assigned by the committee for this recommendation was on account of the action of Hyde Park, which has spent a great deal of time on the subject, and after a thorough investigation seems to have abandoned the idea. As the necessity for some change was in Hyde Park, a great deal more urgent than in Lake View the committee was of the opinion that it was best to wait and see, and if possible learn something from the action finally taken by the Hyde Park people.[17]

The debate on city incorporation continued in both towns for several years. Discussion centered not only on representation, costs, and services, but also on the appropriateness of a suburb incorporating as a city. Some opposed city incorporation, arguing that if an outlying area was so heavily settled it should annex to the center city. Others felt that city government would only bring higher taxes and more corruption. An 1869 proposal to adopt a municipal charter in Evanston brought to light many of the perceived differences between city and suburb. Opponents argued successfully: "Of what use is a city government? . . . The question was aptly answered by the Evanstonian who said that the aim of all cities was to get property up in value by constantly increasing valuation for the purpose of taxation."[18] Corruption was particularly worrisome to Hyde Park residents, who feared that "the political condition of the village will become in time like that of Chicago."[19]

Despite these fears, both Hyde Park and Lake View considered city incorporation several times. Hyde Parkers defeated the question in 1881 and 1885. An analysis of the 1885 vote showed that it was solidly defeated in the southern manufacturing districts, whose voters advocated division of the town into several villages, as well as in the north end of town, where the residential suburbs supported eventual annexation to Chicago. The question carried only in the several communities in the center of town and in small manufacturing areas in the south. Despite these defeats, city incorporation was considered again in 1887, when residents also seriously debated the question of annexation to Chicago. Critics of city incorporation by that time simply argued that it was a means "to forestall a movement for annexation to the city."[20]

Discussion of city incorporation also accompanied the annexation debate in Lake View. By 1885, almost everyone agreed that changes in both representation and service provision were necessary. In 1886, Lake View residents defeated a measure that would have annexed their township to Chicago. Months later, weary Lake View residents finally agreed on a change by voting affirmatively on city incorporation.[21]

All of these alternatives promised better representation or services but presented other problems. Although only Cicero adopted separation, it was considered numerous times in both Lake and Hyde Park. Perhaps this was because separation in these communities solved only problems with representation. Similarly, combined projects for adjoining townships addressed demands for better services but did not improve representation. The Hyde Park/Lake waterworks was the only combined project completed. Bickering between the towns, neither of which felt it was adequately represented, coupled with significant population increases, led to the dissolution of the partnership. Only city incorporation claimed to provide better representation and service provision, and even here adoption proved difficult. Fear of higher taxes and political corruption, as well as its perceived inappropriateness, defeated its adoption in most townships. Lake View reincorporated as a city, but only after all other alternatives had been roundly defeated.

The Annexation Alternative

In the alternatives discussed above, the collar townships remained discrete entities; another way to achieve better services and representation was by annexation to Chicago. Bitterly opposed by some and strongly supported by others, the annexation debate raged in most communities for years before finding resolution. Underlying this debate was the commonly held belief expressed in an 1885 *Tribune* article:

It is the history of all American municipalities that they absorb their populous suburbs. The gravitation is resistless. The ancient cities in the cininiage [sic] of Boston, proud of their charters, rich in their traditions, jealous of their neighbors, all succumbed to the inevitable. So of New York, and Philadelphia and New Orleans, and so in time of Chicago, whose limits will be extended within this generation so as to include all of Cook County worth gathering in.[22]

For those outlying residents most interested in better services, the evidence in favor of annexation was overwhelmingly apparent by the 1880s. It was generally acknowledged that improvements in serviced areas of Chicago were as good or superior to any found in outlying areas. A proponent of annexation in Jefferson explained the reasons why he foresaw the eventual absorption of his town: "Water is a necessity, but sewers are much more so, and the more water there is the more sewers are needed to carry it off. These the village is unable to furnish."[23]

Township residents found annexation to Chicago particularly appealing during the mid-1880s because the city had been rapidly extending its infrastructure. Chicagoans financed much of this work through bond issues and general funds, contrasting with the special assessments method in suburban areas. Outlying residents found not only water and sewerage extension from Chicago attractive, but also improved fire and police protection. Numerous times newspapers cited the fire that had destroyed the Lake View High School in 1885 as evidence of poor fire protection in that township.[24] Many felt not only that services were superior in Chicago but also that they were less expensive: "The people of Lake View are not getting the return on their money which they would get were they annexed to Chicago. Most of them do business in Chicago, but live in Lake View. They pay high taxes and get—what? Bad water, poor schools, worse sewerage."[25]

The projected impact of better services and perhaps higher taxes for those services on real-estate values also entered into the annexation debate. Most real-estate men thought that annexation would increase property values. One agent, dealing mainly in Hyde Park property, figured that real estate would appreciate in value at least 20 to 25 percent with annexation to Chicago.[26] Others, while not so optimistic, were in favor of annexation. Developers, like residents seeking better services, looked longingly at extension of the city infrastructures to their subdivisions.

Of course, not all developers wanted a full range of improvements. There were those who made developments beyond city improvements, out of reach of city taxes, to attract buyers of limited means. One developer who was against annexation was Samuel E. Gross. Gross argued that it would bring an increase in land values *and* taxes, which would adversely affect the chances for workingmen to own their own homes. One 1885 newspaper account explained that "he takes a benevolent view of matters. He wants to keep property cheap so that people of moderate means may be able to purchase homes."[27]

The issue of representation was also crucial to the annexation question. On one hand, many outlying residents argued that they were functionally a part of Chicago, and should be represented as such. One resident of Lake View complained, "nineteen twentieths of our people do business in Chicago. What they want to support a separate city government for is something I cannot understand."[28] Most residents of collar communities identified with the city when traveling, and this was cited as evidence of the inevitable link between Chicago and the collar townships: "If we go up to Milwaukee, we don't sign our names as coming from Austin, but we sign ourselves as coming from Chicago as we ought to be."[29]

As well as advocating metropolitan solidarity, many argued that annexation would actually foster better representation for individual communities within the collar townships. As a part of Chicago, they would be divided into wards on the basis of population, thereby increasing local representation in all the townships except Lake View, which itself had been divided into wards upon its city incorporation. A loss of township autonomy could thus bring better representation for areas within a collar township that had no direct voice in a board of trustees elected at large. The issue of better representation surfaced not only in these ways but more indirectly, in questions of local prerogative and in discussions of corruption in local government.

One issue of local prerogative that concerned outlying residents was the extension of the fire limits into annexed areas. Those limits, encompassing much of the settled area inside Chicago, prohibited frame building as a precaution against a repetition of the 1871 fire. This was a sore issue with many residents of the outlying townships, particularly those who had left the city because of this prohibition. While, on one hand, better water and fire protection were of the utmost importance to owners of frame structures in heavily settled subdivisions outside the city limits, on the other, they were afraid of an extension of the prohibition of frame buildings. It was not until 1889 that the city council explicitly exempted all new territory from the fire limits.

Another issue of local prerogative that led residents to oppose annexation was the existence of liquor prohibition ordinances in many of the collar townships. Residents were not sure that their prohibition ordinances would be honored upon annexation. This was a problem in the early years of discussion concerning annexation, but by 1889 local control on this issue had been established through city ordinance. Outlying prohibition areas would remain dry after annexation, and in fact the provision gave each precinct within Chicago the right to determine whether or not liquor would be sold in their locale. Of course, this did not dissuade opponents of annexation from continuing to use it in their arguments, playing on voters' fears of change.[30]

Residents also considered political corruption in the context of local control. Those in favor of annexation argued that the corrupt actions of local township politicians would be ended only by eliminating the governments they controlled. As one Englewood resident in favor of the annexation of Lake explained: "The Town of Lake is a well squeezed orange, and so long as there is any juice left in its chartered privileges, it will not be forsaken by the politicians and demagogs [sic], nor will their undying love for the people cease to reverberate in our ears."[31] Yet of course annexation to Chicago did not necessarily mean better local control. Many commentators were quick to point out that Chicago's municipal government was far from spotless. The *Real Estate and Building Journal* commented in 1888 that while "the residents of outside towns and villages are cursed with boodlers and want to get out somewhere and somehow," annexation to Chicago would be like jumping "from the frying pan into the fire."[32]

Even in retrospect, it is difficult to evaluate the annexation issue clearly. A whole range of factors had to be considered, including: the economies of scale involved in public improvements; the value of real estate inside and outside the city; the cost of taxes and special assessments; the differential expenses involved with schools, fire, and police forces and other services; the level of corruption and graft in the city and surrounding townships; and the level of representation desired. In each collar township, the positive or negative value of all of these factors might vary from town to town, and also over the time that annexation was being discussed.[33]

The Actual Annexation Process

As with the alternatives considered for improving government in the collar townships, annexation to Chicago was neither a simple nor a clear choice. Not only were the issues surrounding annexation controversial, but the legal and financial issues concerning consolidation were complex. Even the state legislators responsible for framing the annexation law had difficulty sorting out the process. It changed a number of times over the course of the last century.

Initially, annexation was enacted by the state legislature, upon the petition of the local government. No referendum vote was necessary. Several times before 1880, the City of Chicago requested annexations of contiguous unincorporated territory. No attempts were made to annex already incorporated territory. About twenty-five square miles of territory were added to Chicago between 1837 and 1869 simply by acts of the state legislature.[34]

Although there was tremendous population expansion into areas beyond the city limits during the 1870s, no further territory was annexed to Chicago. Instead, as has been outlined in this and preceding chapters, citizens looked to incorporated townships and villages to provide services and amenities such as those found in Chicago. Once incorporated, the annexation of outlying areas became a *considerably* more complicated process. Annexations then required the consolidation of two incorporated governments, and annexation by act of the legislature gave way to annexation only by approval of the populace within the incorporated areas involved.

It was not until 1887 that the state legislature passed an annexation bill which, according to Chicago historian Bessie Louise Pierce, "clarified various questions involved in the annexation of territory, such as the assumption of debts, the retention of prohibition ordinances, and the reformation of boundaries."[35] This bill was sponsored by supporters of annexation in Hyde Park who wanted the procedure to move as smoothly as possible. This bill required that the majority of residents, both in the area to be annexed and the area annexing, approve the move in a referendum vote. Once approval had been established by the county courts, the annexation was put in force. No further action by the state legislature was necessary. This was the basic way in which *all* future annexations of incorporated territory proceeded in Cook County.

The scope of the 1887 legislation was limited; it provided only a means by which portions of an incorporated township could annex to Chicago. Voters chose whether or not to join one of the townships within the city, not the city itself. This was due, at least in part, to controversy over a more straightforward annexation law. Savvy legislators attached this provision to a more general township reorganization bill. A majority of votes in each of the affected townships (one inside, one outside the city) triggered a consolidation.[36] The boundaries of the townships shifted, and a partial annexation resulted.

Small areas of Jefferson and Cicero townships came under an annexation vote in 1887. The first election was held in Jefferson, in the extreme southeast corner of the township near Humboldt Park. Annexation was approved and terms of settlement were reached between Chicago and the Village of Jefferson concerning the assets and debts of the section.[37] Later that same year, a successful annexation vote was taken in the easternmost section of Cicero, comprised of Central Park and portions of Brighton Park.[38]

The most heavily settled areas of Hyde Park, Lake, and Lake View also considered annexation in 1887; it was approved in Hyde Park but was defeated in Lake and Lake View. Reasons for the failure in Lake View centered on the fact that its residents wanted to give "its new city government a more extended trial." Likewise, the ring-ridden Lake Township sought city incorporation rather than annexation. Only in Hyde Park was annexation approved. There residents hoped that it would bring both better services and representation.[39]

Annexation reduced the area to be governed by the town officers, increasing representation for the areas remaining in the town. Opponents to partial annexation pointed out that the unannexed portions of the towns would be left without much of their most valuable taxable property, while assuming the problems in Chicago itself.[40]

The 1887 annexation was immediately contested in the state courts. Hyde Park officeholders—who stood to lose most of their constituents and territory—filed this contestation on a technical point: that the 1887 law was unconstitutional because it involved the consolidation of townships, not incorporated areas. In 1888, the state supreme court ruled the 1887 law unconstitutional, making all the 1887 annexations invalid, including the partial annexations in Jefferson and Cicero townships.

In 1889, the state legislature passed a law that specifically dealt with the annexation of incorporated areas. Written by proponents of annexation in the collar townships, this law led to another set of elections on the annexation of Lake, Jefferson, Lake View, Hyde Park, and the Central Park section of Cicero. Residents in Chicago voted on the issue, as well as those in these outlying areas. Those in favor of annexation banded together in the weeks before the June election to promote their cause. Their efforts were rewarded when all of the annexation measures passed. [41] The area of the city increased from 43 square miles to over 168 square miles. Chicago's population of 900,000 was increased by 225,000 in a single day.

Repercussions of Annexation

The impact of this enormous annexation on individual outlying communities varied. The experience of Ravenswood, however, provides some insight into the process. Ravenswood, to the north of Chicago in Lake View Township, was developed after the Civil War as a commuter suburb at the first outlying stop of the Northwestern Railroad. Until 1880, improvements remained basic and informal. During the 1880s, the township became more and more involved in providing services in Ravenswood, primarily through special assessments. Sewers and the paving of streets were tackled in this manner. Therefore, Ravenswood residents, while unable to make these improvements independently of the township government, were able to determine their timing. The incorporation of Lake View as a city in 1887 facilitated the assessment process, making it easier and quicker for Ravenswood residents to receive improvements.

Already used to dealing with a local government removed from their community, residents of Ravenswood were not heavily involved in the annexation debate. Some felt that annexation would improve the kinds of services they could receive through local government. In particular, the laying of sewers had been hampered by an argument between the towns of Lake View and Jefferson, and it was thought (correctly it turned out) that annexation of the whole area to Chicago would allow for the most rational system of sewer extensions.

Annexation to Chicago did not bring the immediate end of Ravenswood as a distinct entity. As in the decades when the settlement was a part of Lake View Township, it maintained an independent identity for some years after annexation. In 1898, it remained a self-described suburb:

> The constantly enlarging business interests of Chicago
> . . . has been a boon to Chicago suburbs, and Ravens-
> wood being one of the nearest, has had a very fair share
> of the increase. . . . Sometimes the claim is made that
> Ravenswood is not only the representative Chicago sub-
> urb, but also that she presents the truest type of purely
> American civilization, with characteristics unimpaired
> by foreign influence and ideas.[42]

At the same time that residents touted its attributes as a suburb, its
Chicago services were also highlighted. The end to the consideration of
Ravenswood as a suburb came not from annexation or the extension of
city services, but from the encroachment of high-density settlement in
the early twentieth century. As one turn-of-the-century resident
explained: "The smoking, clattering, hungry city of Chicago has swal-
lowed another demure village, whose first and only claim to distinction
was its remoteness from bustle."[43]

One further partial annexation took place in the remaining collar,
incorporated township of Cicero, which pointed up a remaining problem
with the 1889 annexation law. The annexation of Brighton Park and
Central Park put Austin on the border of Chicago in Cicero Township.
In April 1899, Austin was annexed to Chicago on the majority vote of
the entire township plus the majority vote of the residents of Chicago.
(A majority vote was needed in both to secure annexation.) However,
the particular area to be annexed had no special voice in the matter. In
this instance, both the township and the city voted for annexation, but
the residents in the area to be annexed, Austin, voted against the proposal.
A local paper at the time acknowledged that this vote showed "conclu-
sively that such a union is in direct opposition to the public sentiment
of the territory under consideration."[44] Contemporary discussion about
this annexation pointed to another reason beyond better representation
for the move: hostilities among communities within the incorporated
township. By 1899, Cicero residents perceived Austin as significantly
more urban than the rest of the town, and more heterogeneous. They
were willing and able to disassociate themselves from this "urbanization."
Both these characterizations also fueled the annexation move.[45] This
partial annexation was the last in the collar townships.

Annexation Beyond the Collar Townships

The year 1901 marks the end of the large incorporated town in Cook County. Hyde Park, Lake, Jefferson, and Lake View had been completely annexed to the city. Through partial annexation, portions of Cicero had also been annexed to Chicago, and the remaining area was separated into three distinct townships. These developments dramatically changed the areas bordering the city. No longer ringed by incorporated townships, incorporated villages along with unincorporated tracts composed the border to the city. These areas for the first time became potential candidates for consolidation with the city. Immediate momentum for further annexations came both from plans for the 1893 Columbian Exposition and large initial expenditures for city-service extensions into the newly annexed collar townships.[46] Chicago annexed six contiguous incorporated suburbs between 1890 and 1894 (table 27).

The annexation of Washington Heights and West Roseland in 1890, and Fernwood in 1891, illustrates the impact of these factors. Days before the 1890 annexation election, the *Chicago Tribune* commented:

> The experience of the districts that have been already annexed ought to encourage the annexationists in the three villages now concerned. They have better police protection, better protection against fire, gas, water, and all other municipal advantages. All are proud to be a part of the World's Fair City, as Washington Heights, Fernwood, and West Roseland will be after next Tuesday.[47]

While Washington Heights and West Roseland joined the city in 1890, Fernwood had literally to be boxed in before its residents voted in favor of annexation.[48]

Many residents in West Ridge were still farmers who were generally opposed to annexation on the grounds that it would increase taxes and provide services they did not want. One farm worker remembered that taxes were higher the year after annexation, and that the first improvement installed was sewers. He felt decades later that "it would have been just as good if we never went into Chicago."[49] Still, West Ridge annexed in time to become part of the World's Fair City. Another resident at the time of annexation remembered:

> The reason West Ridge annexed at the time that it did

was that there was a regular fever for it. I helped in the campaign that began about 1889 to annex territory around Chicago. People did it because the World's Fair was thought to bring prosperity to those within the city limits. They did it for the hurrah of the thing.[50]

Rogers Park, immediately to the east of West Ridge, had a more suburban orientation. It also had a wide range of home values. During the early 1890s, its village government tried to provide basic services such as sewers, water, paving, electric streetlights, and gas mains. A private company provided water for the village, and boosters claimed that the waterworks was one of the best of its capacity in the state. In 1892, plans were made to lay sewers in the western part of the village. Annexation to Chicago became an attractive alternative to providing these services independently, as the costs of village government increased during these years.[51]

After its 1893 annexation, Rogers Park residents anxiously awaited the benefits of being a part of the magical fair city. For Rogers Park, the wait was a long one. While city improvements began to arrive in Rogers Park by the turn of the century, they did not appear magically. Residents organized the Rogers Park Improvement Association, which lobbied hard for improvements from the city, including water, sewerage, and electricity. They were largely responsible for the 1905 takeover of the expensive private water company by the city.[52]

The 1893 annexation of Norwood Park also occurred because residents wanted better services. As in Rogers Park, those services did not come immediately, and residents were forced to band together to demand their due from the Chicago City Council by the early years of the twentieth century. It was decades into the twentieth century before the area considered itself transformed from a suburb to a contiguous part of the city of Chicago, and, indeed, many residents to this day consider the area more suburban than urban.[53]

Problems with Annexation

The problems faced in Norwood Park and Rogers Park were indicative of the difficulty the city had in providing services in its greatly expanded area. Hundreds of miles of water pipe, sewer mains, streets, sidewalks, and streetlights were extended into these new territories (table 28). By 1902, only Rogers Park, Norwood Park, and Austin remained outside the bounds of possible sewer and water extensions. The cost of extending improvements to these outlying areas was great, and was not matched by the taxes collected in them. In 1895 alone, the city suffered a total shortage of $6,156,269 "due to improvements necessitated by expansion as well as from inequalities in the taxation system."[54] The amount of work completed is reflected in the jump in special assessments of over ten million dollars between 1889 and 1891.[55] Many Chicagoans viewed the difficulties which the city had in providing and financing improvements during these years as a result of the fact that "the City resembles a poor parent who must provide for a large family of growing children."[56]

As these extensions strained city coffers, Chicagoans became increasingly disinterested in annexing more territory. While commentators have often represented cities as land-hungry and eager for annexation, this was *not* the case at the turn of the century in Chicago. Already in 1890, Mayor DeWitt Cregier felt that the city had "reached a limit when it will be well to defer the annexation of more territory until the ways and means can be discovered for extending necessary public improvements and building up some of the extensive areas not under municipal control."[57] This sentiment was echoed nine years later by Mayor Carter Harrison:

> Personally I am unalterably opposed to any scheme of consolidation depending for its accomplishment upon an addition to Chicago's present territorial limits. This city is to-day so spread over an extensive and unproductive territory as to render an extension of its territorial limits absolutely out of the question. Before we add to our territory we should build up and provide for what we have to-day.[58]

Very little territory was added to Chicago after 1893, while there was still much unsettled territory within the city at the turn of the century (map 12).

The city was reaching a mature stage, where the addition of unserviced areas was not appealing to a constituency that had been paying large bills for infrastructure improvements for decades. The switch from general funds to special assessments to finance sewerage extensions after

1889 indicated the growing antipathy of city residents concerning the extension of services into new areas.[59] Most city residents balked at the prospect of extending services across the newly annexed territory that were not paid for by special assessments.

As well as straining city coffers, the annexation of these new areas was a bookkeeping nightmare. The confusion which reigned concerning the debts and assets of the annexed areas took years to sort out. Problems with special assessment accounts were most severe, and were sorted out only after an outside accounting firm was called in. Hundreds of thousands of dollars were involved in the 1901 audit, including rebates due residents and uncollected assessments. In many of the annexed territories, no records were kept for special assessments for several years after annexation. Worst among these records were those for Fernwood: "The primitive methods of accounting in use in this village are best exemplified by their rebate accounts, which were kept on both sides of a number of loose sheets of paper and referred to the names of persons entitled to rebates, but gave no indication of the property in interest."[60]

It was well into the twentieth century before these annexed areas were financially integrated into the city and receiving municipal services. By that time, the number of incorporated suburbs in Cook County had increased substantially. Only a very few annexations took place to counterbalance this tendency toward incorporation. These annexations did not significantly augment either the population or the area of Chicago. The county had come to look very much as it does today: a city government at Chicago surrounded by an increasing number of suburban governments and special function districts (table 29).

Along with problems the city had in servicing annexed areas, there was a fundamental change in the form of outlying government. Until 1889, all areas adjacent to the City of Chicago were incorporated townships, each composed of many distinct settlements. The majority of settlements annexed to Chicago by 1902 came from the five incorporated collar townships (table 30). After that, the city was surrounded either by incorporated villages, composed primarily of a single settlement, or unincorporated territory. Only a very few incorporated villages ever annexed to Chicago. This shift in the forms of outlying government ended all major annexations in Chicago.[61]

Unable to respond adequately either to demands for better representation or services, the incorporated township virtually disappeared from the local government scene in Cook County. Instead, the smaller village government, embracing one settlement or a few subdivisions, responded more easily to the differential service levels fostered by developers and residents and also provided a smaller unit for representation. Developers and early commuters shaped the original suburban governments, but it was the inability of the incorporated townships to resolve their service/representational crises which solidified the hold of small incorporated villages on suburban government. The township as a failed form strikingly reveals the emerging attitudes toward, and demands on, suburban government.

Beyond Chicago

A look at other metropolitan areas indicates that similar processes were taking place in other cities across the country during the nineteenth century. Suburban governments first emerged in response to new settlement patterns. Some were successful, while others were short-lived and soon abandoned. Annexation in the nineteenth century often involved unsuccessful suburban forms.

Brooklyn, like Chicago, was originally formed from three towns and incorporated as a city in 1872.[62] The introduction of a street railway network and the opening of the Brooklyn Bridge in 1883 spurred suburban settlement in the rural townships surrounding the city. These townships, like those around Chicago, were composed of multiple settlements that competed for limited town funds. The fledgling suburban communities turned first to these rural townships with their demands for improvements. They received only limited satisfaction. In order to receive better services and representation, the four adjacent towns were annexed to Brooklyn between 1886 and 1894, leaving the boundaries of the City of Brooklyn coterminous to that of Kings County until the 1898 consolidation with New York City.[63]

In New York, the incorporated townships and the incorporated village emerged in the closing decades of the nineteenth century to serve an increasing number of suburban communities. The forms were not unlike those discussed for Chicago. As in Chicago, the contiguous townships providing suburban services were eventually annexed to the center city.[64] At the same time that the adjacent towns were being absorbed by the city, a number of outlying suburbs began to incorporate as villages. Mount Vernon, just outside the Bronx towns which annexed to New York City, incorporated in 1892 and avoided annexation. Nearby Bronxville was developed as an exclusive suburb after 1890, incorporating as a distinct village in 1898, to facilitate the orderly development of the area.[65] The end result of these annexations and incorporations was a metropolitan area composed of a central city surrounded by incorporated suburbs, much as in Chicago.

To the north, as Boston grew to metropolitan status, a similar process was taking place in the townships adjacent to the city proper, the major difference being that village incorporation was not an option in Massachusetts. Many of these outlying townships possessed a unique, independent history until the mid-nineteenth century, when commuter railroads and streetcar lines drew them into a suburban orbit. Charlestown, Cambridge, and Roxbury were among the towns that incorporated during the 1840s. Like the towns surrounding Chicago, they were composed of multiple settlements joined in a single incorporated government. For instance, the town of Cambridge was composed of at least three settlements: Old Cambridge, Cambridgeport, and East Cambridge. Some of these modified rural governments became successful suburban forms, while Boston annexed others. As outlined in the previous chapter, suburbanites also created new townships, which could more easily provide suburban services and representation.[66] In contrast to New York, Brooklyn, and Chicago, incorporated townships became the most familiar suburban form, as well as the government involved in annexations.

While the township was an important form for suburban governance in the nineteenth century (and beyond, for Boston), it played virtually no role in metropolitan areas in the south and west. For instance, the State of California did not use the township except as a judicial unit. Nor did townships exist as intermediate forms as cities like Los Angeles and San Francisco grew; instead, the county was the basic unit of local government in California. There, as in some other western and southern states, a chartered county form evolved that was employed in urban areas, where more functions were demanded of local government.[67]

The city and county of San Francisco were made coterminous in 1856, after the first spurt of urban growth. Subsequently no significant area has been annexed to San Francisco. Surrounding the city were chartered counties which absorbed further metropolitan growth. Within these counties, however, were found incorporated villages and cities. In the Los Angeles metropolitan area today, numerous chartered counties form the basis of government, with incorporated suburbs and cities—including

Los Angeles proper—serving parts of the counties.

In each metropolitan area, alternative forms of suburban governance emerged during formative periods. In Chicago, Boston, Brooklyn, and New York, the township was the form modified to serve the earliest suburbs in these metropolitan areas. Annexation provided one means by which unsuccessful suburban governments could be eliminated. In contrast, the county was the focus of adaptation in San Francisco and Los Angeles. The larger unit for organization on the West Coast aided in consolidation efforts and provided larger base units for service provision. Fewer suburban forms emerged, either successful or unsuccessful.

Implications

By looking at the forms of government which annexed to Chicago in the nineteenth century, we have seen that annexation was closely tied to maturing suburban government forms. Put simply, most annexations involved incorporated townships, an unsuccessful form of suburban governance in nineteenth-century Cook County. From the immediately preceding paragraphs it is also clear that a similar connection between large-scale annexation and transitory suburban government forms is found in other metropolitan areas. Because the forms available in other metropolitan areas were different, varying suburban forms were accepted or abandoned.

While unsuccessful suburban forms were eliminated through annexations, consolidations, and transformations, successful forms became entrenched in the metropolitan governance scene during these same years. Successful suburban government forms (in Cook County, the incorporated village or city) were able to provide the services and representation demanded by outlying residents. There, annexation was not necessary for these reasons.

It is also clear from the discussion in this chapter that the consolidation of two incorporated governments presented a myriad of problems. It was a far more complicated process than the annexation of unincorporated territory into the central city. Public improvements and debts had to be absorbed into one system. Also, suburban officeholders did not easily relinquish their power. The collar townships annexations make this clear.

In a real sense, the maturation of suburban government forms that successfully provided services and representation made the difficult road to annexation unnecessary in most respects. The "bureaucratic wall" created by suburban governments, their services, and their debts, no longer had to be attacked.

CHAPTER 7

THE SUBURB ARRIVED

The emergence of the improved subdivision on the outskirts of cities like Chicago over the second half of the nineteenth century signaled the arrival of the modern suburb. Because these improvements were new to most nineteenth-century residents, only slowly did a consensus concerning what constituted a core of basic services in outlying areas emerge. Improvements provided a means of sorting urbanites as they moved outward from city centers. A variety of improvement packages provided a crude method of class segregation that would be refined, but not substantially altered, in the twentieth century.[1]

Suburban government in Cook County evolved in both form and function in response to these increasingly homogeneous subdivisions. Real-estate interests, along with outlying residents, fostered suburban government as a means of satisfying service demands. At the same time, the ability of local government to respond to changing settlement patterns fostered further suburban growth, for suburban government provided a stability that institutionalized developers' patterns.

The entrenchment of suburban governments was perhaps most strongly exhibited in the increasing failure of annexation attempts. Annexation decelerated in Chicago, as contiguous residential growth hit the ring of incorporated villages and cities beyond the annexed incorporated townships after 1890, and came to a halt by 1930.[2] With the end to annexation debates in Chicago and other cities that had grown quickly in the late nineteenth century, reformers turned to other ways to achieve consolidation of local governments within metropolitan governments.

The growing power of suburban governments was acknowledged by their inclusion in metropolitan government schemes. Neither suburban nor city government distinctions were wholly eliminated. Some plans went so far as to advocate separate statehood for metropolitan areas like Chicago, to promote a more rational approach to government.[3] Unsuccessful in cities like Chicago, metropolitan government plans were replaced by an increasing number of metropolitan-wide special districts that provided single services to both urban and suburban governments.[4]

In a similar way, regional planning also indicated the growing acceptance of suburbs as distinct entities. The city-planning movement took hold across the country in the early decades of the twentieth century. While Burnham and Bennett's 1909 *Plan of Chicago* considered areas outside of the city limits, implicit was the idea that planning was for cities. This concept changed quickly, so that by the 1920s *regional* planning, not city planning, emerged in metropolitan areas across the country. New regional planning associations acknowledged that much of a metropolitan area was beyond the center city and expanded their planning to include urban, suburban, and even rural areas.[5]

Indications that both suburbs and their governments were entrenched forms in metropolitan areas are also found in the real-estate industry. The growing standardization of the outlying subdivison in the first decades of the twentieth century provided one such indicator. The improved subdivision became the predominant means by which real-estate developers created new residential areas across the country. By the 1920s, they had found that:

> A few years ago people were content with board and cinder sidewalks and dirt streets, plus city water in occasional cases. Today they require sidewalks, water, gas or electric lights—not always sewers, but macadam streets at least. If you are dealing with people who are living in present quarters that contain so-called city improvements, it is practically out of the question to get them to buy property, unless you can give reasonable assurance of being able to provide these same facilities.[6]

The growing interest of developers is evident in the wide variety of professional publications and conferences concerning subdivision development. In the Chicago area, a local real-estate board and special supplements in several of the daily papers provided developers with specific information about the latest trends in subdivision work. Nationally, several architectural and building journals included regular pieces concerning subdivision and building news of interest to realtors. The National Association of Real Estate Boards had by the 1920s a thriving division devoted specifically to disseminating information to homebuilders and subdividers.[7]

The segregation fostered by early improved subdivisions was refined through a variety of means. More and more developers built homes as well as installed infrastructure improvements in their subdivisions. Zoning was increasingly used by suburban communities to ensure their continued development along prescribed lines. In Cook County, at least twenty-four suburban governments adopted zoning ordinances in the 1920s, at the same time that zoning was first widely used by Chicago.[8] Both home construction before land sale and the introduction of zoning further embedded the suburban form in the metropolitan landscape.

Critical Social Scientists

The arrival of suburbs and their governments by the turn of the century did not go unnoticed by social scientists. They, too, provide a record of the institutionalization of forms. One of the first to describe the modern suburb was Adna Ferrin Weber, in his 1899 study of city growth. According to Weber, a suburb combined "at once the open air and spaciousness of the country with the sanitary improvements, comforts and associated life of the city." Weber's suburb was an area with a lower population density than the city, and was distinguished from the surrounding countryside by the existence of city improvements, comforts, and society.[9]

Suburbs were seen by many early social scientists and reformers as a means to humanizing the city. Ebeneezer Howard's garden city idea was essentially a plan for moving individuals, as well as industry, out from the city center in order to provide a more healthful environment. Like Weber, Howard called for further suburbanization (deconcentration), in order that more metropolitan residents could take advantage of the benefits of suburban living.[10]

In contrast to this positive reaction of suburbs themselves, few heralded the arrival of suburban government as a stunning achievement for modern American society. Instead, critics such as Roderick D. McKenzie viewed it as "little short of disastrous," because "every great city now has around it a metropolitan area, one with it economically and socially, but without political unity."[11] Critics blamed political fragmentation both for the inadequate provision of basic services to protect the health and safety across entire metropolitan regions, and for widely varying tax rates. Contemporary and historical commentators argued against the exclusivity of suburban government and wanted services and their costs distributed equally across a metropolitan area.

Underlying all of these criticisms was an indictment of the segregation institutionalized by suburban government.[12] This situation placed a considerable strain on the competing tensions between local control and equal opportunity. These tensions had grown considerably since the founding of the United States. The local community in preindustrial society necessarily contained a wide range of people and economic functions. The separation of work and home made possible through new industrial techniques and transportation advances fostered the separation of residential from industrial and commercial areas, as well as the creation of class-segregated neighborhoods. It was suddenly feasible for local governments to serve these class-segregated residential areas exclusively, thereby linking segregation by class, race, and ethnicity to questions of local control.

Suburban government to many of its critics was (and is) local control run amok. Suburbanites exploited the concept of local autonomy, gaining charters from state governments.[13] Local control of this sort is argued to hinder equal opportunity.[14] It remains a pressing conflict even today. Perhaps no issue illustrates the strength of the tensions as much as the school desegregation plans enacted since the 1954 Brown decisions, underscoring the importance of class and race to the discussion.[15] At the root of the debate lies the fact that, for better or worse, metropolitan residents find their housing (and choose it) segregated on the basis of class, race, and ethnicity. Because of this segregation, differential access to services can be argued as a legitimate product of local prerogative, *or* as a hindrance to equal access to services and programs within a metropolitan area.

Getting away from this indictment of suburban government in order to understand it is a difficult task. But suburban governments, as I have shown in this study, are not in themselves the problem. To say they are would be somewhat on the order of blaming the messenger for the bad news. Local government, more than any other facet of our public life, closely reflects forms of settlement and community demands. Suburban governments emerged in response to suburban settlement, which in turn was based quite clearly on the emergence of the homogeneous residential subdivision as the preferred form of real-estate development.

The problem is, then, *not* simply suburban governance, but the segregated settlement patterns fostered by nineteenth-century real-estate developers, and ultimately preferred by their customers. If suburban areas were microcosms of a city's heterogeneity, there would be little problem with suburban governments (at least in principle), especially regarding the issue of equal opportunity. Instead, the emergence of suburban governance is closely tied to the development of the homogeneous residential subdivision, which was based on differences from, not similarities to, other areas across a metropolitan area. A real-estate developer sought ways of making his subdivision especially marketable to a homogeneous group of purchasers, who made similar demands for improvements and amenities and had the means to provide them. This homogeneity of settlement did not disappear when the original developer faded from the scene. Rather, it became the basis for the future.

The critical role of the homogeneous subdivision in the emergence of suburban governments is often overlooked because few developers constructed homes in nineteenth-century subdivisions. Instead most residential construction in the United States, as in England, was the work of small builders. This has led to the misperception that the residential patterns of the nineteenth century were the result of thousands upon thousands of individual decisions.

I have stressed here that the city building process consists of two distinct procedures: the initial subdivision and improvement of a tract of land, and the actual construction of buildings. I have shown that service improvements were used in the nineteenth century to sort out suburbanites before tract housing was common. In fact, sorting began before the advent of tract housing, with sewers, water, and street improvements. Real-estate developers offered outlying residents service packages, which became more sophisticated in the twentieth century, culminating in completely planned communities.

In this context, the real criticism of suburban government becomes the fact that it was responsive to newly emerging, homogeneous subdivisions, allowing the institutionalization of segregation. Suburban governments did not *create* segregation, they responded to and then fostered it.

Varieties of Suburban Government

Another important point which I hope this study has highlighted is that there is no *one* kind of suburban government. The evolution of suburban government is not the same in other places or times. Local government traditions, settlement patterns, and the attractiveness of amenity packages shape a particularistic history in every metropolitan area across the country. Suburban governments must be defined by function rather than form.

This is clear even from the specific case of Chicago, where two kinds of suburban government emerged to cater to the needs and demands of nineteenth-century suburbanites. The transformation of the rural villages and townships into suburban governments illustrates both successful and unsuccessful adaptations made in nineteenth-century Cook County. Over the course of the nineteenth century it was found that village incorporations "fit" the communities that emerged from developers' subdivisions better than the larger township jurisdictions, but both emerged in response to similar factors.

From a cursory look at other metropolitan areas, a similar process appears to have taken place in them. Early suburbanites used local governmental forms available within their states to create suburban governments. A variety of forms emerged across the country. Of course, to understand their evolution fully, a more detailed look at settlement patterns fostered by developers and at emerging demands of residents for services and improvements is needed. Those cities, like Chicago, which saw tremendous growth in the nineteenth century faced similar circumstances.

While my findings are not directly applicable elsewhere, they point to many of the variables central to understanding the evolution of suburban government across the country. Perhaps most fundamental is the crucial role that the original forms of local government in an area play in later developments in suburban government. Each government's adaptability is determined not only by area residents but by the bounds placed on the expansion of the powers and representation of the form by state government. The state legislature, inadvertently or deliberately, made some governmental forms more responsive to suburbanization.

Flexibility in local government is most important in the period when a city is first growing quickly and initial suburbanization is taking place. Having the flexibility to provide services and respond to the demands of new suburbanites was crucial to governmental success. Once patterns were set, they were not easily changed.

The amenity orientation of outlying government reflected the role that real-estate developers played in its evolution. Over the course of the late nineteenth and early twentieth centuries, developers planned outlying subdivisions and attracted urban residents by presenting them with a variety of improvement packages. Some worked closely with nascent suburban governments to provide the services that would make their property marketable, while others worked on their own. In either case, developers brought urban services to the suburbs.

As the twentieth century unfolded, basic services became virtually ubiquitous, not only over metropolitan areas, but also in rural districts. Distinctive services remained a focal point of suburban government, though, and other amenities emerged. For instance, the development of private-school standards for suburban public schools resulted from the changing amenity orientation of suburban residents in the early twentieth century. The homogeneous subdivision remains the means by which metropolitan residents are segregated on the basis of class, ethnicity, and race. Because of the physical sorting out made possible through these subdivisions, service differentials have been, and continue to be, the hallmark of suburban communities and governments.

NOTES

Introduction

1. Adna Ferrin Weber, *The Growth of Cities in the Nineteenth Century* (Ithaca, N.Y.: Cornell University Press, 1963; originally published in 1899), was among the first social scientists to attempt a definition of a suburb. His final chapter "Tendencies and Remedies" attempted to sort through the impact of deconcentration on the city. Harlan Paul Douglass, "Suburbs," *Encyclopedia of the Social Sciences*, ed. Edwin R. A. Seligman (New York: MacMillan, 1934), p. 433, identified suburbs as fragments of cities, unable to survive independently. A more recent attempt has been made by Herbert Gans, "Urbanism and Suburbanism as Ways of Life: A Reevaluation of Definitions," in *Human Behavior and Social Processes*, ed. Arnold M. Rose (Boston: Houghton Mifflin, 1962). Gans is specifically reacting to the work of Louis Wirth on the distinctiveness of urban life. See Wirth, "Urbanism as a Way of Life," *American Journal of Sociology* 44 (July 1938): 1–24. Gans identifies the fact that little distinguishes urban neighborhoods from suburbs except for the political discreteness of suburbs.

2. Carol A. O'Connor emphasizes the fact that suburbs comprise relatively homogeneous local areas. She stresses that "differences . . . have always existed among suburbs." She is also quick to point out, however, that while individually homogeneous, as a group suburbs are quite heterogeneous. See "Sorting Out the Suburbs: Patterns of Land Use, Class and Culture," *American Quarterly* 37 (Bibliography 1985): 393.

3. Sam Bass Warner's classic study of *Streetcar Suburbs* (Cambridge: Harvard University Press, 1962) in Boston considers areas which today are seen as urban neighborhoods, but which began their existence as suburbs.

4. One such suburban community was founded by Charles Cleaver in 1851 along the Illinois Central Railroad to the south of the city, as a site for his slaughterhouse and soap factory. See Charles Cleaver, *Early Chicago Reminiscences* (Chicago: Fergus Printing Co., 1882), p. 44.

5. See Jean Block, *Hyde Park Houses* (Chicago: University of Chicago Press, 1978), p. 3. To the north of Fernwood, John Wentworth, antebellum mayor, congressman, and newspaper editor, built his retreat in an area known as Brighton. See Joseph Hamzik, "Gleanings of Archer Road" (typescript, December 1961), Chicago Historical Society, pp. 43–69.

6. Chicago was by no means atypical in this regard. There have been residents in the outlying areas of cities for thousands of years. Many were involved in garden farming or mining/processing, producing products that were marketed in the city center. Others, however, inhabited the country estates of the wealthy elites. These houses were located on the outskirts of cities—far enough away to avoid city problems but close enough for leisured men and women to travel back and forth to town. These estates had many of the amenities available in city homes, because large retinues of servants accompanied the wealthy to the country, insuring the provision of basic comforts such as heated rooms, baths, and lighting. Elite families with many servants operated as self-contained islands with regard to basic services, regardless of whether they were in the city or the countryside. Lewis Mumford, *The City in History* (New York: Harcourt, Brace, 1961), pp. 482–524.

7. By 1866, a newspaper headline for an article about towns along railroad lines up to forty miles being a "haven for homes" for Chicagoans read "Our Suburbs." *Chicago Daily Tribune,* December 31, 1866.

8. The radius of suburban settlement was expanding rapidly, and it was not clear how far suburbs would extend. For instance, the *Chicago Times* regularly ran a column titled "Suburban," which contained local news from areas outside Chicago in the decades after the Civil War. Many of the communities considered are familiar ones today, but it also contained items on communities that were far-flung from Chicago. Milwaukee, Waukegan, Racine, and Kenosha—all communities either in Wisconsin or in the far northern reaches of Illinois and at least fifty miles from the center of Chicago—were regularly included in the "Suburban" column. See *Chicago Times,* January 25, 1880, "Suburban."

9. *Chicago Daily Tribune,* September 29, 1872, "Hyde Park." The article specifically considers the settlements along the railroad in Hyde Park which had benefited from the availability of commutation tickets: Oakland, Kenwood, South Park, Woodlawn, Oakwood, South Chicago, Wildwood, Englewood, Kensington, and Cornell. All these communities had populations between 800 and 1,500.

10. Everett Chamberlin, *Chicago and Its Suburbs* (Chicago: T. A. Hungerford & Co., 874), p. 385.

11. Jon Teaford has examined the transformation of urban government as it confronted growing industrialization and modernization. Merchants gave way to speculators, businessmen, and early industrialists, while concern with wharves and markets gave way to interest in infrastructure improvements and fire and police protection. See Teaford, *The Municipal Revolution in America* (Chicago: University of Chicago Press, 1975), and *The Unheralded Triumph: City Government in America, 1870–1900* (Baltimore: Johns Hopkins Press, 1984).

12. Chicago was among the very first cities in the U.S.A. to develop a sewerage system in the years just before the Civil War. For more information on these achievements, see Jon C. Teaford, *The Unheralded Triumph,* pp. 217–50. See also: Nelson Blake, *Water for the Cities* (Syracuse: Syracuse University Press, 1968); Charles Rosenberg, *The Cholera Years* (Chicago, University of Chicago Press, 1968); and Jon A. Peterson, "The Impact of Sanitary Reform upon American Urban Planning, 1840–90," *Journal of Social History* 13 (1979): 87–88.

13. David P. Handlin, *The American Home: Architecture and Society, 1815–1915* (Boston: Little, Brown, 1979), p. 452.

14. Olmstead, Vaux and Company, "Proposed Suburban Village at Riverside, Illinois," pp. 6–7.

15. Only a few years earlier, "Hyde Park was not of much note, except as a cheap and convenient suburban residence where persons doing business in Chicago could live and be free from city taxes and the excitement of political contests." *Chicago Daily Tribune,* April 20, 1874, "Hyde Park Corporation Election."

16. In 1869, Evanston, a suburb to the north of Chicago, voted on a move to adopt a city form of government. The move was resoundingly defeated, because even though Evanstonians wanted many urban amenities, they wanted them without city government. *Chicago Times,* April 7, 1869, p. 4.

17. Among the historians who have devoted their attention to suburbs are: Kenneth T. Jackson, *The Crabgrass Frontier: The Suburbanization of the United States* (New York: Oxford University Press, 1985); Zane Miller, *Suburb: Neighborhood and Community in Forest Park, Ohio* (Knoxville: University of Tennessee Press, 1976); Henry Binford, *The First Suburbs:*

Residential Communities on the Boston Periphery, 1815–1860 (Chicago: University of Chicago Press, 1985); Sam Bass Warner, *Streetcar Suburbs* (Cambridge: Harvard University Press, 1962); Carol O'Connor, *A Sort of Utopia: Scarsdale, 1891–1981* (Albany: State University of New York, 1983); and Michael Ebner, *Creating Chicago's North Shore: A Suburban History* (forthcoming, University of Chicago Press).

18. Jackson, like others before him, accepts suburban government as a largely static form, accepted or rejected by outlying residents in varying degrees. He devotes a chapter to the failure of annexation movements in the twentieth century. Implicit in this discussion is a stable set of governmental forms that can be rejected or accepted by a changing society. Jackson does acknowledge, however, the growing ease of incorporation of outlying areas and the rapidly improving ability of suburban governments to meet the service demands of residents, both factors indicating that local government is responsive to societal change and urban growth. See pp. 138–156.

19. Michael Ebner, in a 1979 review article on urban government, complained that historical research was missing "at the nexus of municipalism, urbanism, and the emergent modernization process." Ebner reiterated Eric Lampard's earlier complaint: "Precisely what is lacking is a good political history of American cities . . . political in the larger sense, not just elections and running for office, who governs, but the nature of urban government." Their challenge, if conceived a bit more broadly to include all government found within metropolitan areas, is to tie the development of metropolitan government to the modernization and urbanization that transformed nineteenth-century society. See Ebner, "Urban Government in America, 1776–1876," *Journal of Urban History* 5 (1979): 512.

Chapter 1

1. Kenneth T. Jackson, *The Crabgrass Frontier* (New York: Oxford University Press, 1986), chaps. 2, 4–6, provides an overview of nineteenth century suburban growth. Case studies include: Sam Bass Warner, *Streetcar Suburbs,* (Cambridge: Harvard University Press, 1962), especially pp. 54–58; Henry Binford, *The First Suburbs* (Chicago: University of Chicago Press, 1985); Henry D. Shapiro and Zane L. Miller, *Clifton: Neighborhood and Community in an Urban Setting* (Cincinnati: The Laboratory in American Civilization, 1976), esp. pp. 30–32; and Robert Fogelson, *The Fragmented Metropolis* (Cambridge: Harvard University Press, 1967), esp. chaps. 5, 8. Miller has also explored the role of transportation in residential growth in the whole of Cincinnati. See *Boss Cox's Cincinnati* (New York: Oxford University Press, 1968), esp. chaps. 1–3. Binford challenges the notion that transportation improvements were necessary for suburban growth in the antebellum Boston suburbs of Cambridge and Somerville.

2. This chapter builds on the work of other historians, especially: Harold M. Mayer and Richard C. Wade, *Chicago: Growth of a Metropolis* (Chicago: University of Chicago Press, 1969); Bessie Louise Pierce, *History of Chicago,* 3 vols., (Chicago: University of Chicago Press, 1937–57); Louis Carroll Wade, *Chicago's Pride: The Stockyards, Packingtown, and Environs in the Nineteenth Century* (Urbana: University of Illinois Press, 1987); Michael Ebner, *Creating Chicago's North Shore: A Suburban History* (forthcoming, University of Chicago Press); Barbara Mercedes Posadas, "Community Structures of Chicago's Northwest Side, The Transition from Rural to Urban, 1830–1889," (Ph.D. diss., Northwestern University, 1976); Homer Hoyt, *One Hundred Years of Land Value in Chicago* (Chicago: University of Chicago Press, 1933); and Helen Monchow, *Seventy Years of Real Estate Subdividing in the Region of Chicago* (Evanston: Northwestern University Press, 1939).

3. For further description of life at Fort Dearborn, see Jacqueline Peterson, "Wild Chicago: The Formation and Destruction of a Multiracial Community on the Midwestern Frontier," in *The Ethnic Frontier,* ed. Melvin H. Holli and Peter d'A. Jones (Grand Rapids, Mich.: William B. Eerdmans Publishing Co., 1977), pp. 26–71.

4. Chicago was chosen as the county seat in 1831, and the U.S. Land Office for the region was opened there in 1835. Chicago began to develop as a port after the federal government agreed to finance harbor improvements there in 1834. Pierce, 1: 90–92.

5. For more information, see Harold M. Mayer, "The Launching of Chicago: The Situation and the Site," *Chicago History* 9 (Summer 1980): 68–80, and James A. Clifton, "The Last Great Indian Treaty in the Old Northwest," *Chicago History* 9 (Summer 1980): 86–96.

6. Mayer and Wade, p. 20.

7. John Silk Buckingham, as cited in Bessie Louise Pierce, *As Others See Chicago* (Chicago: University of Chicago Press, 1933), p. 89.

8. Residential segregation increased in Chicago between 1837 and 1850. For more information, see Ann Durkin, "Housing and Residential Patterns in Early Chicago, 1830–1850" (seminar paper, University of Chicago, 1979).

9. As well, the middle decades of the nineteenth century witnessed a growing interest in nature on the part of urban intellectuals. Leaders of this arcadian movement included Ralph Waldo Emerson and William Cullen Bryant, who "travelled near to home and not alone and were articulate commentators on the tamed wilderness around them." See Peter J. Schmitt, *Back to Nature: The Arcadian Myth in Urban America* (New York: Oxford University Press, 1969), p. 22. The writings of Andrew Jackson Downing emphasized the moral advantages of country living as the ideal environment for the family. Downing wrote that country living was not only more healthful and pleasant than city living, but also more morally sound . See Downing, *The Architecture of Country Houses* (New York: D. Appleton & Co., 1850), pp. 257–70.

10. The information on Brighton Park is taken from three sources: A. T. Andreas, *History of Cook County* (Chicago: A. T. Andreas, 1884), pp. 796–98; Joseph Hamzik, "Gleanings of Archer Road" (typescript, Chicago Historical Society, December 1961), pp. 43–69; and *The Kelly Community* (Chicago: Thomas Kelly High School, 1938), passim. The information on Wentworth is from Hamzik, pp. 46–47.

11. Hamzik, pp. 45–49; Andreas, p. 497.

12. *Chicago Democratic Press,* October 29, 1854, as in Hamzik, p. 46. It is well to keep in mind that Wentworth, an investor in this venture, was also the publisher and editor of this newspaper.

13. Louise Carroll Wade devotes several chapters to exploring the growth of stockyards and meatpacking, as well as adjoining communities. See *Chicago's Pride,* especially chapters 2, 3, 5, 11–13. Some of this settlement was the result of omnibus and horsecar lines, but Chicago was still primarily a walking city. In 1860, 70 percent of the city's population lived within two miles of the downtown area. The population within a four-mile radius of State and Madison was 112,000; within a two-mile radius, 79,000. See Jerome Fellman, "Pre-Building Growth Patterns of Chicago," *Annals of the Association of American Geographers* 47 (March 1957): 74; also Hoyt, p. 66.

14. In 1850, the population of Cook County outside of Chicago was 14,000. By 1860, this population had reached close to 33,000.

15. For Palatine, see Andreas, *History of Cook County* (Chicago: A. T. Andreas, 1884), p. 830; for Barrington, see Bateman, p. 773; for Jefferson, see Everett Chamberlin, *Chicago*

and Its Suburbs (Chicago: T. A. Hungerford, 1874), p. 447.

16. Hamzik, pp. 48–61. At the turn of the century, it was already closely tied to the city center by streetcar lines. Some residents continued to farm, others worked as brick makers (a traditional fringe occupation), while an increasing number worked for the railroads and in small local factories. A business directory published in 1906 shows a variety of businesses, many of which catered to residents who worked in local industry or commuted to jobs closer to the city. Among those listed were 13 grocers, 2 undertakers, 18 liquor dealers, 3 real-estate dealers, 2 plumbers, 8 contractors, 3 dry goods store owners and 2 dealers of flour, feed, and coal. The area was on the verge of a building boom, which would fill in much of the vacant land and tracts used for farming. With about 1,000 dwelling units in 1899, there would be over 6,000 by 1920, and over 10,000 by the 1929 crash. By then, it was hard to imagine that only a little under a hundred years before the area had been open prairie. *The Kelly Community,* passim, and Louis Wirth and and Eleanor H. Bernert, eds., *Local Community Fact Book of Chicago* (Chicago: University of Chicago Press, 1949).

17. S. Ella Wood Dean, *Kay Wood's Chicago* (Paris: Imprimere Le Moil and Pascaly, 1930).

18. Chamberlin, p. 357.

19. Andrew Yox, "Hyde Park Politics, 1861–1919," *Hyde Park History,* no. 2, 1980, p. 2.

20. *Chicago Press Tribune,* July 4, 1860, "Hyde Park," p. 1.

21. See Jean Block, *Hyde Park Houses* (Chicago: University of Chicago, 1978), p. 3. Similar efforts were made to the north of the city a few years before Cornell's, in Hyde Park. The Lake View House, to the north of the city along the lakeshore, was built in 1854. See Vivien Marie Palmer, "The Primary Settlement as a Unit of Urban Growth and Organization" (Ph.D. diss., University of Chicago, 1932), p. 122, and A. T. Andreas, *History of Cook County,* pp. 708–9.

22. As well as building for themselves, several wealthy Chicagoans also bought extensive outlying tracts with the intention of subdividing them into lots suitable for summer estates or more modest cottages. To the north of the city, near the Lake View House, Joseph Waller subdivided an area named Buena Park in the late 1850s. Just north of the city, near Fullerton and Clark, an area known as Wrightwood was subdivided by the heirs of John S. Wright in 1860 as resort property. See Palmer, "The Primary Settlement," pp. 145–46, and Block, pp. 4–10.

23. "Our Suburbs," *Chicago Tribune,* December 31, 1866.

24. James B. Runnion, *Out of Town* (Chicago: The Western News Company, 1869), p. 50.

25. "Cheap Transportation," *Real Estate and Building Journal,* February 12, 1876, p. 141, and February 26, 1876, p. 186.

26. "Maywood," *The Landowner,* July 1869, p. 4.

27. "Englewood," *The Landowner,* August 1869, p. 37.

28. Runnion, p. 15. Other sources on Ravenswood include Chamberlin, pp. 370–71; Andreas, pp. 712–16; Helen Zattenberg, *Old Ravenswood and Lake View* (Chicago: Ravenswood-Lake View Historical Association, 1941); and the collection of typescript descriptions by early residents and newspaper clippings compiled by the Ravenswood Lake View Historical Association, Special Collections, Hild Regional Public Library.

29. Chamberlin, p. 370.

30. The 1869 figures were supplied by Mrs. Alben Young, "Family and Social Life of Early Ravenswood" (typescript, 1935), Ravenswood Historical Collection, Hild Regional Public Library, Chicago. Mrs. Young came to Ravenswood as a young girl in 1873. The 1874 figures are from Chamberlin, p. 370.

31. Chamberlin, p. 370.

32. This was also the case for several of the settlements in Jefferson Township. One of the largest communities in the township was at the market town called Jefferson, in the northwest corner of the township. It was at the nexus of several roads and a station of the Northwestern Railroad by the early 1870s. *The Landowner* reported that by 1870 Jefferson had been transformed into "one of our regular suburbs" through the interest of capitalists who had improved its land as suburban residence property (see *The Landowner,* February 1879, p. 40). Of course, praise for suburban development from *The Landowner* was only slightly above self-advertisement, since the publication appears to have been controlled by real-estate interests in Chicago.

33. Information about Glenview comes primarily from: Isabel Ernst, ed., *Roots: A Glenview Bicentennial* (Glenview: Glenview Bicentennial Commission, 1976); Glenview Area Historical Society, *Glenview at 75* (Melrose Park, Ill: Union Press, 1974); A. T. Andreas, *History of Cook County,* pp. 868–70; and newspaper collections, interview files, and other materials of the Glenview Area Historical Society. Kennicott quote from *Roots,* p. 6.

34. Local History File, biographical information on early residents, compiled by their descendants 1971–73, Glenview Public Library.

35. The area was known first as South Northfield and then as Oak Glen until 1895, when the village name was changed to Glenview.

36. Nicholas Haupt, an early farmer, spent much of his time during the 1860s "on the road to and from Chicago, as they improved their opportunities in that market." Local History File, typescript of an article in the *Glenview View,* June 13, 1925, on Nicholas Haupt and his family, Glenview Historical Society.

37. *Glenview at 75,* n.p., "Early Communication and Travel." The commute in the 1890s took one hour each way.

38. *Roots: A Glenview Bicentennial,* pp. 39–40.

39. *Glenview at 75,* remembrances of Miss Gladys Blackman, unpaginated.

40. Taken from typescript by Fred Homan identifying the buildings in Glenview in 1903. Compiled in January 1973. Glenview History Files, Glenview Public Library.

41. Anne Lunde, "Early Families Learned Different Sense of 'Community' in Monroe Precinct," *The Review,* February 29, 1985, p. 16. This article was one in a series of twenty-four on the history of Norwood Park, published in its local newspaper in conjunction with a survey by the Commission on Chicago Historical and Architectural Landmarks. Other sources on Norwood Park include: Andreas, pp. 481–90; Chamberlin, pp. 448–51; and Edward T. Scholl, *Seven Miles of Ideal Living* (Berwyn, Ill.: Norman King, Co., 1957).

42. Scholl, pp. 64–65.

43. Elizabeth K. Burns, "Subdivision Activity on the San Francisco Peninsula: 1860–70," *Yearbook of the Association of Pacific Coast Geographers* 39 (1977): 17–39, points out a similar progression for the San Francisco peninsula.

44. Barbara Posadas, "Community Structures of Chicago's Northwest Side: The Transition from Rural to Urban, 1836–1889" (Ph.D. diss., Northwestern University, 1976), pp. 108, 132.

45. Advertisement for Irving Park, *Real Estate and Building Journal,* March 29, 1873, p. 6. The most expensive home in the area remained Race's, which was valued around $20,000. See *The Landowner,* July 1869, p. 7.

46. Mrs. Louisa Roberts, a resident of Grand Crossing for nearly sixty years, interviewed

in February 1928. History of Grand Crossing, Document #3, Local Community Documents, Vivien Marie Palmer, compiler, Chicago Historical Society.

47. Mrs. J. Keller, Born in Grand Crossing in 1883, interviewed in February 1928, History of Grand Crossing, Document #4, Local Community Documents, Vivien M. Palmer, compiler, Chicago Historical Society.

48. Everett Chamberlin, *Chicago and Its Suburbs,* pp. 357–59. The plat filed in 1871 bore the name Cornell.

49. D. H. Horne, *History of Grand Crossing* (Cleveland: Nevins Steam Printing House, 1876), p. 9.

50. *Chicago Daily News,* November 14, 1930, "Eleven Mile House," as in Box 2, Roseland Community Collection, Special Collections, Chicago Public Library. A variety of interviews, reminiscences, newspaper clippings, and typescript histories are found in the Roseland Community Collection.

51. Lewis Sprietsma, "Roseland Community Study" (typescript, June 1938), Box 5, Roseland Community Collection, Special Collections, Chicago Public Library. Roseland was originally known as High Prairie.

52. *Onze Toekomst (The Holland-American Weekly)* (Chicago) 48, no. 6 (February 5, 1941), Roseland Community Collection, Box 5, Special Collections, Chicago Public Library. The translator for the English version is not given.

53. Ibid. Also Wirth and Bernert, "Roseland," unpaginated.

54. *Onze Toekomst* (Chicago) 48, no. 6 (February 5, 1941).

55. Harry Eenigenburg, "The Calumet Region and Its Early Settlers" (typescript, 1935), pp. 26–27, Box 4, Roseland Community Collection, Special Collections, Chicago Public Library. Eenigenburg's parents were early Dutch settlers in the region.

56. Sprietsma identifies an 1882 migration of a group of Roseland farmers to South Dakota after their lands were purchased for residential and industrial purposes and speculation.

57. Anne E. Dannegar, *Early Austin from Its Beginnings until the Time of Annexation to the City of Chicago, 1899* (Austin: Austin Friends of the Library, 1944), pp. 3–8. Danneger was the assistant librarian at the Austin Branch of the Chicago Public Library, which during the 1940s was the center for a local historical society. The files from this organization, including clipping files of local newspapers, are now a part of the Austin Community Collection, Special Collections, Chicago Public Library.

58. Ibid.

59. Chamberlin, p. 424.

60. *Austinite,* December 26, 1924, Box 4, Austin Community Collection, Special Collections, Chicago Public Library.

61. A. T. Andreas, *History of Chicago* (Chicago: A. T. Andreas, 1887), 2: 119–21. See also Hoyt, p. 295. He estimated that the range of settlements was approximately one hour via any means of transportation from the place of work to the place of residence. Therefore the settlement radius was 3 miles for those walking, 6 miles with horsecars, 12 miles with electric and cable cars, and 25 to 30 miles for the elevated and steam railroads.

62. "Cheap Transportation," *Chicago Tribune,* December 1, 1873, p. 3.

63. Ibid.

64. Wages for unskilled workers during this period reached a high in 1872 of $25 per week and fell to $9 per week at the bottom of the depression in 1879. See Bessie Louise Pierce, 3: 240.

65. Block, p. 81; and Wirth and Bernert, "Hyde Park," unpaginated.

66. Block, pp. 33–34, and passim.

67. Arthur B. Tebbets and Frank M. Simons, *History of Ravenswood* (Chicago: The Mirror Publishing Company, 1898), p. 9.

68. "Ravenswood One of First Subdivisions," *Chicago Tribune,* October 6, 1929, p. 1, as in the typescript of John B. Stone, "Ravenswood Now Only a Memory," Ravenswood Historical Society Collection, Hild Regional Branch, Chicago Public Library.

69. Wirth and Bernert, *Local Community Fact Book of Chicago,* "Uptown," unpaginated.

70. Mrs. Lyman A. Martin, resident of Ravenswood from 1898, Document #60, History of Uptown, vol. 2, Local Community Documents, Vivien Marie Palmer, compiler, Chicago Historical Society.

71. The growth in Norwood Park reflected similar developments in communities surrounding it, and by 1930 the boundaries of these settlements were blurred. See Scholl, pp. 73, 83; Anne Lunde, "Public Transportation Adds Street Car Service Along Milwaukee Avenue Corridor," *The Review,* June 19, 1985, p. 14; and "Community Definitions Change as Area Enters First Decades of Twentieth Century," *The Review,* July 10, 1985, p. 16; and Wirth and Bernert, "Norwood Park," unpaginated.

72. Wirth and Bernert, "Austin," unpaginated.

73. Z. T. Egartner, student at the University of Chicago, 1924, History of Grand Crossing, Document #1, Local Community Documents, Chicago Historical Society.

74. Mrs. J. Keller, born in Grand Crossing in 1878, interviewed in February 1928, History of Grand Crossing, Document #4, Local Community Documents, Chicago Historical Society.

75. Andreas, *History of Cook County,* p. 865.

76. Harvey was named for Turlington Harvey, but it appears that Harvey Hopkins, the owner of the Hopkins Mower Company may also have been an intended namesake. See First National Bank of Harvey, *History, The City of Harvey, 1890–1962,* (Harvey, Ill.: n.p., 1962), pp. 14–16. See also *The Town of Harvey, Illinois* (Harvey, Ill.: Harvey Land Association, 1892), pp. 3–4.

77. Recollections of Horace Holmes, who came to Harvey from Missouri with his family in 1892. *History, City of Harvey,* p. 32. See also pp. 15–37. Also *The Town of Harvey, Illinois,* frontispiece for the quotes on success and prosperity.

78. Monchow, p. 44.

79. Brookfield Area Diamond Jubilee, *The History of Brookfield* (Brookfield, Ill.: Brookfield Area Diamond Jubilee, 1968).

80. Ibid.

81. A problem faced by a number of Chicago suburbs that were expanding during the 1890s was the large number of lots which had been sold to nonresidents, particularly during the fair year. This was clearly a problem in Harvey and was shared by Brookfield, according to a local history: "Many buyers apparently went back home and forgot all about Grossdale (Brookfield)." This sort of speculative buying held up both settlement of and improvements in these suburban towns, particularly because local governments installed them only after property owners raised special assessments. It could easily take years for properties to be confiscated due to delinquent taxes and assessments. See *Brookfield Area Diamond Jubilee,* unpaginated.

82. For a more detailed discussion on the creation of Kenilworth, see Ebner, pp. 171–81, and Mary Corbin Sies, "American Country House Architecture in Context: The Suburban

Ideal of Living in the East and the Midwest, 1877–1917" (Ph.D. diss., University of Michigan, 1987). See also Anne Higginson Spicer, *Kenilworth: The First Fifty Years* (Kenilworth, Ill.: n.p., 1947), and Colleen Browne Killner, *Joseph Sears and Kenilworth* (Kenilworth, Ill.: Kenilworth Historical Society, 1969).

83. See Appendix 1 for more details on how these communities were chosen.

84. History of Cook County Folder, A. T. Andreas Collection, Manuscripts, Chicago Historical Society. Also A. T. Andreas, *History of Cook County*, pp. 631, 814–15.

85. As a close neighbor of DesPlaines, Riverview had few market functions. Background on DesPlaines and Riverview can be found in DesPlaines Historical Society, *DesPlaines Historical Quarterly, 1939–1944* (mimeographed), passim.

86. Runnion, publishers note, p. i.

Chapter 2

1. A British observer James Bryce claimed in 1888 that "there is no denying that the government in cities is the one conspicuous failure of the United States." Progressive urban reformers continued this attack, leveling particularly virulent attacks against the boss politics and corruption of the era. The standard account of city government of the late nineteenth century, Ernest S. Griffith's *A History of American City Government: The Conspicuous Failure, 1870–1900* (New York: Praeger, 1974), continued this indictment. Only recently have the accomplishments of the era been acknowledged. See Jon Teaford, *The Unheralded Triumph: City Government in America, 1870–1900* (Baltimore: Johns Hopkins Press, 1984), esp. chap. 1; Harold L. Platt, *City Building in the New South: The Growth of Public Services in Houston, Texas, 1830–1915* (Philadelphia: Temple University Press, 1983); Eugene Moehring, "Space, Economic Growth and the Public Works Revolution in New York," in *Infrastructure and Urban Growth in the Nineteenth Century*, Essays in Public Works History, no. 14, December 1985, pp. 29–59; and Joel A. Tarr, "Building the Urban Infrastructure in the Nineteenth Century, An Introduction," in *Infrastructure and Urban Growth in the Nineteenth Century*, Essays in Public Works History, no. 14, December 1985, pp. 61–85. Bryce qoute as in Teaford, p. 1.

2. Schools and fire and police protection were other areas of municipal expansion during these years, but their impact on the physical distinction between urban and rural life was less dramatic, and so less important to the story at hand.

3. James C. O'Connell, "Technology and Pollution: Chicago's Water Policy, 1833–1930" (Ph.D. diss., University of Chicago, 1980), p. 22.

4. William Ferguson, a Scottish scientist and author, visited Chicago in 1855. As quoted in Bessie Louise Pierce, *As Others See Chicago* (Chicago: University of Chicago Press, 1933), p. 149.

5. Hugo S. Grosser, *Chicago: A Review of Its Governmental History* (Chicago: n.p., 1906), p. 10, and Faith Fitzgerald, "Growth of Municipal Activities in Chicago, 1833 to 1875" (Ph.D. diss., University of Chicago, 1933), p. 155.

6. Fitzgerald, p. 38. For boosters in other cities, see Alan J. Artibise, "Boosterism and the Development of Prairie Cities, 1871–1913," in Artibise, ed., *Town and City* (Regina, Sasketchewan: Canadian Plains Research Center, 1981), pp. 209–36.

7. Michael Frisch, *Town into City: Springfield, Massachusetts 1840–1880 and the Meaning of Community* (Cambridge: Harvard University Press, 1972), p. 159. The quote was taken from an article in the *Springfield Republican* following the Civil War.

8. Stanley K. Schultz and Clay McShane, "To Engineer the Metropolis: Sewers, Sanitation and City Planning in Late Nineteenth Century America," *Journal of American History* 65 (1978): 389–411; and Anthony Sutcliffe, "The Growth of Public Intervention in the British Urban Environment during the Nineteenth Century: A Structural Approach," in *The Structure of Nineteenth Century Cities,* ed. James H. Johnson and Colin C. Pooley (New York: St. Martin's Press, 1982), pp. 107–24.

9. For a concise account of these achievements, see Teaford, pp. 217–50. See also: Nelson Blake, *Water for the Cities* (Syracuse, N.Y.: Syracuse University Press, 1968); Charles Rosenberg, *The Cholera Years* (Chicago: University of Chicago Press, 1968); and Jon A. Peterson, "The Impact of Sanitary Reform Upon American Urban Planning, 1840–90," *Journal of Social History* 13 (1979): 87–88.

10. A. T. Andreas, *History of Cook County,* p. 358. See also Samuel Edwin Sparling, *Municipal History and Present Organization of the City of Chicago* (Madison: University of Wisconsin, 1898), pp. 17–18, and Hugo S. Grosser, *Chicago: A Review of Its Governmental History from 1837 to 1906* (Chicago: Municipal Information Bureau, 1906), pp. 1–2.

11. A. T. Andreas, *History of Chicago* (Chicago: A. T. Andreas, 1884), 1: 177–78.

12. Fitzgerald, p. 254, and Sparling, pp. 111–30.

13. For the relationships of cities and their state legislatures in other cases, see Hendrik Hartog, *Public Property and Private Property, The Corporation of New York in American Law* (Chapel Hill: University of North Carolina Press, 1983), pp. 85–86, 193–95, 206–07; and Edwin A. Gere, Jr., "Dillon's Rule and the Cooley Doctrine," *Journal of Urban History* 8, no. 3 (May 1982): 271–98.

14. Edmund J. James, *The Charters of the City of Chicago* (Chicago: University of Chicago Press, 1898), pp. 80–81.

15. Bessie Louise Pierce, *History of Chicago* (Chicago: University of Chicago Press, 1933–57) 2: 308–12; 3: 303–6.

16. Pierce, 2: 312–15; 3: 307–9.

17. Pierce, 2: 391–96; 3: 381–90.

18. The form was chosen more in response to the limited power granted the city under its 1851 charter with regard to water provision than in an attempt to bypass city control. Andreas, *History of Cook County,* pp. 186–87; O'Connell, pp. 13–14.

19. McAlpine had apprenticed on the Erie Canal. See O'Connell, p. 14, and McAlpine, *Report Made to the Water Commissioners of the City of Chicago on Supplying the City with Water* (Chicago: City of Chicago, 1851).

20. Board of Water Commissioners, *Ninth Semi-Annual Report* (Chicago: City of Chicago, 1856), p. 15. *Industrial Chicago,* vol. 2: *The Building Interests* (Chicago: Goodspeed Publishing Company, 1891), pp. 309–10, gives the 1856 water rates for Chicago. The rates ranged from $5 to $28 per year for dwelling units determined by street frontage. There was an additional $3 yearly charge for bathing tubs or water closets. The charges for saloons or groceries ranged anywhere from $6 to $100.

21. Chicago Board of Public Works, *Eleventh Annual Report* (Chicago: City of Chicago, 1872), p. 16; and Chicago Department of Public Works, *Third Annual Report* (Chicago: City of Chicago, 1878), p. 10. In 1878, there was a $51,718.60 surplus and 307 water bonds were retired. The water system was administered by a number of different administrative bodies over the nineteenth century—including first the Chicago Board of Public Works and later the Chicago Department of Public Works. See pp. 15–16 for more information on this transition.

22. Chicago Board of Public Works, *Third Annual Report* (Chicago: City of Chicago, 1864), p. 5.

23. Board of Water Commissioners, *Ninth Semi-Annual Report*, 1856, p. 7.

24. Louis P. Cain, *Sanitation Strategy for a Lakefront Metropolis* (DeKalb, Ill.: Northern Illinois University Press, 1978).

25. Mayor Carter H. Harrison, as quoted in the *Chicago Tribune*, March 1, 1882.

26. Chicago Department of Public Works, *Fourth Annual Report* (Chicago: City of Chicago, 1879), p. 99.

27. Department of Public Works, *Fourth Annual Report*, 1879, p. 99. Permits for drain connection cost around $2.00 in 1872; and close to half a million dollars was collected in water rents in that year, Board of Public Works, *Eleventh Annual Report*, 1872, pp. 119–20.

28. Chicago Board of Public Works, *First Annual Report* (Chicago: City of Chicago, 1862), p. 48. The owners of rented buildings composed the group that was, however, subject most heavily to the scrutiny of the Department of Health's Tenement House Inspectors who by the late 1870s were making house-by-house checks and enforcing drain, garbage, and water ordinances. See Sparling, pp. 125–28.

29. For instance, in 1864, 222 property owners were ordered to connect private drains from their property to the sewer mains, *Third Annual Report*, 1864, p. 53. See also *Industrial Chicago*, 2: 167.

30. Chicago Board of Public Works, *Fifth Annual Report* (Chicago: City of Chicago, 1866), p. 16.

31. *Chicago Tribune*, March 18, 1871. The change ultimately came with the massive annexation of 1889, which turned the city finally to making sewer extensions by special assessment.

32. During the early years of the city corporation, Chicagoans assumed that the liability for accidents lay with those involved in the accident or on abutting property owners. A series of court decisions, however, made it clear by the 1850s that the city was liable for accidents caused by poorly maintained or nonexistent streets or sidewalks. See "City News," *Chicago Daily News*, June 8, 1858, p. 3.

33. "Our Heavy Assessments," *Chicago Press Tribune*, November 19, 1859; Grosser, p. 24; Fitzgerald, pp. 166–67.

34. "Paving Streets By Private Contract," *Chicago Tribune*, September 5, 1875.

35. "Scammon as a Taxpayer," *Chicago Tribune*, July 20, 1872.

36. Board of Public Works, *Eleventh Annual Report*, 1872, pp. 8–9.

37. Department of Public Works, *Second Annual Report*, 1878, p. 26.

38. *Chicago Daily Times*, September 8, 1857, contained in notes on the council meeting an example of the owners on a street receiving permission to do their own paving. Also *Chicago Daily Times*, April 12, 1855, reported that the property owners on Wells Street investigated and found a lower bid for macadamizing their street than that given by the city appointed contractor.

39. For example, see "The City," *Chicago Tribune*, January 6, 1862; *Chicago City Council Proceedings*, April 5, 1858, p. 5; and *Chicago Daily Times*, May 2, 1856, p. 2.

40. For examples of these situations, see *Chicago Daily Tribune*, April 12, 1855, September 20, 1858.

41. Fitzgerald, appendix A; Andreas, p. 56.

42. *Chicago Daily Times*, August 28, 1857.

43. *Chicago Tribune,* June 7, 1876, p. 2.

44. See Christine Rosen, *The Limits of Power* (New York: Cambridge University Press, 1986), for a later-day reaffirmation of this progressive approach.

45. The study of Charles T. Yerkes and local transportation in the closing decades of the nineteenth century point up time and time again how Yerkes "greased the wheels" of legislation favorable to his traction companies. Similar charges have been made with regard to gas franchises in the city and suburbs. See Homer Charles Harlan, "Charles Tyson Yerkes and the Chicago Transportation System" (Ph.D. diss., University of Chicago, 1975), pp. 187–223.

46. "Wasting Public Money," *Chicago Tribune,* June 22, 1884.

47. Citizens Association of Chicago, *Annual Report* (Chicago: Citizen's Association of Chicago, 1885).

48. *Chicago Sunday Times,* February 1, 1880, p. 10.

49. *Chicago Tribune,* June 18, 1885.

Chapter 3

1. Aspects of the changes in homes have been explored by a number of historians. Among them: David P. Handlin, *The American Home, Architecture and Society, 1815–1915* (Boston: Little, Brown, 1979); Alan Gowans, *The Comfortable House* (Cambridge: MIT Press, 1987); and Gwendolyn Wright, *Building the Dream: A Social History of Housing in America* (New York: Pantheon, 1981). By and large, however, these authors have not moved beyond homes to the implications of these changes for settlement patterns and local government.

2. Real Estate Account Books, vols. 5 and 7, Potter Palmer Papers, Chicago Historical Society.

3. Siegfried Giedion, *Mechanization Takes Command* (New York: Oxford University Press, 1948), pp. 684–711.

4. Alex W. Murray, "The Sanitation of Cities: Essay Assigned to Chicago Master Plumbers' Association by the National Association," *The Inland Architect and Builder* 3, 6 (July 1884): 76.

5. Handlin, pp. 459–65. The earth closet was one alternative to the water closet proposed by the sanitarian George Waring and others during the second half of the nineteenth century, but it did not gain public support.

6. For more information on the extension of gas for lighting see Handlin, pp. 473–74.

7. A. E. Kennelly, "Electricity in the Household," *Scribner's Magazine* 7, 1 (January 1890): 102–15.

8. *Industrial Chicago: The Building Interests* (Chicago: Goodspeed Publishing Co., 1891), 2: 272, 300–1, and Helen Campbell, *Household Economics* (New York: G. P. Putnam and Sons, 1896), pp. 72–73.

9. Handlin, pp. 475–80.

10. *The Home Guide* (Chicago: J. Fairbanks, 1878).

11. Campbell, p. 77.

12. Ellen Richards, *The Cost of Shelter* (New York: John Wiley & Sons, 1905), p. 84. See also *The Cost of Living* (New York: John Wiley & Sons, 1905), pp. 66–67. Richards was an instructor of sanitary chemistry at the Massachusetts Institute of Technology.

13. Richards, *The Cost of Living*, p. 57.

14. See Gervase Wheeler, *Homes for the People* (New York: Scribner, 1858), p. 304. Also Andrew Jackson Downing, *The Architecture of Country Houses* (New York: D. Appleton & Co., 1850) and J. H. Hammong, *The Farmers and Mechanics Practical Architect* (Boston: J. P. Jewett, 1858), passim.

15. Daniel Atwood, *Country and Suburban Houses* (New York: Orange Judd, 1871), pp. 17–18, gives an elaborate description of running water in the rural kitchen. Gervase Wheeler, *The Choice of a Dwelling* (London: John Murray, 1871), includes a special section on plumbing, water service, gas lighting, heating, and ventilation in urban, suburban, and rural homes, pp. 239–54.

16. *Industrial Chicago,* 2: 31–32.

17. Ibid., 2: 91–122.

18. *Industrial Chicago,* 2: 300–01.

19. Mathew L. Mandable, paper read before the Chicago Local Association of Master Plumbers, June 24, 1890, "In What Relation Should the Intelligent and Trustworthy Plumber Stand Towards His Customers in the Selection of Sanitary Appliances?" quoted in *Industrial Chicago,* 2: 142–43.

20. *Industrial Chicago,* 2: 143. Sanitarian George Waring was an important participant in the sewer gas debate. For his view, see *Modern Methods of Sewage Disposal* (New York: D. Van Nordstand, 1896).

21. *Industrial Chicago,* 2: 101. From a reprint of a paper by Martin Moylan, "Extras in Plumbing Work," presented to the National Association of Master Plumbers Convention at Deer Park, Maryland, June 1886.

22. *Industrial Chicago,* 2: 33–38, gives descriptions of "model architects" by a plumber and "model plumbers" by an architect.

23. William L. B. Jenney, "A Reform in Suburban Dwellings," *The Inland Architect and Builder* 1, no. 1 (February 1882): 2.

24. One example of an article designed to inform architects of the most up-to-date information on sanitation is Dr. Ross, "Sanitary Suggestions for Architects." *The American Architect and Building News,* January 15, 1876. Ross was the Medical Officer of Health for St. Giles, London.

25. For instance, Alex W. Murray, "The Sanitation of Cities," *The Inland Architect and Builder* 3 (July 1884): 75.

26. Eugene Robinson, *Domestic Architecture* (New York: MacMillan Company, 1926), pp. x–xii.

27. Murray, p. 76.

28. W. B. Gray, "Practical Gas-fitting," as quoted in *Industrial Chicago,* 2: 282.

29. Handlin, p. 452.

30. Chicago Department of Public Works, *Eighth Annual Report* (Chicago: City of Chicago, 1883), p. 73.

31. Carter H. Harrison, *Growing Up with Chicago* (Chicago: Ralph Fletcher Seymour, 1944), p. 19; Thomas E. Tallmage, *Architecture in Old Chicago* (Chicago: University of Chicago Press, 1941), p. 184.

32. Joseph L. Arnold found a similar development in Baltimore. He explains that "local facilities and services proved critical in the development of neighborhood associations." See "The Neighborhood and City Hall: The Origin of Neighborhood Associations in

Baltimore, 1880–1911," *Journal of Urban History* 6, no. 1 (November 1979): 7.

33. *Real Estate and Building Journal,* February 5, 1876, p. 118.

34. Ibid., March 22, 1873, p. 1.

35. Ibid., May 17, 1873, p. 6.

36. Ibid., May 31, 1873, p. 10, and *Chicago Tribune,* June 2, 1872, p. 4, for examples of other associations dedicated to petitioning the city for improvements.

37. "West Side Growlers," *Chicago Tribune,* April 26, 1873, p. 4.

38. "North Side Improvement Committee," *Chicago Tribune,* September 15, 1870.

39. For example, Alderman Woodward presented an ordinance for street improvements within his ward. See *Chicago Tribune,* September 8, 1868.

40. *Chicago Tribune,* February 17, 1877, p. 4.

41. Fred Nelson, History of Uptown, Document #19, Local Community Documents, Vivien Marie Palmer, compiler, Chicago Historical Society. Roger Simon found similar sentiments among working-class families in Milwaukee. See *The City Building Process: Housing and Services in New Milwaukee Neighborhoods 1880–1910* (Philadelphia: American Philosophical Society, 1978).

42. Mrs. Louisa Roberts, resident of Grand Crossing for sixty years, interviewed February 1928, History of Grand Crossing, Local Community Documents, Chicago Historical Society.

43. "Early Austin History," *Austinite,* December 26, 1924.

44. Miss Gladys Blackman, resident of Glenview from 1894, as in *Glenview, 1899–1974* (Melrose Park, Ill.: Union Press, 1974), unpaginated.

45. "Suburban—Irving Park," *Chicago Tribune,* March 27, 1887, p. 15.

46. Helen Zattenberg, *Old Ravenswood and Lake View* (Chicago: Ravenswood-Lake View Historical Association, 1941), p. 12.

47. *Chicago Tribune,* September 12, 1886, p. 16.

48. Chicago Department of Public Works, *Nineteenth Annual Report* (1894), p. 3.

49. Arnold also found this to be the case in Baltimore. First, outlying residents came to expect urban services. Then "the demand for large houses and back gardens, plus the cost of connecting the houses to the urban service system, precluded the old pattern of street/alley dwellings." This led to increasing homogeneity within neighborhoods. See "The Neighborhood and City Hall," pp. 8–9.

Chapter 4

1. In the nineteenth century, newspapers and chroniclers often described the individuals involved in this process as speculators. I employ this term freely in this manuscript, using it synonymously with developer. I do not mean to make a value judgment about the work of speculators through this term. I wholeheartedly agree with Paul-André Linteau, who sees land development as an industry "in which, in the best capitalist tradition, numerous entrepreneurs, often in a very competitive environment, try to create, organize and sell a town, a subdivision, a building, or simply a lot and to obtain the greatest possible profit out of it." See "Canadian Suburbanization in a North American Context: Does the Border Make a Difference?" *Journal of Urban History,* 13 (May 1987): p. 255.

2. Sam Bass Warner, *Streetcar Suburbs, The Process of Growth in Boston, 1870–1900*

(Cambridge: Harvard University Press, 1962), p. 117. Marc Weiss has more recently shown the rise of large-scale "community builders" in the early twentieth century, generally agreeing with Warner's thesis, in *The Rise of the Community Builders* (New York: Columbia University Press, 1987). Besides Warner and Weiss, other historians who have considered residential construction at the turn of the century are: Martha J. Vill, "Speculative Building Enterprise in late Nineteenth Century Baltimore," unpublished conference paper, University of Guelph Conference on Comparative Canadian-American Urban Development, August 24–28, 1982, and "Residential Development on a Landed Estate: The Case of Baltimore's 'Harlem,' " *Maryland Historical Magazine* 77 (Fall 1982): 266–78. A comparable literature also exists for British examples: H. J. Dyos, "The Speculative Builders and Developers of Victorian London," *Victorian Studies* 11 (1968): 641–90, and *Victorian Suburb: A Study of the Growth of Camberwell* (Leicester: Leicester University Press, 1961). For a review article on the British literature on city building, see J. W. R. Whitehead, "The Changing Nature of the Urban Fringe: A Time Perspective" in *Geographical Processes at the Edge of the Western City,* James H. Johnson, ed. (New York: John Wiley and Sons, 1974), pp. 31–52. Also Peter J. Aspinall, "The Internal Structure of the Housebuilding Industry in the Nineteenth Century," in James H. Johnson and Colin C. Pooley, eds., *The Structure of Nineteenth Century Cities* (New York: St. Martin's Press, 1982).

3. Warner, Chapter Five title. Warner acknowledges but minimizes the importance of the creation of manufactured lots to the city building process in his streetcar suburbs. He does so because he found that in Boston services quickly followed the extension of streetcars (see esp. p. 31). This close correlation between the extension of transportation and urban services has not been found in other cities. Peter W. Moore, "Public Services and Residential Development in a Toronto Neighborhood, 1880–1915," *Journal of Urban History* 9, no. 4 (August 1983): 446, found that infrastructure did not necessarily follow streetcar extensions in Toronto. Roger Simon also found a variable pattern in Milwaukee. See "Housing and Services in an Immigrant Neighborhood: Milwaukee's Ward 14," *Journal of Urban History* 2, no. 4 (August 1976): 450. It is clear that while transportation/service extensions were related, they were not necessarily interchangeable in all cities. See chap. 2 for more discussion of other relevant factors.

4. Matthew Edel, Elliott D. Sclar, and Daniel Luria, *Shaky Palaces: Homeownership and Social Mobility in Boston's Suburbanization* (New York: Columbia University Press, 1984), p. 198.

5. Herma Clark, *The Elegant Eighties* (Chicago: A. C. McClurg, 1941), letter of January 16, 1887. Clark, the longtime companion of wealthy Chicago dowager Mrs. William Blair, wrote a series of fictional letters about her life, first published in the *Chicago Tribune* and later compiled as a book.

6. See Eugene Moehring, "Public Works and the Patterns of Urban Real Estate Growth in Manhattan, 1835–1894," (Ph.D. diss., City University of New York, 1976), pp. 10–41, and Charles Lockwood, *Manhattan Moves Uptown* (Boston: Houghton Mifflin, 1976).

7. The large number of unimproved outlying tracts in his possession at death demonstrates Ogden's approach. See William B. Ogden Papers, Manuscript Collections, Chicago Historical Society.

8. "Old and New Real Estate Methods," *Real Estate and Building Journal,* March 12, 1892, p. 331.

9. Homer Hoyt, *One Hundred Years of Land Values in Chicago* (Chicago: University of Chicago Press, 1933), pp. 91, 345.

10. *Real Estate and Building Journal,* March 12, 1892, p. 331.

11. *The Landowner,* February 1870, p. 31.

12. James B. Runnion, *Out of Town* (Chicago: The Western News Company, 1869), p. 8. Before the 1870 Illinois Constitutional Convention, land companies received special charters under Illinois law. After the Constitutional Convention, a general incorporation act was passed, and companies were no longer granted special charters. All of the named companies were created before 1870, so each had a special charter. See also Helen Monchow, *Seventy Years of Real Estate Subdividing in the Region of Chicago* (Evanston: Northwestern University, 1939), pp. 121–28.

13. The designation for economic base used in this study is based on actual occupational information for these settlements in 1880. This should be distinguished from the projected economic base which developers anticipated. Basic market functions and agricultural processing characterize eight of these settlements in 1880, but only two—the Union Stock Yards and South Chicago—were not originally conceived as commuter settlements. The six intended as commuter suburbs were not initially successful as such but survived by servicing the agricultural hinterland until commuters arrived later in the last century.

14. Hoyt, p. 117, and Jerome Fellman, "Pre-Building Growth Patterns in Chicago," *Annals of the Association of American Geographers* 47 (March 1957): 70–71, "municipal parks and outlying settlements had a strong influence on both initial subdivision and individual lot sales."

15. Levi Z. Leiter, a leading Chicago businessman, documents this through the account book he kept for all taxes paid on his Chicago real estate. See Box 187, v. 8, Leiter Papers, Manuscript Collections, Chicago Historical Society.

16. As quoted in "Real Estate," *Chicago Tribune,* July 10, 1872. For a more complete history of the parks development see Everett Chamberlin, *Chicago and Its Suburbs* (Chicago: T. A. Hungerford and Company, 1874), pp. 313–40.

17. Chamberlin, p. 319.

18. Ibid., p. 434.

19. Ibid., p. 326.

20. See papers dated August 29, 1866, Chicago City Railway Company Papers, Chicago Surface Lines, Folder 13, Manuscript Collections, Chicago Historical Society.

21. See the reminiscences of a German saloonkeeper, Lou Schmitt, who came to the Gross Park area in 1882, History of Hamlin Park, v. 3, pt. 1, Document #1, Local Community Documents, Vivien Marie Palmer, compiler, Chicago Historical Society, for the connections between Yerkes and Gross in the development of Gross Park on the city's northwest side. Yerkes ran a car line to the subdivision and also subdivided adjoining property to take advantage of increasing land values.

22. *Real Estate and Building Journal,* August 14, 1875, p. 506. Samuel S. Hayes, Charles W. Rigdon, Samuel Walker, and Samuel Eastman were among the other speculative builders working on the west side during the decades after the Civil War. Each had a company that was involved in at least one project with over seventy-five houses.

23. As early as 1855, the *Chicago Tribune* commented that: "Every dwelling place in the city of Chicago is occupied . . . so long as men perceive a chance, or are made to believe there is one, of realizing 300–400% profit in a single twelvemonth upon their money invested in 'real estate' so long will they not build houses and so long will the city suffer for want of them." *Chicago Tribune,* May 3, 1855, p. 1.

24. Franklin Park, to the west of Chicago, is an example of this sort of development. Laid out in 1872, a discount was given to those who were prepared to build immediately on their land. See Chamberlin, p. 437.

25. Chicago Plan Commission, *Forty Four Cities in the City of Chicago* (Chicago: City

of Chicago, 1942), p. 76. Other subdivisions which soon offered this option were South Lynne, Austin, Cummings, and Central Park.

26. Chamberlin, p. 405, and Blue Island Land and Building Company, *Homes for the People* (Chicago: n.p., n.d.), p. 10. The price of homes ranged from $1,200 to $4,000. The company employed the auction method quite successfully by sponsoring daylong excursions to the subdivision with free transportation and lunches. See also *Forty Four Cities*, p. 76.

27. Of course, this was by no means a fail-safe method of directing growth. Residents sometimes purchased double lots in subdivisions with mid-size lots (for instance, with a 30-foot frontage), creating a more spacious community initially, and allowing for "filling in" as transportation advances and population growth pushed contiguous settlement further outward. Ravenswood was one such community, Rogers Park another.

28. Palmer, Local Community Documents, History of Hamlin Park, vol. 3, pt. 1, Documents #1, 2, 3; Homer Hoyt, *One Hundred Years of Land Values in Chicago* (Chicago: University of Chicago Press, 1933), p. 166; and *Real Estate and Building Journal*, September 30, 1890, advertisement and December 28, 1889, p. 918.

29. Chicago Department of Public Works, *Twentieth Annual Report* (Chicago: City of Chicago, 1895), "Commissioner's Report," p. xvii.

30. Chamberlin, p. 370. Other improvement companies whose methods were similar to those of the Ravenswood Improvement Company, although not nearly so successful, were the Norwood Park Land and Building Company and the Maywood Company.

31. Gustavus Anderson, quoted in Palmer, Local Community Documents, History of Uptown, Document #55, Chicago Historical Society.

32. *Prospectus of the Calumet and Chicago Canal and Dock Company* (Chicago: Calumet and Chicago Canal and Dock Company, 1874), pp. 4–8.

33. Runnion, p. 17. For more information on romantic suburbs, see John Archer, "Country and City in the American Romantic Suburb," *Journal of the Society of Architectural Historians*, 42, no. 2 (May 1983): 142–65.

34. The population only reached 1,500 by 1900. Other suburbs along the Chicago, Burlington, and Quincy Railroad grew equally slowly, including Clyde, Hawthorne, and Berwyn. See Chamberlin, pp. 412–15.

35. Runnion, p. 20. *The New York Evening Post* in 1871 commented on this method of service provision, comparing it to the scramble for improvements from local governments: "[T]his is no job, no 'great public work'; there are no politics in it. It is a commercial venture, conceived in a vivid spirit and admirably carried out." Quoted in Herbert J. Bassman, ed., *Riverside: Then and Now* (Riverside, Ill., n.p.; 1936), p. 84.

36. Information contained in an advertisement for Kenilworth, *Chicago Tribune*, September 21, 1890, and Anne Higginson Spicer, *Kenilworth: The First Fifty Years* (Kenilworth, Ill.: n.p., 1947), p. 21.

37. Colleen Browne Killner, *Joseph Sears and Kenilworth* (Kenilworth, Ill.: Kenilworth Historical Society, 1969), pp. 81–94, 145. Among the residents of Kenilworth were Samuel Insull, the electric power magnate, and neighbors of Sears's from the Prairie Avenue district.

38. Paul Swartzlose, employed by Cochran until 1903, gave a December 1927 interview in which he commented: "The main feature about Edgewater in the first days of its growth was the Edgewater Light Company which provided light. It was organized and the plant built as much for advertising as to give good lighting. It was quite a thing then to have electricity out in the country." Cochran came to Chicago from Philadelphia in 1881 to work as the Chicago manager for a tobacco company. He developed clever advertising

techniques for it, which were quite useful in the development of subdivisions. A promotional pamphlet published by Cochran's real-estate firm explained that after only a few years in Chicago he had entered the real-estate business because "the optimistic spirit of this energetic, hustling city seized the young man." See Document #13, vol. 2, pt. 1, History of Uptown, Local Community Documents, Vivien Marie Palmer, compiler, Chicago Historical Society.

39. *The Town of Harvey, Illinois* (Harvey, Ill.: Harvey Land Association, 1892), pp. 3–4.

40. *History of the City of Harvey, 1890–1962* (Harvey, Ill.: First National Bank of Harvey, 1962), pp. 16–17.

41. *Real Estate and Building Journal,* August 22, 1891, p. 1209.

42. Palmer, Local Community Documents, History of Hamlin Park; vol. 3, pt. 1, Documents #1 and 2; Hoyt, p. 166; and *Real Estate and Building Journal,* September 30, 1890, advertisement for Grossdale (Brookfield).

43. *Real Estate and Building Journal,* January 1, 1887, p. 5.

44. *Real Estate and Building Journal,* January 1, 1888, supplement.

45. *Real Estate and Building Journal,* February 6, 1892, p. 172, letter to the editor.

46. Harrison R. Baker, "The Broker's Interest in the Subdivision," *California Real Estate* 11, no. 2 (November 1930): 53, as in Marc Allan Weiss, "The Rise of the Community Builders: Real Estate Developers, Urban Planners and the Creation of Modern Residential Subdivisions," paper delivered at the Urban History Seminar, Chicago Historical Society, January 16, 1986, p. 6. See also Catherine Bauer, *Modern Housing* (Boston: Houghton, Mifflin Co., 1934), p. 30.

47. Ira D. Malbrough, "The Magician," *The Economist,* August 25, 1925, p. 25. As in Monchow, p. 159.

48. Another factor to keep in mind is that in many subdivisions, settlement took place over decades, not years, and transportation and other infrastructure advances changed the relative attractiveness of an area for particular sorts of settlement. The case of Ravenswood is an important one in this regard. While the initial subdivision around a railroad station was sold out rather quickly, the area became more thickly settled with the advent of streetcar and elevated lines. Apartment buildings and smaller homes surrounded the original settlement by the turn of the century, and changed its overall character. Michael McCarthy has stressed the heterogeneity of suburban communities in Philadelphia in "Corrupt and Contented? Philadelphia Stereotypes and Suburban Growth on the Main Line," Suburbia Re-Examined Conference, Hofstra University, Long Island, New York, June 1987.

49. Marc Weiss discusses the disdain which the community builders, the manufacturers of finished lots, had for curbstoners—those who simply platted and sold lots by the 1930s. This disdain reflected a growing consensus concerning a basic set of infrastructure services demanded by urban and suburban residents. It does not reflect the situation in the late nineteenth century, when curbstoners catered to those who wanted few services and societal norms did not view this as remiss. See "The Rise of the Community Builders: The American Real Estate Industry and Urban Land Planning," American Historical Association, Chicago, December 1986, pp. 5–8.

Chapter 5

1. This is a little-studied but important area for the historian or political scientist who is concerned with comparing local governments in different states. Designations as cities,

villages, and towns have very different meanings in different states, as far as functions and forms are concerned. This makes generalization very difficult and risky. Hendrik Hartog, *Public Property and Private Property: The Corporation of the City of New York in American Law* (Chapel Hill: University of North Carolina Press, 1983), attempts to generalize beyond the case of New York. He does not take into account the very real differences that Massachusetts local governmental law presents. See Joan Williams, "Review—The Development of the Public/Private Distinction in American Law," *Texas Law Review* (August 1985): 230–31.

2. This is similar to the situation in New York and very different from the situation in Massachusetts, where townships were deemed corporate entities. See Joan C. Williams, "The Invention of the Municipal Corporation: A Case Study in Legal Change," *The American University Law Review* (Winter 1985): 370–438.

3. James B. Runnion, *Out of Town* (Chicago: The Western News Agency, 1869), p. 4.

4. Michael J. Doucet, "Urban Land Development," *Journal of Urban History*, 8, no. 3 (May 1982): 299.

5. D. C. M. Platt, "Financing the Expansion of Cities," *Urban History Review* 11 (February 1983): 5.

6. "Westside Improvements," *Chicago Tribune*, October 18, 1874. See also Homer Hoyt, *One Hundred Years of Land Values in Chicago* (Chicago: University of Chicago Press, 1933), p. 343.

7. The exception to the townships' rural orientation were the three townships which comprised the city of Chicago: North Chicago, West Chicago, and South Chicago.

8. A. T. Andreas, *History of Cook County* (Chicago: A. T. Andreas, 1884), p. 478.

9. Weston A. Goodspeed and Daniel D. Healy, *History of Cook County* (Chicago: Goodspeed Historical Association, 1909), pp. 281–82.

10. *Industrial Chicago*, vol. 4: *The Commercial Interests* (Chicago: Goodspeed Publishing Company, 1894), p. 23.

11. For a study of this widespread use of the chartered urban form across New York State, see Hendrik Hartog, *Public Property and Private Property, The Corporation of the City of New York in American Law*. New England was an exception. There the incorporated village did not exist. See Williams, "The Invention of the Municipal Corporation," p. 399.

12. It is crucial to note the distinction between townships and incorporated towns. All incorporated towns, like incorporated villages and cities, remained a part of some township. For Evanston, see Viola Crouch Reeling, *Evanston, Its Land and People* (Evanston: n.p., 1928), pp. 344–45. For DesPlaines, A. T. Andreas, *History of Cook County*, pp. 493–94.

13. *Real Estate and Building Journal*, September 13, 1873, p. 2.

14. Donald Foster Stetzer, "Special Districts in Cook County: Toward a Geography of Local Government," (Ph.D. diss., University of Chicago, 1975), p. 123. For a copy of the general incorporation act, see Henry V. Freeman, *Municipal Code of Hyde Park* (Hyde Park, Ill.: Village of Hyde Park, 1887), p. 137. All of the special charters granted in Cook County were published in the annual volume of the *Private Laws* printed by the State of Illinois.

15. "Further Improvements at Harvey," *Real Estate and Building Journal*, November 18, 1893, pp. 13–15.

16. Ibid.

17. By 1905, Brookfield had at least three subdivisions, all platted by Gross. Gross's problems continued after he withdrew from Grossdale, and it appears he went bankrupt

before his death in 1913. See *Brookfield Diamond Jubilee, 1893–1968* (Brookfield, Ill., 1968). Other suburbs whose initial developers had close ties to early government were Riverside and Norwood Park, where some of the original development company members also served as first town officers. Zane L. Miller found a similar digression from the developers' original plans in the twentieth-century development of Forest Park, Ohio. See *Suburb: Neighborhood and Community in Forest Park, Ohio, 1935–1976* (Knoxville: University of Tennessee Press, 1981).

18. Vivien Marie Palmer, Local Community Documents, History of Rogers Park, clerk of the village before annexation, interviewed December 1927.

19. Ibid.

20. Palmer, "The Primary Settlement as a Unit of Urban Growth and Organization" (Ph.D. diss., University of Chicago, 1932), p. 174.

21. Glenview Historical Society, *Glenview at 75* (Melrose Park, Ill.: Union Press, 1974).

22. Barrington, Palatine, Arlington Heights, and LaGrange were among incorporated villages that sought incorporation primarily to regulate liquor sales.

23. Andreas, p. 503; Newton Bateman, *Historical Encyclopedia of Illinois* (Chicago: Munsell Publishing Company, 1905), p. 798.

24. For the powers of towns, see Edwin C. Crawford, *Civil Government of Illinois* (Chicago: George Sherwood & Co., 1882), pp. 8–21.

25. This is in fact what happened to Cicero Township in 1906, when it became Cicero, Oak Park, and Berwyn Townships, and each new town incorporated separately following the division.

26. "1869 Annual Report, Hyde Park Treasurer," *Chicago Tribune,* October 15, 1869.

27. "Minutes of the Hyde Park Trustees Meeting," *Chicago Tribune,* September 2, 1874. For more information on waterworks, see Letty Anderson, "Hard Choices: The Water Supply Decision in New England Towns," presented at the meeting of the Social Science History Association, Washington, D.C., October 1983.

28. *Chicago Tribune,* July 16, 1880. The City of Chicago was having its own problems supplying water to the westside. The new Hyde Park waterworks was under the direction of John A. Cole. Cole came to Chicago after training as a consulting engineer in Boston and Charleston, and was soon embarked on a successful consulting career in these collar towns, as they began to develop waterworks systems. By the 1880s, he was the official consulting engineer for Jefferson, as well as Lake View and Hyde Park, involving himself in many projects besides the waterworks. See *Chicago Tribune,* April 2, 1881, and Andreas, p. 546. For work Cole did in Lake View, see Edgar Sanders Papers, Chicago Historical Society.

29. *Real Estate and Building Journal,* July 28, 1883, p. 383; also March 17, 1883, p. 108.

30. City of Lake View, *Annual Report of the City Officers of Lake View,* (Lake View, Ill.: Eaton Bros., 1888), pp. 31–33.

31. City of Lake View, *Annual Report of the City Officers of Lake View,* 1888, pp. 15, 31, 33.

32. He did, however, draw a salary for this work, as well as for being a bailiff in the local courts. Edgar Sanders, Correspondence from June 16, 1887; April 12, 1887; Edgar Sanders Papers, Chicago Historical Society.

33. For more information on Cochran and his subdivision work, see Palmer, Local Community Documents, vol. 2, pt. 1, History of Uptown, Document #13, interview with a Cochran employee held in 1927; Document #15, 1927 interview with Cochran's son; Document #16, 1927 interview with the president of Cochran's real-estate company.

34. *Chicago Tribune,* November 18, 1884.

35. It was not until the late 1880s that Jefferson considered alternatives for a township water system. See *Real Estate and Building Journal,* March 16, 1889, p. 162; *Chicago Tribune,* January 15, 1887. Sewers were constructed in some of the suburban settlements within the township. In 1880, the town board approved plans for sewers to be constructed at the suburban settlements of Maplewood and Montrose. The projects did not extend over the entire town, though, and were in direct response to the demands of residents of particular communities within the town. See *Chicago Tribune,* January 15, 1887.

36. *Chicago Tribune,* May 9, 1885.

37. *Chicago Tribune,* June 3, 1883.

38. *Austinite,* February 19, 1926. In 1884, Austin "lacked sewer, streetcars, phones, and electric lights." See *Austinite,* December 1924.

39. Besides Scoville in Cicero, the minutes of the village board meeting in Hyde Park in May 1885 included the approved request for a connection to the water system by the Cheltenham Improvement Company for their subdivision in the south of the village. The petition passed, no doubt aided by the fact that the work was sponsored by A. Hegewisch, a trustee on the village board and an investor in Cheltenham. See "Suburban Improvements—Hyde Park," *Real Estate and Building Journal,* May 23, 1885, p. 245.

40. The three exceptions were the special cases of Norwood Park, Evanston, and Riverside. Five of the developed settlements were founded after the incorporation of townships in which they were located. This eliminated the possibility of influence by these developers on the initial incorporated form. They, like other latecomers, attempted to receive desired services and improvements through established forms.

41. "Real Estate," *Chicago Tribune,* March 23, 1873.

42. Ibid.

43. For Cambridge and Somerville, see Henry Binford, *The First Suburbs* (Chicago: University of Chicago Press, 1985), esp. chap. 7. Robert Dale Karr outlines a similar development in nearby Brookline. See "Brookline and the Making of an Elite Suburb," *Chicago History* 13, no. 2 (Summer 1984): 36–47.

44. Matthew Edel, Elliott D. Sclar, and Daniel Luria, *Shaky Palaces: Homeownership and Social Mobility in Boston's Suburbanization* (New York: Columbia University Press, 1986), esp. chapter 8.

Chapter 6

1. Jon Teaford and Kenneth Jackson have provided two of the most succinct discussions concerning annexation: Jon Teaford, *City and Suburb: The Political Fragmentation of Metropolitan America, 1850–1970* (Baltimore: Johns Hopkins, 1979), esp. chaps. 1 and 2; and Kenneth T. Jackson, *Crabgrass Frontier: The Suburbanization of the United States* (New York: Oxford University Press, 1986), pp. 138–56. As Teaford explains: "By 1910 suburban America was a segregated collection of divergent interests, industrial and residential, Protestant and Catholic, truck farmer and commuter, saloon habitué and abstainer. . . . Each of these segments sought to escape from others and to achieve its goals by taking advantage of the state's willingness to abdicate its control over the creation of municipalities" (p. 12). Kenneth Jackson identifies a similar trend that heightened racial, ethnic, and class distinctions (p. 150).

2. Teaford, pp. 31, 39, 78. Jackson, p. 150. For discussion on specific annexation fights

outside Chicago, see: Ronald Dale Karr, "Brookline and the Making of an Elite Suburb," *Chicago History* 13, no. 2 (Summer 1984): 36–47; Henry D. Shapiro and Zane L. Miller, *Clifton: Neighborhood and Community in an Urban Setting* (Cincinnati: The Laboratory in American Civilization, 1976), pp. 18–21; and Sam Bass Warner, *Streetcar Suburbs* (Cambridge: Harvard University Press, 1962), pp. 163–64.

3. Michael P. McCarthy, "The New Metropolis: Chicago, The Annexation Movement, and Progressive Reform," in *The Age of Urban Reform: New Perspectives on the Progressive Era*, eds. Michael H. Ebner and Eugene M. Tobin (Port Washington, N.Y.: Kennikat Press, 1977), pp. 43–54, provides an important overview of the annexation process in Chicago during the late nineteenth century. Among the reasons which McCarthy saw as critical for approval of annexation was the perception that it would provide improved water, fire, and police, as well as better administration (pp. 45–46). See also Louis P. Cain, "To Annex or Not? A Tale of Two Towns: Evanston and Hyde Park," *Explorations in Economic History* 20 (1983): 58–72.

4. For more information on waterworks in other areas, see Letty Anderson, "Hard Choices: The Water Supply Decision in New England Towns," Social Science History Association Annual Conference, October 1983, Washington, D.C.

5. A. T. Andreas, *History of Cook County* (Chicago: A. T. Andreas, 1884), pp. 341–42; 660–61, and *Chicago Tribune*, August 23, 1881. In 1870, the combined populations of Lake and Hyde Park had been about 7,000, but by 1880 the population of Hyde Park was 15,716, and Lake had 18,380 residents. Hyde Park did not completely abandon the idea of a combined venture when it built a new waterworks. It agreed to sell water to Pullman, which had originally been served by a private system based on well water. They also made a contract with the South Parks Board to provide their water supply. These agreements provided Hyde Park with cash to pay expenses, as well as allowing the town to build a system bigger than necessary, in the hopes that it would not be quickly outgrown. For more on the politics of these discussions, see Andrew P. Yox, "Hyde Park Politics, 1861–1919: Suburban Protection and Urban Progress," *Hyde Park History* 2 (1980): 1–84.

6. *Real Estate and Building Journal,* March 16, 1889, p. 162.

7. *Real Estate and Building Journal,* November 10, 1883, p. 572, and *Chicago Tribune,* April 15, 1885. Annexation to Chicago was viewed as another, but less acceptable, alternative.

8. *Real Estate and Building Journal,* February 23, 1889, p. 114; March 16, 1889, p. 162. Efforts of local governments to combine extended beyond the collar townships. For instance, South Evanston tried to reach an agreement with the Village of Evanston in 1883 concerning the provision of Evanston water to South Evanston. See *Chicago Tribune,* March 30, 1883.

9. See Louis P. Cain, *Sanitation Strategy for a Lakefront Metropolis* (DeKalb, Ill.: Northern Illinois University Press, 1978) and James C. O'Connell, "Technology and Pollution: Chicago's Water Policy, 1833–1930" (Ph.D. diss., University of Chicago, 1980), for more on the development of the Metropolitan Sanitary District.

10. The only exception was the Lincoln Park Board, which was only semiautonomous from Chicago and Lake View. There were more and more special districts in the twentieth century. By 1973, there were 196 special districts within Cook County. See Donald Foster Stetzer, "Special Districts in Cook County: Toward a Geography of Local Government" (Ph.D. diss., University of Chicago, 1975).

11. *Real Estate and Building Journal,* June 19, 1880, p. 36. See Louise Wade, *Chicago's Pride* (Urbana: University of Illinois, 1987), pp. 72–73, for a discussion of the creation of the South Parks Board.

12. *Chicago Tribune,* January 26, 1883.

13. "Divide the Town of Lake," *Chicago Tribune,* September 12, 1880.

14. It was thought that the northern section might eventually be annexed to Chicago, because of the strong ties of commuters to the city. See "Division of Hyde Park," *Chicago Tribune,* January 23, 1883.

15. Ibid.

16. Walter B. Spelman, *The Town of Cicero* (Cicero: n.p., 1921), pp. 17–18.

17. "Summary of Hyde Park Annual Report," *Chicago Tribune,* April 2, 1881.

18. "Suburban Ambition," *Chicago Tribune,* April 7, 1869. However, in 1892 the residents of Evanston approved a change to city government. During that same year, the village of South Evanston was consolidated with Evanston, following the lead of North Evanston. In 1894, Evanstonians rejected consolidation with the City of Chicago. Issues of representation and better services at a cheaper rate were central to these moves. See Michael H. Ebner, *Creating Chicago's North Shore: A Suburban History* (University of Chicago Press, forthcoming), chap. 4.

19. Letter against Hyde Park becoming a city, *Chicago Tribune,* March 20, 1885.

20. "City Incorporation in Hyde Park," *Chicago Tribune,* April 12, 1885; January 5, 1887.

21. *Chicago Tribune,* April 12, 1887; November 2, 1887; December 22, 1887. Complaints concerning the new government soon surfaced. Some argued that the level of corruption and unnecessary spending had risen from the moment the city administration took over. Concern was also expressed that the town government had not been abandoned, even though administration had been turned over to city officials.

22. "Great Expense of City Government," *Chicago Tribune,* March 29, 1885.

23. William Baragwanath, *Chicago Tribune,* March 25, 1885.

24. Cain, "To Annex or Not?" pp. 58–72.

25. Peter Buschwah, *Chicago Tribune,* May 4, 1889. For a careful study of annexation issues in two communities, see Louis P. Cain, "To Annex or Not?" pp. 58–72.

26. "Annexation," *Chicago Tribune,* December 6, 1885.

27. Ibid.

28. C. J. Shubert, *Chicago Tribune,* May 4, 1889.

29. George E. Plumb, pro-annexationist in Austin, *Chicago Tribune,* May 15, 1889.

30. This issue was particularly addressed in the 1889 annexation law (see *Chicago Tribune,* January 17, 1889). McCarthy discusses the fire limits and prohibition in both the 1887 and the 1889 annexation campaigns, p. 46.

31. A. H. Champlin, a resident of Englewood, in a letter to the editor in favor of annexation, *Chicago Tribune,* January 1, 1888.

32. *Real Estate and Building Journal,* March 17, 1888, p. 134.

33. For instance, pro-annexationists in Lake View discussed not the whole tax rate but only the part expended for schools—which was higher in Lake View than in Chicago (see *Chicago Tribune,* December 6, 1885, p. 18). At other points, the higher tax rates outside the city were argued across the board; and even at other times, pro-annexationists claimed that Chicago taxes were as high or higher than in the outlying incorporated areas, but that the city resident received more for his money (see *Chicago Tribune,* October 23, 1887). Barry J. Kaplan described the 1897 New York City consolidation "as a leap in the dark." Clearly, many felt the same way about the 1889 annexations to Chicago. See "Metropolitics, Administrative Reform and Political Theory: The Greater New York City Charter of

1897," *Journal of Urban History* 9, no. 2 (February 1983): 166–67.

34. This is a more widespread approach to annexation across the country. Jackson had found that the "predominant view in the nineteenth century was the doctrine of forcible annexation" (p. 147). In Cook County during these decades, the annexation *was forced* for the unincorporated territory added to Chicago, but the annexations were requested by Chicago. However, by 1852 this doctrine of forcible annexation was *not* found in Ohio. There annexation could not take place without the concurrence of voters in the territory to be annexed. But this did not stop Cincinnati from threatening a forced annexation in 1868–69. See Shapiro and Miller, p. 19.

35. Bessie Louise Pierce, *History of Chicago* (Chicago: University of Chicago Press, 1957), 3: 331.

36. Pierce, 3: 331–32.

37. Barbara Mercedes Posadas, "Community Structures of Chicago's Northwest Side: The Transition from Rural to Urban, 1830–1889" (Ph.D. diss., Northwestern University, 1976), pp. 164–66.

38. "The Triumph of Annexation," *Chicago Tribune,* November 9, 1887.

39. Ibid.

40. Pierce, 3: 332. The 1887 annexation attempt excluded southwestern Hyde Park, western Lake, and northern Lake View. See McCarthy, pp. 46–47, and Pierce, pp. 332–33.

41. Pierce, 3: 333; *Real Estate and Building Journal,* March 17, 1888; *Chicago Tribune,* November 9, 1887; April 7, 1888; May 5, 1889.

42. Arthur B. Tebbets and Frank M. Simons, *History of Ravenswood* (Chicago: The Mirror Publishing Company, 1898), p. 7.

43. John B. Stone, "Ravenswood Now Only a Memory," typescript, around 1930, Local History Collection, Hild Regional Public Library, Chicago.

44. *Oak Park Vindicator,* April 7, 1899.

45. *Austinite,* February 19, 1926.

46. Report of the Finance Committee, Chicago City Council, March 24, 1889, "Appropriation for 1889."

47. *Chicago Tribune,* November 2, 1890.

48. See James A. Todd, *A Sketch of the Fernwood Park District* (Chicago: Board of Commissioners of the Fernwood Park District, 1929), pp. 22, 29.

49. Palmer, History of West Rogers Park, vol. 1, pt. 1, Document #7, Chicago Historical Society, quotation from a man who worked for a West Ridge farmer in the 1890s.

50. A legal advisor to West Ridge during annexation debate as quoted in Vivien Marie Palmer, Local Community Documents, History of West Rogers Park, vol. 1, pt. 1, Document #4A, Chicago Historical Society.

51. Palmer, History of Rogers Park, vol. 1, pt. 1, Document #2, Chicago Historical Society: notes of the Village Board of Trustees meeting, October 28, 1892; clippings from the *Rogers Park News,* July 17, 1891; November 6, 1891, .

52. Hugo S. Grosser, *Chicago, A Review of Its Governmental History from 1837 to 1906* (Chicago: City of Chicago, 1906), p. 109. The other private system was located in Austin.

53. A 1907 promotional booklet described Norwood Park as having "the finest system of macadamized streets of any *suburb* of Chicago," and the title of the pamphlet was "Norwood Park—The Ideal Suburb, Its Residents and Their Homes." See Anne Lunde,

"Norwood Park Aims for Suburban Ideal Long After 1893 Annexation to Chicago," *The Review*, July 17, 1895.

54. Ellen Josephine Beckman, "The Relationship of the Government of the City of Chicago to Cook County from 1893 to 1916." (M.A. Thesis, University of Chicago Press, 1940), p. 7.

55. Chicago Department of Public Works, *Nineteenth Annual Report* (Chicago: City of Chicago, 1894), p. 207. The amount of special assessments increased from $3,655,956.78 in 1889 to $14,505,701.79 in 1894.

56. Chicago Department of Public Works, *Twenty First Annual Report* (Chicago: City of Chicago, 1896), p. vii.

57. Mayor Cregier, Chicago Department of Public Works, *Fifteenth Annual Report*, 1890, p. vi.

58. Mayor Carter Harrison, Chicago Department of Public Works, *Twenty Fourth Annual Report*, 1899, p. 14. Kenneth Jackson cites yet another occasion in 1902 when Harrison again argued against further annexation. Jackson points out that "the core areas themselves occasionally rejected consolidation" (pp. 149–50). Clearly, in Chicago this was a view held during critical years for further annexation around the turn of the century.

59. *Chicago Tribune*, December 9, 1889; December 31, 1889; March 15, 1890; May 9, 1890; see also *Real Estate and Building Journal*, January 4, 1890.

60. Haskins and Sells, *Report on the Special Assessment Accounts of the City of Chicago, October 9, 1871 to April 20, 1901* (Chicago: John F. Higgins, 1903), p. 18.

61. The repeated failures to annex Evanston to Chicago at the turn of the century are often cited as the end to the annexation movement in the area. Evanston provides a fascinating case unto itself with regard to developments in suburban government. Consolidations—and attempted consolidations, city incorporation, and the expansion of public services—characterized the closing decades of the last century. All these moves allowed Evanston to respond successfully to demands for better services and representation. See Cain, "To Annex or Not?" and Ebner, "The Result of Honest Hard Work." *Chicago History* 13, (Summer 1984): 48–65.

62. Brooklyn 1976 Symposium, *Brooklyn USA* (New York: Brooklyn College Press, 1978), pp. 22–23.

63. Alter F. Landesman, *A History of New Lots, Brooklyn* (Port Washington, N.Y.: Kennikat Press, 1977), esp. pp. vii, 114.

64. The 1898 Consolidation of Greater New York ended this township annexation, as the city's boundaries solidified. Stephen Jenks, *The Story of the Bronx* (New York: G. P. Putnam's Sons, 1912), pp. 2, 7.

65. Anita Inman Comstock, *Bronxville in the Good Ol' Days* (Bronxville, N.Y.: n.p., 1982). For information on nearby Scarsdale, see Carol A. O'Connor, *A Sort of Utopia, Scarsdale, 1891–1981* (Albany: State University of New York Press, 1982), pp. 1–15.

66. Henry Binford, *The First Suburbs* (Chicago: University of Chicago Press, 1985), chap. 7; Warner, *Streetcar Suburbs*, and Karr, "Brookline." See also Justin Winsor, *Memorial History of Boston* (Boston: James R. Osgood, 1881), pp. 569–600; S. B. Sutton, *Cambridge Reconsidered* (Cambridge: MIT Press, 1976), p. 45; and Francis S. Drake, *The Town of Roxbury* (Roxbury: n.p., 1878).

67. John C. Bollens and John R. McKinley, *California City Government* (Berkeley: Bureau of Public Administration, 1948), p. 10; John C. Bollens, *The Problem of Government in the San Francisco Bay Area* (Berkeley: Bureau of Public Administration, 1948), pp. 10, 25, 31.

Chapter 7

1. David Ward argues that by the turn of the century a "minimum of utilities and paving was necessary to attract the middle-class clientele. Inadequate utilities in a subdivision usually reflected the intention of the developer to cater to low-income groups." See "A Comparative Historical Geography of Streetcar Suburbs in Boston, Massachusetts and Leeds, England, 1850–1920." *Annals of the Association of American Geographers* 54, no. 4 (1964): 487. This study concurs with this finding, although I have argued that there was not a strict class/improvement package correlation in the early decades of outlying improved subdivisions.

2. Roderick D. McKenzie, *The Metropolitan Community* (New York: McGraw-Hill, 1933), p. 307. McKenzie felt in 1933 that it was "safe to say that the tendency of today is toward less annexation," especially of already incorporated territories.

3. Separate statehood or federal districts for the government of metropolitan regions were considered by Albert Lepawsky, *Home Rule for Metropolitan Chicago* (Chicago: University of Chicago, 1935), especially p. xiii. In 1861, Mayor Fernando Wood proposed that New York City withdraw from the Union and form a free state, both to protect its trading relationship with the South and to eliminate the power of the state legislature. See George J. Lankevich and Howard B. Furer, *A Brief History of New York City* (Port Washington, N.Y.: Associated Faculty Press, 1984), pp. 164–65. The shift from annexation to consolidation/metropolitan-wide governments is seen in Jon Teaford, *City and Suburb: The Political Fragmentation of Metropolitan American, 1850–1970* (Baltimore: Johns Hopkins, 1979). He argues that annexation largely ended in 1910, to be replaced by metropolitan government schemes.

4. Another area in which the growing influence of suburban forms may have exerted itself was in progressive reforms to government. The referendum was pioneered by Winnetka residents, including Henry Demarest Lloyd, at the turn of the century. See Michael H. Ebner, *Creating Chicago's North Shore: A Suburban History* (University of Chicago Press, forthcoming), p. 217. Connections can also be seen with the commission and city manager forms of government. For instance, suburban-elected officials served on a part-time basis and left the actual administration of government to paid specialists. Elected suburban officials in both the Town of Hyde Park and the Village of Norwood Park held other full-time jobs and employed workers as needed. Politicians were not usually involved in the day-to-day operations of these suburban communities. The city manager and commission forms formalized the way in which government had been executed in many suburbs for decades. While the history of the commission and city manager forms has been written largely from the perspective of cities, many suburbs provided examples of how politics and administration in local government could be accomplished. In the early twentieth century in Illinois and many other states, legislation was passed making it possible for incorporated places to adopt a commission or city manager form of government similar to the emerging suburban forms that fostered a separation of politicians and a paid professional staff. See Bradley Robert Rice, *Progressive Cities, The Commission Government Movement in America, 1901–1920* (Austin: University of Texas Press, 1977), for an account of the rise of the commission and city manager forms.

5. See Mel Scott, *American City Planning since 1890* (Berkeley: University of California Press, 1969), esp., pp. 183–270.

6. William E. Harmon, "Suburban Real Estate: Financing, Development, and Selling," *Proceedings of the National Association of Real Estate Boards, Home Builders, and Subdividers Division,* 1924, pp. 30–41.

7. For instance, the *Chicago Herald and Examiner* published for a number of years in

the 1920s *Chicago Skylines, A Magazine of Real Estate,* devoted to providing information to all those active in Chicago real estate (and to increasing the advertisements placed in the newspaper, of course). *The Architectural Forum* for May 1935 devoted the entire issue to subdivisions and their development. They provided perspectives from city planners, architects, the public, realtors, and bankers. The 1924 meeting of the Homebuilders and Subdividers Division of the National Association of Real Estate Boards contained committee reports on subdivision legislation nationwide and on factors in subdivision location, as well talks by two prominent real-estate developers. J. C. Nichols of Kansas City discussed "Suburban Subdivisions with Community Features," and William E. Harmon of New York City, "Suburban Real Estate—Financing, Developing and Selling."

8. McKenzie, p. 299, and J. M. Albers, "Zoning Ordinances, A Charted Summary of Regulations in the Chicago Region," *Chicago Skylines* 2, no. 4 (April 20, 1927): 12–13.

9. Adna Ferrin Weber, *The Growth of Cities in the Nineteenth Century* (Ithaca, N.Y.: Cornell University Press, 1899), p. 459. His final chapter, "Tendencies and Remedies," attempted to sort through the impact of deconcentration on the city. Other early observers of suburbs included Graham Taylor, *Satellite Cities: A Study of Industrial Suburbs* (New York: Appleton & Co., 1915), and Harlan Paul Douglass, *The Suburban Trend* (New York: Arno Press, 1925). As Carol A. O'Connor has aptly pointed out, "all these early observers note the existence of relatively homogeneous local units within heterogeneous suburban regions." See "Sorting Out the Suburbs: Patterns of Land Use, Class and Culture," *American Quarterly* 37 (Bibliography 1985): 382–94.

10. Ebeneezer Howard, *Garden Cities of Tomorrow* (Cambridge, Mass.: MIT Press, 1965).

11. McKenzie, *The Metropolitan Community,* p. 303. This monograph was a part of the series Recent Social Trends in the United States, prepared in the 1920s under the direction of the President's Research Committee on Social Trends. A more recent account that takes essentially the same line is Jon Teaford, *City and Suburb* (Baltimore: Johns Hopkins Press, 1980), p. 1: "The result of this fragmentation is inefficiency, confusion of authority, and disparity in shouldering the burdens of the metropolis." Other social scientists who have criticized suburban government include: John C. Bollens and Henry J. Schmant, *The Metropolis: Its People, Politics and Economic Life* (New York: Harper & Row, 1975); John H. Jackson, ed., *Public Needs and Private Behavior in Metropolitan Areas* (Cambridge: Ballinger Publishing Co., 1975); Amos Hawley and Basil G. Zimmer, *The Metropolitan Community* (Beverly Hills, Calif.: Sage Publications, 1970); and Robert C. Wood, *Suburbia: Its People and Their Politics* (Boston: Houghton Mifflin, 1962).

12. The Chicago School of Sociology did identify the increasing segregation of metropolitan areas by the 1920s. Patricia Mooney Melvin provides an important discussion on these issues in "Changing Contexts: Neighborhood Definition and Urban Organization," *American Quarterly* 37 (Bibliography 1985): 357–67.

13. As Jon Teaford describes it, "Pliant legislators handed out acts of incorporation with no questions asked and enacted general incorporation measures that gave localities a carte blanche. Suburbanites had exploited this privilege because a climate of social and economic diversity made political separatism seem increasingly desirable" (Teaford, p. 31). He contrasts this view with that taken in Britain, where local control is not nearly so strong: "English law did not allow every race track promoter, tax evading industrialist, or community of teetotalers to create its own municipality." See *City and Suburb,* p. 70.

14. Equality is as fundamental to the American political process as local prerogative. Initially perceived as an individual right, as U.S. society was transformed by industrialization and urbanization, many argued that government would have to regulate and promote equality aggressively. The concern with trusts at the turn of the century was an early

attempt on the part of the federal government to protect equal access to the economic system. The affirmative action program was another attempt on the part of the government to promote equal opportunity for all citizens in the workplace.

15. J. Anthony Lukas, *Common Ground* (New York: Knopf, 1985) considers this conflict between local autonomy and equal opportunity, as well as attendant class and race issues in the busing program for Boston in the 1970s. It is also critical to the Mt. Laurel, New Jersey, decision, which established the concept that each community must provide for its "fair share" of low-income housing, and that local zoning could *not* be used to exclude certain classes of people. While a more general application of this court decision has not been established, it highlights the continuing tension between local autonomy and equal opportunity. See Roger Lowenstein, "Another Long Battle Ending in Low-Income Housing Fight," *Wall Street Journal,* June 10, 1987, p. 25, for a more recent test of this concept in Brookhaven, Long Island.

SELECTED BIBLIOGRAPHY

Published Sources

Abbott, Carl. " 'Necessary Adjuncts of Its Growth': The Railroad Suburbs of Chicago." *Journal of the Illinois State Historical Society* 73, no. 2 (Summer 1980): 117–31.

Anderson, Alan. *The Origin and Resolution of an Urban Crisis: Baltimore 1890–1930*. Baltimore: The Johns Hopkins Press, 1977.

Andreas, A. T. *History of Chicago*. 3 vols. Chicago: A. T. Andreas, 1882–86.

———. *History of Cook County*. Chicago: A. T. Andreas, 1884.

Archer, John. "Country and City in the American Romantic Suburb." *Journal of the Society of Architectural Historians* 42, no. 2 (May 1983): 139–56.

Arnold, Joseph L. "The Neighborhood and City Hall: The Origin of Neighborhood Associations in Baltimore, 1880–1911." *Journal of Urban History* 6, no. 1 (November 1979): 3–30.

Artibise, Alan J., ed. *Town and City*. Regina, Saskatchewan: Canadian Plains Research Center, 1981.

Atwood, Daniel. *Country and Suburban Houses*. New York: Orange Judd, 1871.

Bassman, Herbert J., ed. *Riverside, Then and Now*. Riverside, n.p., 1936.

Bateman, Newton. *Historical Encyclopedia of Illinois*. Vol. 1, Cook County. Chicago: Munsell Publishing Company, 1905.

Bender, Thomas. *Community and Social Change in America*. Baltimore: The Johns Hopkins Press, 1978.

Bennett, Fremont O. *Politics and Politicians of Chicago, Cook County and Illinois, 1787–1887*. Chicago: The Blakely Printing Company, 1886.

Binford, Henry. *The First Suburbs: Residential Communities on the Boston Periphery, 1815–1860*. Chicago: University of Chicago Press, 1985.

Blake, Nelson. *Water for the Cities: A History of the Urban Water Supply Problem in the United States*. Syracuse, N.Y.: Syracuse University Press, 1956.

Block, Jean. *Hyde Park Houses*. Chicago: University of Chicago Press, 1978.

Bollens, John C., and John R. McKinley. *California City Government*. Berkeley: Bureau of Public Administration, 1948.

Brookfield Area Diamond Jubilee. *The Histoy of Brookfield*. Brookfield, Ill.: n.p., 1968.

Brooklyn 1976 Symposium. *Brooklyn USA*. New York: Brooklyn College Press, 1978.

Burns, Elizabeth K. "Subdivision Activity on the San Francisco Peninsula: 1860–70." *Yearbook of the Association of Pacific Coast Geographers* 39 (1977): 17–39.

Cain, Louis P. *Sanitation Strategy for a Lakefront Metropolis*. DeKalb, Ill.: Northern Illinois University Press, 1978.

———. "To Annex or Not? A Tale of Two Towns: Evanston and Hyde Park." *Explorations in Economic History* 20 (1983): 58–72.

Campbell, Helen. *Household Economics*. New York: G. P. Putnam, 1896.

Carpenter, William Seal. *Problems in Service Level*. Princeton, N.J.: Princeton University Press, 1940.

Chamberlin, Everett. *Chicago and Its Suburbs*. Chicago: T. A. Hungerford and Co., 1874.

Chesbrough, Ellis S. *Chicago Sewerage: Report of the Results of Examinations Made in Relation to Sewerage in Several European Cities in the Winter of 1856–57*. Chicago: City of Chicago, 1858.

———. *Report and Plan of Sewerage for the City of Chicago*. Chicago: City of Chicago, 1855.

Chicago. *Board of Public Works Annual Report*. 1861–1872.

———. *Board of Water Commissioners Annual and Semi-Annual Report*. 1852–1860.

———. *City Council Minutes*. 1872–1902.

———. *Department of Public Works Annual Report*. 1861–72.

The Chicago Blue Book of Selected Names of Chicago and Suburban Towns. Chicago: The Chicago Directory, Co., 1894.

Childs, May Louise. *Actual Government in Illinois*. New York: The Century Company, 1914.

Citizen's Association of Chicago. *Annual Report*. 1874–1900.

Cleaver, Charles. *Early Chicago Reminiscences*. Fergus Historical Series, no. 9. Chicago: Fergus Printing Company, 1882.

Clifton, James A. "The Last Great Indian Treaty in the Old Northwest." *Chicago History* 9 (1980): 86–96.

Colbert, Elias. *Chicago, Historical and Statistical Sketch of the Garden City*. Chicago: n.p., 1868.

Colbert, Elias, and Everett Chamberlin. *Chicago and the Great Conflagration*. Cincinnati, Ohio: C. F. Vent, 1891.

Cook County. Board of Commissioners *Annual Report*. 1872–1902.

Conzen, Kathleen Neils. *Immigrant Milwaukee, 1836–60, Accommodation and Community in a Frontier City*. Cambridge, Mass.: Harvard University Press, 1976.

Crawford, Edwin C. *Civil Government of Illinois*. Chicago: George Sherwood and Company, 1882.

Dannegar, Anne E. *Early Austin from Its Beginnings until the Time of Annexation to the City of Chicago, 1899*. Austin, Ill.: Austin Friends of the Library, 1944.

Doucet, Michael. J. "Urban Land Development in Nineteenth Century North America." *Journal of Urban History* 8 (1982): 299–342.

Douglass, Harlan Paul. *The Suburban Trend*. New York: Arno Press, 1925.

Downing, Andrew Jackson. *The Architecture of Country Houses*. New York: D. Appleton & Co., 1850.

Duis, Perry. *Chicago: Creating New Traditions*. Chicago: Chicago Historical Society, 1976.

Dyos, H. J. "The Speculative Builders and Developers of Victorian London." *Victorian Studies* 11 (1968): 641–90.

————. *Victorian Suburb*. Leicester, Eng.: University Press, 1961.

Ebner, Michael H. *Creating Chicago's North Shore: A Suburban History*. Chicago: University of Chicago, forthcoming.

————. "The Result of Honest Hard Work: Creating a Suburban Ethos for Evanston." *Chicago History* 13 (Summer 1984): 48–65.

————. "Urban Government in America, 1776–1876." *Journal of Urban History* 5 (1979): 501–19.

Edel, Mathew, Elliot D. Sclar, and Daniel Luria. *Shaky Places: Homeownership and Social Mobility in Boston's Suburbanization*. New York: Columbia University Press, 1984.

Ernst, Isabel, ed. *Roots: A Glenview Bicentennial*. Glenview, Ill.: Glenview Bicentennial Commission, 1976.

Fellman, Jerome. "Pre-Building Growth Patterns of Chicago." *Annals of the Association of American Geographers* 47 (1957): 59–82.

Finn, John J. *Chicago*. Chicago: The Standard Guide, 1892.

Fogelson, Robert M. *The Fragmented Metropolis: Los Angeles, 1850–1930*. Cambridge, Mass.: Harvard University Press, 1967.

Foster, Clyde D. *Evanston's Yesterdays*. Evanston, Ill.: Evanston Historical Society, 1956.

Frisch, Michael. *Town into City: Springfield, Massachusetts and the Meaning of Community, 1840–1880*. Cambridge, Mass.: Harvard University Press, 1972.

Gans, Herbert. *The Levittowners: Ways of Life and Politics in a New Suburban Community*. New York: Pantheon Books, 1967.

———. "Urbanism and Suburbanism as Ways of Life: A Reevaluation of Definitions." In *Human Behavior and Social Processes*, edited by Arnold M. Rose. Boston: Houghton Mifflin, 1962.

Gere, Edwin A., Jr. "Dillon's Rule and the Cooley Doctrine." *Journal of Urban History* 8 (1982): 271–98.

Gideon, Siegfried. *Mechanization Takes Command*. London: Oxford University Press, 1969.

Glenview Area Historical Society. *Glenview at 75*. Melrose Park, Ill.: Union Press, 1974.

Goodspeed, Weston A., and Daniel D. Healy. *History of Cook County*. Chicago: Goodspeed Historical Association, 1909.

Gowans, Alan. *The Comfortable House*. Cambridge, Mass.: MIT Press, 1986.

Griffiths, Ernest S. *A History of American City Government, The Conspicuous Failure, 1870–1900*. New York: Praeger, 1974.

———. *A History of American City Government: The Progressive Years and Their Aftermath, 1900–1920*. New York: Praeger, 1974.

Grosser, Hugo S. *A Review of Its Governmental History from 1837 to 1906*. Chicago: City of Chicago, 1906.

Haeger, John Denis. *Chicago: The Investment Frontier: New York Businessmen and the Economic Development of the Old Northwest*. Albany: State University of New York Press, 1981.

Handlin, David R. *The American Home: Architecture and Society, 1815–1915*. Boston: Little, Brown & Co., 1979.

Harmon, William E. "Suburban Real Estate: Financing, Development, and Selling." *Proceedings of the National Association of Real Estate Boards, Home Builders and Subdividers Division*, 1924.

Harris, Carl V. *Political Power in Birmingham, 1871–1921*. Knoxville: University of Tennessee Press, 1977.

Harris, Chauncey D. "Suburbs." *American Journal of Sociology* 49, no. 1 (July 1943): 1–13.

Hartog, Hendrik. *Public Property and Private Property, The Corporation of the City of New York in American Law*. Chapel Hill: University of North Carolina Press, 1983.

Holli, Melvin H., and Peter d'A. Jones, eds. *Ethnic Chicago*. Grand Rapids, Mich.: Eerdmans Publishing Co., 1977.

Horne, H. D. *History of Grand Crossing*. Cleveland, Ohio: Nevins Steam Printing House, 1876.

Howard, Ebeneezer. *Garden Cities of Tomorrow*. Cambridge, Mass.: MIT Press, 1965.

Hoyt, Homer. *One Hundred Years of Land Values in Chicago*. Chicago: University of Chicago Press, 1933.

Illinois. *Constitutional Convention Debates and Proceedings*, 1870.

———. *Counties and Incorporated Municipalities*, 1971.

———. Supreme Court. *The Village of Morgan Park vs. City of Chicago*, 1912.

Industrial Chicago. 4 vols. Chicago: The Goodspeed Publishing Company, 1891. Vol. 2, *Building Interests*. Vol. 4, *Commerical Interests*.

Jackson, Kenneth T. *The Crabgrass Frontier: The Suburbanization of the United States*. New York: Oxford University Press, 1985.

James, Edmund J. *The Charters of the City of Chicago*, parts 1 and 2. Chicago: University of Chicago, 1898.

Jenney, William L. B. "A Reform in Suburban Dwellings." *The Inland Architect and Builder* 1, no. 1 (February 1882).

Jeter, Helen R. *Trends of Population in the Region of Chicago*. Chicago: University of Chicago Press, 1927.

Johnson, James H. *Geographical Processes at the Edge of the Western City*. New York: St. Martin's Press, 1982.

Johnson, James H., and Colin C. Pooley, eds. *The Structure of Nineteenth Century Cities*. New York: St. Martin's Press, 1982.

Kaplan, Barry J. "Metropolitics, Administrative Reform and Political Theory: The Greater New York City Charter of 1897." *Journal of Urban History* 9, no. 2 (February 1983): 165–94.

Karr, Robert Dale. "Brookline and the Making of an Elite Suburb." *Chicago History* 13, no. 2 (Summer 1984): 36–47.

The Kelly Community. Chicago: Thomas Kelly High School, 1938.

Kenilworth. *First Fifty Years*. Kenilworth: Kenilworth Historical Society, 1947.

Kerr, Alec C. *The City of Harvey, 1890–1962*. Harvey, Ill.: First National Bank in Harvey, 1962.

Kilner, Colleen Browne. *Joseph Sears and Kenilworth*. Kenilworth: Kenilworth Historical Society, 1969.

Landesman, Alter F. *A History of New Lots, Brooklyn*. Port Washington, N.Y.: Kennikat Press, 1977.

Lepawsky, Albert. *Home Rule for Metropolitan Chicago*. Chicago: University of Chicago Press, 1935.

Linteau, Paul-André. "Canadian Suburbanization in a North American Context: Does the Border Make a Difference?" *Journal of Urban History* 13, no. 3 (May 1987): 252–74.

Lockwood, Charles. *Manhattan Moves Uptown*. Boston: Houghton Mifflin, 1976.

Lotchin, Roger. *San Francisco, 1846–1856*. New York: Oxford University Press, 1974.

Lukas, J. Anthony. *Common Ground: A Turbulent Decade in the Lives of Three American Families*. New York: Knopf, 1985.

McAlpine, William. *Report Made to the Water Commissioners of the City of Chicago on Supplying the City with Water*. Chicago: City of Chicago, 1851.

McCarthy, Kathleen D. *Noblesse Oblige: Charity and Cultural Philanthropy in Chicago, 1849–1929*. Chicago: University of Chicago Press, 1982.

McCarthy, Michael P. "The New Metropolis: Chicago, The Annexation Movement and Progressive Reform." In Michael H. Ebner and Eugene M. Tobin, eds. *The Age of Urban Reform: New Perspectives*. Port Washington, N.Y.: Kennikat Press, 1977: 43–54.

McKenzie, Roderick D. *The Metropolitan Community*. New York: McGraw-Hill Book Company, 1933.

McShane, Clay. *Technology and Reform: Street Railways and the Growth of Milwaukee, 1877–1900*. Madison: State Historical Society of Wisconsin, 1974.

Mayer, Harold M. "The Launching of Chicago: The Situation and the Site." *Chicago History* 9 (1980): 68–80.

Mayer, Harold M., and Richard C. Wade. *Chicago: Growth of a Metropolis*. Chicago: University of Chicago Press, 1969.

Melvin, Patricia Mooney. "Changing Contexts: Neighborhood Definition and Urban Organization." *American Quarterly* 37 (Bibliography 1985): 357–67.

Merriam, Charles Edward. *Chicago*. New York: The MacMillan Company, 1929.

———. *Government of the Metropolitan Region of Chicago*. Chicago: University of Chicago Press, 1933.

Miller, Zane L. *Boss Cox's Cincinnati, Urban Politics in the Progressive Era*. New York: Oxford University Press, 1968.

———. *Suburb: Neighborhood and Community in Forest Park, Ohio, 1935–1976*. Knoxville: University of Tennessee Press, 1981.

Moehring, Eugene P. *Public Works and Urban History: Recent Trends and New Directions*. Chicago: Public Works Historical Society, 1982.

———. "Space, Economic Growth and the Public Works Revolution in New York." *Infrastructure and Urban Growth in the Nineteenth Century*, pp. 29–59. Chicago: Public Works Historical Society, 1985.

Monchow, Helen Corbin. *Seventy Years of Real Estate Subdividing in the Region of Chicago*. Evanston, Ill.: Northwestern University, 1939.

Moore, Peter W. "Public Services and Residential Development in a Toronto Neighborhood, 1880–1915." *Journal of Urban History* 9 (1983): 445–71.

Mumford, Lewis. *The City in History*. New York: Harcourt, Brace, 1961.

O'Connor, Carol A. "Sorting Out the Suburbs: Patterns of Land Use, Class, and Culture." *American Quarterly* 37 (Bibliography 1985): 382–94.

———. *A Sort of Utopia: Scarsdale, 1891–1981*. Albany: State University of New York, 1982.

Owen, David Edward. *The Government of Victorian London, 1885–89*. Cambridge, Mass.: Harvard University Press, 1982.

Park, Robert E., Ernest W. Burgess, and Roderick D. McKenzie. *The City*. Chicago: University of Chicago Press, 1925.

Peterson, Jon A. "The Impact of Sanitary Reform upon American Urban Planning, 1840–90." *Journal of Social History* 13 (1979): 83–103.

Pierce, Bessie Louise. *As Others See Chicago*. Chicago: University of Chicago Press, 1933.

———. *History of Chicago*. 3 vols. Chicago: University of Chicago Press, 1933–57.

Platt, D. C. M. "Financing the Expansion of Cities." *Urban History Review* 11 (1983): 1–34.

Platt, Harold. *City Building in the New South: The Growth of Public Services in Houston, Texas, 1830–1915*. Philadelphia: Temple University Press, 1983.

Posadas, Barabara M. "Suburb into City: The Transformation of Urban Identity on Chicago's Periphery—Irving Park as a Case Study, 1870–1910." *Journal of the Illinois State Historical Society* 86, no. 3 (Autumn 1983): 162–76.

Reeling, Viola Crouch. *Evanston, Its Land and People*. Evanston, Ill.: Fort Dearborn Chapter of the Daughters of the American Revolution, 1928.

Rice, Bradley Robert. *Progressive Cities: The Commission Government Movement in America, 1901–1920*. Austin: University of Texas Press, 1977.

Richards, Ellen. *The Cost of Living*. New York: John Wiley and Sons, 1905.

———. *The Cost of Shelter*. New York: John Wiley and Sons, 1905.

Rosen, Christine Meisner. *The Limits of Power: Great Fires and City and the Process of Growth in America*. New York: Cambridge University Press, 1986.

Rosenberg, Charles. *The Cholera Years*. Chicago: University of Chicago Press, 1962.

Runnion, James B. *Out of Town*. Chicago: Western News Company, 1868.

Scholl, Edward T. *Seven Miles of Ideal Living*. Berwyn, Ill.: Norman King, 1957.

Schultz, Stanley K., and Clay McShane. "To Engineer the Metropolis: Sewers, Sanitation and City Planning in Late Nineteenth Century America." *Journal of American History* 65 (1978): 389–411.

Scott, Mel. *American City Planning since 1890*. Berkeley: University of California Press, 1969.

Shapiro, Henry A., and Zane L. Miller, *Clifton: Neighborhood and Community in an Urban Setting*. Cincinnati, Ohio: The Laboratory in American Civilization, 1976.

Simon, Roger. *The City Building Process: Housing and Services in New Milwaukee Neighborhoods, 1880–1910*. Philadelphia: American Philosophical Society, 1978.

———. "Housing and Services in an Immigrant Neighborhood: Milwaukee's Ward 14." *Journal of Urban History* 2 (August 1976): 435–58.

South Park Commissioners. *Annual Report*. 1869–85.

Sparling, Samuel Edwin. *Municipal History of Chicago*. Madison: University of Wisconsin, 1898.

Spelman, Walter B. *The Town of Cicero*. Cicero, Ill., 1921.

Spicer, Anne Higginson. *Kenilworth: The First Fifty Years*. Kennilworth, Ill.: n.p., 1947.

Studenski, Paul. *The Government of Metropolitan Areas in the United States*. New York: National Municipal League, 1930.

Tarr, Joel A. "Building the Urban Infrastructure in the Nineteenth Century, An Introduction." *Infrastructure and Urban Growth in the Nineteenth Century*, pp. 61–85. Chicago: Public Works Historical Society, 1985.

———. "The Separate Vs. Combined Sewer Problem." *Journal of Urban History* 5 (May 1979): 308–39.

———. *Transportation Innovation and Changing Spatial Patterns in Pittsburgh, 1850–1934*. Chicago: Public Works Historical Society, 1978.

Teaford, Jon C. *City and Suburb: The Political Fragmentation of Metropolitan America, 1850–1970*. Baltimore: The Johns Hopkins Press, 1979.

———. *The Municipal Revolution in America*. Chicago: University of Chicago Press, 1975.

———. *The Unheralded Triumph: City Government in America, 1870–1900*. Baltimore: The Johns Hopkins Press, 1984.

Tebbetts, Arthur B., and Frank M. Simons. *History of Ravenswood*. Chicago: The Mirror Publishing Company, 1898.

The Town of Harvey, Illinois. Harvey, Ill.: Harvey Land Association, 1892.

Vill, Martha J. "Residential Development on a Landed Estate: The Case of Baltimore's 'Harlem.'" *Maryland Historical Magazine* 77 (1982): 266–78.

Wade, Louis Carroll. *Chicago's Pride: The Stockyards, Packingtown and Environs in the Nineteenth Century*. Urbana: University of Illinois, 1987.

Ward, David. "A Comparative Historical Geography of Streetcar Suburbs in Boston, Massachusetts and Leeds, England, 1850–1920." *Annals of the Association of American Geographers*, 1964, vol. 54, no. 4.

Waring, George. *Modern Methods of Sewage Disposal*. New York: D. Van Nostrand, 1896.

Warner, Sam Bass. *Streetcar Suburbs: The Process of Growth in Boston, 1870–1900*. Cambridge, Mass.: Harvard University Press, 1962.

Weber, Adna Ferrin. *The Growth of Cities in the Nineteenth Century*. New York: MacMillan Company, 1899.

Weiss, Marc Allan. *The Rise of the Community Builders: The American Real Estate Industry and Urban Land Planning*. New York: Columbia University Press, 1987.

West Chicago Park Commissioners. *Annual Report*, 1872–90.

Williams, Joan C. "The Invention of the Municipal Corporation: A Case Study in Legal Change." *American University Law Review* (Winter 1985): 370–438.

Wirth, Louis. "Urbanism as a Way of Life." *American Journal of Sociology* 44 (July 1938): 1–24.

Wirth, Louis, and Eleanor H. Bernert, eds. *Local Community Fact Book of Chicago*. Chicago: University of Chicago Press, 1949.

Wood, Robert. *Suburbia, Its People and Politics*. Boston: Houghton Mifflin, 1962.

Wright, Gwendolyn. *Building the Dream: A Social History of Housing in America*. New York: Pantheon Books, 1981.

———. *Moralism and the Model Home*. Chicago: University of Chicago Press, 1980.

Wright, John S. *Chicago: Past, Present and Future*. Chicago: Chicago Board of Trade, 1870.

Yox, Andrew. "Hyde Park Politics, 1861–1919: Suburban Protection and Urban Progress." *Hyde Park History* 2 (1980): 1–84.

Zattenberg, Helen. *Old Ravenswood and Lake View*. Chicago: Ravenswood-Lake View Historical Association, 1941.

Newspapers

The Austinite (Cicero, Ill.), 1890–1926.

Chicago Tribune, 1837–1902.

The Economist (Chicago), 1890–1902.

The Landowner (Chicago), 1869–70.

Oak Park Vindicator (Cicero, Ill.), 1895–1900.

Real Estate and Building Journal (Chicago), 1871–93.

The Review (Norwood Park-Chicago), 1895.

Unpublished Sources

Anderson, Letty. "Hard Choices: The Water Supply Decision in New England Towns." Presented at the Social Science History Association Conference, Washington, D.C., October 1983.

Beckman, Ellen Josephine. "The Relationship of the Government of the City of Chicago to Cook County from 1893 to 1916." M.A. thesis, University of Chicago, 1940.

Bixler, William Shelton. "The Government of Cook County, Illinois." M.A. thesis, University of Chicago, 1904.

Chicago Historical Society. Chicago, Illinois. A. T. Andreas Papers.

———. Chicago City Railway Company Papers.

———. Levi Leiter Papers.

———. William B. Ogden Papers.

———. Potter Palmer Papers.

———. Vivien Marie Palmer. Local Community Documents, Chicago, Illinois.

———. Edgar Sanders Papers.

Chicago Public Library. Special Collections. Roseland Community Collection.

———. Special Collections. Austin Community Collection.

———. Sulzer Regional Branch. Neighborhood History Research Collection.

Christgau, Eugene Frederick. "Unincorporated Communities in Cook County." M.A. thesis, University of Chicago, 1942.

DesPlaines Historical Society. Quarterly Reports, 1939–44 (mimeographed).

Evanston. Village Trustees Minutes. 1863–71.

Fitzgerald, Faith. "Growth of Municipal Activities in Chicago, 1833 to 1875." M.A. thesis, University of Chicago, 1933.

Glenview Historical Society. Local History File.

Hamzik, Joseph. "Gleanings of Archer Road." Typescript, December 1961. Chicago Historical Society.

Harlan, Homer Charles. "Charles Tyson Yerkes and the Chicago Transportation System." Ph.D. dissertation, University of Chicago, 1975.

Harvey Public Library. Historical Collection.

Historical Society of Oak Park and River Forest. Photography Collection.

Hughes, Everett Cherrington. "A Study of a Secular Institution: The Chicago Real Estate

Board." Ph.D. dissertation, University of Chicago, 1928.

Moehring, Eugene P. "Public Works and the Patterns of Urban Real Estate Growth in Manhattan, 1835–1894." Ph.D. dissertation, City Colleges of New York, 1976.

O'Connell, James C. "Technology and Pollution: Chicago's Water Policy, 1833–1930." Ph.D. dissertation, University of Chicago, 1980.

Palmer, Vivien Marie. "The Primary Settlement as a Unit of Urban Growth and Organization." Ph.D. dissertation, University of Chicago, 1932.

Posadas, Barbara Mercedes. "Community Structures of Chicago's Northwest Side, the Transition from Rural to Urban, 1830–1889." Ph.D. dissertation, Northwestern University, 1976.

Stetzer, Donald Foster. "Special Districts in Cook County: Toward a Geography of Local Government." Ph.D. dissertation, University of Chicago, 1975.

University of Chicago Library. Special Collections. Archival Photofiles.

APPENDIX A

TABLES

NOTE ON TABLES

In creating a data base and specific categories for this study, I followed the following rules of definition and assignment.

Universe of Settlements: All communities in Cook County that incorporated by 1900. As well as simply an enumeration of incorporated communities in 1900, the universe includes all those incorporated communities that were annexed in the nineteenth century and a selection of settlements in the collar-incorporated townships that were composed of many settlements. A total of eighty settlements are considered.

Generation of Settlement: Date of plat or earliest settlement. Also used for foundation date.

Kind of Government: The major distinction is between an incorporated township, usually composed of multiple settlements, and an incorporated village, which is composed of one primary settlement. Exceptions to this are Riverside and Norwood Park, which were incorporated townships but composed of only one primary settlement (like incorporated townships). The breakdown of the incorporated township of Cicero in 1901 into three smaller, eventually incorporated, townships also skirts this classification, because the resulting townships had one primary settlement. How these exceptions are categorized is indicated in each table. This categorization ignores the fact that incorporated townships were incorporated as villages or cities, because no general township incorporation existed in Illinois. It is a descriptive rather than a technical categorization.

Economic Base: In order to describe the economic base of each settlement, these categories were created: core market, agricultural market/services, commuter market/services, industrial/agricultural processing, industrial, and not identifiable. In order to assign each community to a category, the entries for each settlement in *Illinois Gazetter and Business Directory,* 1880 (Detroit: R. L. Polk & Co., 1880) — or, if it was not listed there, in A. T. Andreas, *History of Cook County* (Chicago: A. T. Andreas, 1884)—were counted according to the following breakdowns:

Core market	Postmaster, station/express agent, grocer/dry goods/general store owner
Agricultural market/ Services	Elevator/flour and feed dealer Grain or livestock dealer Farm implements dealer
Commuter market/ Services	Real estate/insurance/lawyer/architect/ engineer Plumber/waterworks contractor Fancy dry good/specialty shops Residents who commute to Chicago to management/professional/business jobs
Industrial/agricultural Processing	Brewer/distiller/bottler Miller/buttermaker/pickler/haymaker/ cheesemaker Blacksmith/carriagemaker/wagonmaker/ cooper/harnessmaker Cigarmaker Slaughterhouse/meatpacking/by-product industry
Industrial	Foundry Stone cutter/quarry/brickmaking Manufacturing

The number of entries in each of these categories was counted and taken as a percentage of the total number of entries. The results are presented in the final pages of this appendix. After determining the percentages, the category with the highest percentage was assigned to that settlement—excluding the Core market category, which was only assigned when no other category had entries. When no entries were given for a settlement in either the 1880 *Business Directory* or *History of Cook County,* the category "Not identifiable" was assigned, except in cases where I found strong descriptive evidence for an assignment. Those which I assigned in this fashion were: Gross Point (Market); West Ridge (Market); Kenilworth (Commuter services); Brookfield-Grossdale

(Commuter services); and Riverview (Industrial/agricultural processing). While there are, admittedly, numerous biases in my sources, the category assignments by and large are supported by historical description of the settlements.

TABLE 1

OUTLYING COOK COUNTY SETTLEMENTS TO 1900, BY ECONOMIC BASE

	Blue Island	Wheeling	Gross Point	Brighton	Summit	Thornton	Calumet	Lyons	Niles	Willow Springs
Market	14.6	15.8		20.0	28.6	40.0	100.0	25.9	43.8	33.3
Agricultural market/ Services	3.7	—		—	—	6.7	—	—	—	—
Commuter market/ Services	9.8	—		6.7	—	—	—	—	—	—
Industrial/ Agricultural processing	22.0	31.6		26.7	14.3	13.3	—	26.3	18.8	—
Industrial	—	—			—	6.7		5.3	6.3	22.2
Total Entries	82	19		15	7	15	3	19	16	9

	Barrington	Winnetka	Palatine	DesPlaines	Lemont	Evanston	Niles Center	Homewood	Harlem	Matteson
Market	13.8	16.0	10.0	13.3	13.4	8.4	17.7	16.7		26.3
Agricultural market/ Services	6.9	—	6.0	2.2	—	2.4	—	—		—
Commuter market Services	3.4	12.0	4.0	—	4.5	24.1	7.2	—		—
Industrial/ Agricultural processing	13.8	4.0	12.0	15.6	13.4	7.2	14.3	33.3		26.3
Industrial	—	4.0	—	—	7.4	1.2	—	—		—
Total Entries	58	25	50	45	67	83	28	18		19

Source: Taken from A. T. Andreas, *History of Cook County* (Chicago: A. T. Andreas, 1884).
Note: Category assigned is underlined.

T A B L E 1, *continued*

	Arlington Heights	Oakland*	Grand Crossing	Kenwood*	Hyde Park Center	Wright's Grove	Rosehill	Jefferson	Bowmanville*	South Englewood
Market	44.0	—	23.5	—	22.3	17.9	35.7	13.3	—	20.0
Agricultural market/ Services	—	—	—	—	—	3.6	—	3.3	—	—
Commuter market/ Services	—	63.3	11.8	90.0	22.3	14.3	—	3.3	—	—
Industrial/ Agricultural processing	13.5	—	—	—	—	—	—	20.0	30.0	20.0
Industrial	10.8	—	26.4	—	—	—	14.3	—	—	—
Total Entries	37	30	34	30	18	28	14	30	10	5

	South Holland	Oak Park*	Riverdale	Normalville	Roseland	Pullman*	South Chicago*	Ravenswood	Irving Park	Maplewood
Market	50.0	—	12.5	100.0	17.4	3.1	20.0	22.2	50.0	17.6
Agricultural market/ Services	—	—	8.3	—	—	—	2.0	—	—	5.9
Commuter market/ Services	—	53.3	8.3	—	8.7	3.1	2.0	22.2	—	11.8
Industrial/ Agricultural processing	20.0	—	20.8	—	21.7	—	4.0	—	—	5.9
Industrial	—	—	—	—	—	59.3	2.0	11.1	—	5.9
Total Entries	6	75	24	1	23	32	50	9	4	17

TABLE 1, *continued*

	Austin	Central Park Cicero Berwyn	Union Stock Yards*	Englewood	River Forest*	Glencoe	Wilmette	Riverside	Park Ridge
Market	19.0	<u>29.4</u>	—	6.7	6.7	25.5	26.7	33.3	50.0
Agricultural market/ Services	4.8	—	13.5	4.0	—	—	—	—	—
Commuter market/ Services	<u>14.3</u>	—	2.1	6.7	<u>80.0</u>	<u>18.8</u>	<u>26.7</u>	—	—
Industrial/ Agricultural processing	—	—	69.9	12.0	—	—	—	<u>16.7</u>	<u>20.0</u>
Industrial	—	—	1.0	5.3	—	—	—	—	—
Total Entries	21	17	193	75	15	16	15	6	8

	Roger's Park	La Grange	Washington Heights	South Evanston	Norwood Park	Western Springs*	Bartlett	Morgan Park*	Melrose Park*
Market	57.1	11.5	20.0	19.0	23.5	100.0	16.7	11.1	—
Agricultural market/ Services	—	—	5.0	—	—	—	8.3	11.1	—
Commuter market/ Services	<u>14.2</u>	<u>19.2</u>	2.5	<u>38.1</u>	<u>17.6</u>	—	4.2	<u>44.4</u>	—
Industrial/ Agricultural processing	—	3.8	<u>12.5</u>	—	—	—	<u>25.0</u>	—	—
Industrial	—	3.8	—	4.8	—	—	—	—	100.0
Total Entries	7	26	40	21	17	1	24	9	1

TABLE 1, *continued*

	Lansing	Dolton	Maywood	Fernwood	River Park	West Hammond*	West Ridge	West Roseland	Orland Park	Riverview
Market	28.6	20.0	23.5		11.8	6.7				
Agricultural market/ Services	—	—	—		—	—				
Commuter market/ Services	—	13.3	23.5		—	6.7				
Industrial/ Agricultural processing	50.0	6.7	—		23.5	13.3				
Industrial	—	—	5.9		—	26.7				
Total Entries	14	15	17		17	15			3	

	River Grove	LaGrange Park	Kenilworth	Hodgkins	Harvey	Glenview	Evergreen Park	Chicago Heights	Grossdale	Edison Park
Market		50.0			—	100.0	22.0			100.0
Agricultural market/ Services		—			—	—	11.1			—
Commuter market/ Services		—			—	—	5.6			—
Industrial/ Agricultural Processing		—			—	—	5.6			—
Industrial		50.0			—	—	—			—
Total Entries		2			1	3	18			1

TABLE 2

SELECTED STATISTICS ON ANTEBELLUM CHICAGO

Year	Population	Number of Buildings Constructed	Assessed Value of Real Estate (dollars) (Land and Buildings)
1830	50	12	
1833	350	150	
1835	3,265	270 (1834–35)	
1837	4,170	66	236,842
1842	6,000	845 (1838–42)	108,757
1849	23,047		5,181,637
1851	34,000	1,966 (1846–51)	6,804,262
1854	65,872		18,990,744
1859	95,000	2,400	30,732,313
1861	120,000		31,314,749

Source: Homer Hoyt, *One Hundred Years of Land Values in Chicago* (Chicago: University of Chicago Press, 1933), pp. 474, 483, 487.

TABLE 3

SELECTED ILLINOIS CENTRAL RAILROAD STATIONS
IN THE TOWN OF HYDE PARK, 1869

Station	Distance from City Center (in miles)	Price of Lots Adjacent to Station (dollars per foot)	Commutation Ticket Prices (dollars per one hundred rides)
Oakland	5.0	80	9.00
Kenwood	6.0	50–75	11.00
Hyde Park	7.0	40–60	12.50
Woodville	7.5	20–50	12.50
Woodlawn	9.0	20–25	12.50
Oak Woods	9.5	15–25	12.50

Source: James Runnion, *Out of Town* (Chicago: Western News Company, 1869), p. 50.

TABLE 4

Enumeration of New Outlying Settlement in Cook County, 1831–40*

Settlement	Date of Foundation	Economic Base	Date of Incorporation	Kind of Government	Date of Annexation	1880 Population	1900 Population	1920 Population
Blue Island	1837	Agricultural processing/Industry	1872	Incorporated city		1,542	6,114	11,424
Brighton	1840	Agricultural processing/Industry	1868	Incorporated township (Cicero)	1889	605	—	—
Calumet	1830s	Market	1867	Incorporated township (Hyde Park)	1889	250	—	1,237
Gross Point	1830s	Market	1874	Incorporated village		327	669	—
Lyons	1832–35	Agricultural processing/Industry	1888	Incorporated village		486	951	2,564
Niles	1837	Agricultural processing/Industry	1899	Incorporated village		239	514	1,258
Summit	1836	Agricultural processing/Industry	1890	Incorporated village		272	547	—
Thornton	1835	Agricultural processing/Industry	1900	Incorporated village		401	—	—
Wheeling	1830s	Agricultural processing/Industry	1894	Incorporated village		204	331	313
Willow Spring	1840	Industrial/Market	1892	Incorporated village		378	—	—

*See Note on Tables for an explanation of universe, categories, and sources.

TABLE 5

SUMMARY OF OUTLYING SETTLEMENT IN COOK COUNTY, 1831–40*

Economic Base	*Number of Communities*
Market	2 (20%)
Commuter services/Market	
Agricultural processing/ Related industry/Market	7 (70%)
Industrial/Market	1 (10%)
Not identifiable	—
Total	10 (100%)

*See Note on Tables for an explanation of universe and categories.

TABLE 6

ENUMERATION OF NEW OUTLYING SETTLEMENT IN COOK COUNTY, 1841–60 *

Settlement	Date of Foundation	Economic Base	Date of Incorporation	Kind of Government	Date of Annexation	1880 Population	1900 Population	1920 Population
Arlington Heights	1854	Agricultural processing/Industry	1887	Incorporated village	—	995	1,380	2,250
Barrington	1854	Agricultural processing/Industry	1865	Incorporated village	—	410	770	1,743
Bowmanville	1854	Agricultural processing/Industry	1872	Incorporated township (Jefferson)	1889	337	—	—
DesPlaines	1857	Agricultural processing/Industry	1869	Incorporated village	—	818	1,666	3,451
Evanston	1854	Commuter services	1863	Incorporated city	—	4,400	19,259	37,234
Grand Crossing	1853	Industrial	1867	Incorporated township (Hyde Park)	1889	—	—	—
Harlem	1860	Not identified	1884	Incorporated village	—	—	4,085	—
Homewood	1852	Agricultural processing/Industry	1892	Incorporated village	—	313	352	1,389
Hyde Park Center	1856	Commuter services	1867	Incorporated township (Hyde Park)	1889	—	—	—
Jefferson	1855	Agricultural processing/Industry	1872	Incorporated township (Jefferson)	1889	619	—	—
Kenwood	1856—59	Commuter services	1867	Incorporated township (Hyde Park)	1889	—	—	—
Lemont	1850	Agricultural processing/Industry	1873	Incorporated village	—	2,108	2,449	—
Matteson	1855	Agricultural processing/Industry	1889	Incorporated village	—	451	449	—
Niles Center	1854	Agricultural processing/Industry	1888	Incorporated village	—	293	529	763

Settlement	Date of Foundation	Economic Base	Date of Incorporation	Kind of Government	Date of Annexation	1880 Population	1900 Population	1920 Population
Oakdale†	1851	Commuter services	1867	Incorporated township (Hyde Park)	1889	—	—	—
Oak Park‡	1858	Commuter services	1868	Incorporated township (Cicero)	—	1,888	4,771	39,858
Palatine	1857	Agricultural processing/ Industry	1866	Incorporated village	—	731	1,020	1,210
Rosehill	1854	Industrial	1865	Incorporated township (Lakeview)	1889	—	—	—
South Englewood	1854–57	Agricultural processing/ Industry	1865	Incorporated township (Lake)	1889	—	—	—
South Holland	1847	Agricultural processing/ Industry	1894	Incorporated village	—	—	766	—
Winnetka	1854	Commuter services	1869	Incorporated village	—	584	1,833	6,694
Wright's Grove	1853	Commuter services	1865	Incorporated township (Lakeview)	1889	—	—	—

*See Note on Tables for an explanation of the universe of communities, various categories, and sources.

†Although this began as an industrial site (Cleaverville), by 1880 it had become primarily a commuter area.

‡In 1901, Cicero Township spun off Oak Park and Berwyn as distinct townships, which were subsequently incorporated as villages.

T A B L E   7

SUMMARY OF OUTLYING SETTLEMENT IN COOK COUNTY, 1841–60*

Economic Base	Number of Communities
Market	
Commuter services	7 (31.8%)
Agricultural processing/	
Related industry	12 (54.6%)
Industrial	2 (9.1%)
Not identifiable	1 (4.5%)
Total	22 (100%)

*See Note on Tables for an explanation of universe and categories.

TABLE 8

Enumeration of New Outlying Settlement in Cook County, 1861–80*

Settlement	Date of Foundation	Economic Base	Date of Incorporation	Kind of Government	Date of Annexation	1880 Population	1900 Population	1920 Population
Austin	1866	Commuter services.	1868	Incorporated township (Cicero)	1899	3,000	—	—
Bartlett	1873	Agricultural processing/ Industry	1891	Incorporated village	—	175	360	—
Berwyn†	1872	Not identifiable	1868	Incorporated township (Cicero)	—	—	—	14,150
Central Park	1873	Market	1868	Incorporated township (Cicero)	1889	913	—	—
Cicero	1872–73	Not identifiable	1868	Incorporated township (Cicero)	—	—	—	44,995
Dolton	1868	Commuter services	1892	Incorporated village	—	448	1,229	2,076
Englewood	1867–70	Agricultural processing/ Industry	1865	Incorporated township (Lake)	1889	2,850	—	—
Fernwood	1870s	Not identifiable	1886	Incorporated village	1891	—	—	—
Glencoe	1869	Commuter services	1869	Incorporated village	—	387	1,020	3,381
Irving Park	1869	Market	1865	Incorporated township (Jefferson)	1889	430	—	—
La Grange	1871	Commuter services	1879	Incorporated village	—	531	3,969	6,525
Lansing	—	Agricultural processing/ Industry	1893	Incorporated village	—	218	830	1,409
Maplewood	1869	Commuter services	1872	Incorporated township (Jefferson)	1889	725	—	—
Maywood	1869	Commuter services	1881	Incorporated village	—	716	4,532	12,072
Melrose Park	1873	Industrial	1882	Incorporated village	—	200	2,592	2,147
Morgan Park	1869	Commuter services	1882	Incorporated village	1914	187	2,329	—

Settlement	Date of Foundation	Economic Base	Date of Incorporation	Kind of Government	Date of Annexation	1880 Population	1900 Population	1920 Population
Normalville	1881	Market	1865	Incorporated township (Lake)	1889	352	—	—
Norwood Park	1869	Commuter services	1874	Incorporated village	1893	1,675	—	—
Orland Park	1880	Market	1892	Incorporated village	—	—	366	—
Park Ridge	1873	Agricultural processing/Industry	1873	Incorporated village	—	457	1,340	3,383
Pullman	1880	Industrial	1867	Incorporated township (Hyde Park)	1889	—	—	—
Ravenswood	1869	Commuter services	1865	Incorporated township (Lakeview)	1889	485	—	—
River Forest	1869	Commuter services	1880	Incorporated village	—	162	1,539	4,358
River Park§	1872	Agricultural processing/Industry	1892	Incorporated village	—	—	483	914
Riverdale	1869	Agricultural processing/Industry	1892	Incorporated village	—	450	558	1,166
Riverside	1869	Agricultural processing/Industry	1875	Incorporated township	—	450	1,551	2,532
Rogers Park	1870	Commuter services	1878	Incorporated village	1893	529	—	—
Roseland	1873	Agricultural processing/Industry	1867	Incorporated township (Hyde Park)	1889	772	—	—
South Chicago	1869	Agricultural processing/Industry	1867	Incorporated township (Hyde Park)	1889	1,961	—	—
South Evanston	1868	Commuter services	1873	Incorporated village	1893‡	1,517	—	—
Union Stock Yards	1865	Agricultural processing/Industry	1865	Incorporated township (Lake)	1889	—	—	—

TABLE 8, continued

Settlement	Date of Foundation	Economic Base	Date of Incorporation	Kind of Government	Date of Annexation	1880 Population	1900 Population	1920 Population
Washington Heights	1869	Agricultural processing/Industry	1874	Incorporated village	1890	1,035	—	—
West Hammond§	1875	Industrial	1892	Incorporated city	—	—	2,935	7,492
West Ridge	1874	Market	1890	Incorporated village	1893	—	—	—
West Roseland	1875	Not identifiable	1886	Incorporated village	1890	172	—	—
Western Springs	1871	Market	1886	Incorporated village	—	—	662	1,258
Wilmette	1869	Commuter services	1872	Incorporated village	—	419	2,300	7,814

* See Note on Tables for an explanation of the universe of settlements and categories.

† In 1901, Oak Park and Berwyn townships were spun off from Cicero and subsequently incorporated as distinct incorporated villages. Cicero in this enumeration consists only of that part of the township which remained in Cicero after 1901 (primarily the settlement called Clyde).

‡ Annexation to Evanston.

§ River Park changed its name to Franklin Park; West Hammond, to Calumet City.

TABLE 9

SUMMARY OF OUTLYING SETTLEMENT IN COOK COUNTY, 1861–80*

Economic Base	Number of Communities
Market	6 (16.2%)
Commuter services	13 (35.1%)
Agricultural processing/ Related industry	11 (29.7%)
Industry	3 (8.1%)
Not identifiable	4 (10.9%)
Total	37 (100%)

*See Note on Tables for an explanation of settlement universe and categories.

TABLE 10

ENUMERATION OF NEW OUTLYING SETTLEMENT IN COOK COUNTY, 1881–1900*

Settlement	Date of Foundation	Economic Base	Date of Incorporation	Kind of Government	Date of Annexation	1880 Population	1900 Population	1920 Population
Chicago Heights	1891	Industrial	1891	Incorporated village	—	—	5,100	19,653
Edison Park‡	resettled/ 1880s	Market	1892	Incorporated village	1910	—	—	—
Evergreen Park	1890–93	Market	1893	Incorporated village	—	—	445	705
Glenview‡	1880s	Market	1893	Incorporated village	—	—	652§	760
Grossdale‡	1882–83	Commuter services	1893	Incorporated village	—	—	1,111	3,589
Harvey	1889	Industrial	1891	Incorporated city	—	—	5,395	9,216
Hodgkins	—	Not identifiable	1896	Incorporated village	—	—	195	—
Kenilworth	1890	Commuter services	1896	Incorporated village	—	—	336	—
LaGrange Park	—	Not identifiable	1892	Incorporated village	—	—	730	1,684
River Grove	—	Not identifiable	1888	Incorporated village	—	—	333	484
Riverview	1890s	Agricultural processing/ Industry	1890s	Incorporated village	1900s†	—	406	—

*See Note on Tables for an explanation of settlement universe and categories.

†Riverview annexed to DesPlaines.

‡Edison Park was originally called Canfield. Grossdale's name was changed to Brookfield. Glenview was originally South Northfield.

§In 1910

TABLE 11

SUMMARY OF OUTLYING SETTLEMENT IN COOK COUNTY. 1881–1900*

Economic Base	Number of Communities
Market	3 (27.3%)
Commuter services	2 (18.2%)
Agricultural processing/ Related industry	1 (9.0%)
Industrial	2 (18.2%)
Not identifiable	3 (27.3%)
Total	11 (100%)

*See Note on Tables for an explanation of settlement universe and categories.

TABLE 12

SETTLEMENTS IN COOK COUNTY INCORPORATED, 1881–1900

Economic Base	Generation of Settlement			
	1831–40	*1841–60*	*1861–80*	*1881–1900*
Market	—	—	3 (20%)	3 (27.3%)
Commuter services	—	—	4 (26.7%)	2 (18.2%)
Agricultural processing/ Related industry	5 (83.3%)	5 (83.3%)	4 (26.7%)	1 (9%)
Industrial	1 (16.7%)	—	2 (13.3%)	2 (18.2%)
Not identifiable	—	1 (16.7%)	2 (13.3%)	3 (27.3%)
Total	6 (100%)	6 (100%)	15 (100%)	11 (100%)

*See Note on Tables for an explanation of universe and categories.

TABLE 13

CHICAGO DWELLINGS WITH/WITHOUT WATER, 1856–58

Year	Total Number Dwellings	Dwellings with Water Connections		Dwellings Without Water Connections	
		Number	% of Total	Number	% of Total
1856	5,777	4,821	83.5	956	16.5
1857	6,641	5,640	84.9	1,001	15.1
1858	10,215	7,777	76.1	2,438	23.9

Source: *Semi-Annual Report of the Board of Water Commissioners*, 1857, 1858, 1859.

TABLE 14

CHICAGO INFRASTRUCTURE EXPANSION, 1863–89

Year	Population	Streets★	Paved Streets★	Sidewalks★	Sewers★	Water Pipe★
1863	150,000	400	5			115
1866	200,418		12	470†		152
1871	325,000	533	88		151	288
1875	400,000	609	116	648	263	410
1880	512,060	651	143	721	337	455
1884	704,080				414	543
1889	900,000	2,048	740	2,041	518	730

Sources: Faith Fitzgerald, "Growth of Municipal Activities in Chicago, 1833 to 1875" (Ph.D. diss., University of Chicago, 1933), pp. 169, 170, 173, 174; Department (Board) of Public Works, *Annual Reports*, 1863–89, passim.

★ Each is calculated in miles of improvement.

† This figure is actually for 1867.

TABLE 15

MUNICIPAL EXPENDITURES IN CHICAGO, 1863–73 (In Dollars)

	1863		1873	
	Total	Per Capita	Total	Per Capita
Police	100,031	.62	799,221	2.07
Fire	93,348	.58	586,082	1.51
Health	5,332	.03	91,610	.24
Highways	237,980	1.49	1,609,162	4.20
Education	112,454	.70	1,166,380	3.02
Sanitation	293,491	1.83	1,778,141	4.64
Correctional	39,547	.25	69,337	.18
Public service	216,151	1.39	1,991,174	5.16
General government	252,041	1.57	1,371,210	3.44
Total	1,603,159	10.02	10,921,118	28.33

Source: Faith Fitzgerald, "Growth of Municipal Activities in Chicago, 1833 to 1875" (Ph.D. diss., University of Chicago, 1933), p. 236.

TABLE 16

EXPANSION OF WATER AND SEWER SYSTEMS IN CHICAGO, 1861–1900

Year	Population of Chicago	Miles of Water Pipe		Water Taps		Miles of Sewers		Private Drains	
		Total	Per 100 Population	Total	Per 100 Population	Total	Per 100 Population	Total	Per 100 Population
To 1861	120,000	95.3	.08	6,876	5.73	53.7	.04	2,194	1.83
1865	178,492	141.2	.08	11,406	6.39	62.7	.04	3,850	2.16
1870	298,700	272.4	.09	35,318	8.83	132.1	.04	19,813	6.63
1875	400,000	410.0	.10	55,293	13.82	235.6	.06	40,511	10.13
1880	503,298			67,949	13.50	317.8	.06	51,367	10.21
1885	700,000			98,688	14.10	410.0	.06	77,970	11.14
1890	1,098,570			159,001	14.47	521.5	.05	112,291	10.22
1892	1,425,000	1,402.0	.10	203,954	14.31	993.5	.07	145,444	10.21

Sources: Homer Hoyt, One Hundred Years of Land Values in Chicago (Chicago: University of Chicago Press, 1933), p. 483; Department of Public Works, Annual Reports, 1878, 1883, and 1892.

TABLE 17

CHICAGO LAND VALUES, 1836–79*

Miles from Downtown	1836	1856	1879
1	5,900	51,000	60,000
1–2	2,000	37,000	60,000
2–3	816	18,500	40,000
3–4	416	7,000	30,000
Over 4	1,400	12,000	50,000
Total	10,532	125,500	240,000

Source: Homer Hoyt, *One Hundred Years of Land Values in Chicago* (Chicago: University of Chicago Press, 1933), p. 116.

*Total value for the mile zone in thousands of dollars.

DEVELOPERS INVOLVED IN OUTLYING SETTLEMENT IN COOK COUNTY, 1861– 80*

Developer	Settlement	Number of years between Plat and Incorporation	Kind of Government	Improvements		Economic Base
				Before Incorp.	After Incorp./ by Govt.	
Henry W. Austin	Austin	2	Incorporated township (Cicero)	Limited	Major	Commuter services
West Chicago Land Co.	Central Park	-5	Incorporated township (Cicero)	Limited	Limited	Market
Irving Park Land & Building Co.	Irving Park	-4	Incorporated township (Jefferson)	Major	—	Market
Wing and Farlin	Maplewood	3	Incorporated township (Jefferson)	Major	—	Commuter services
Maywood Company	Maywood	12	Incorporated village	Limited	Limited	Commuter services
Melrose Company	Melrose Park	9	Incorporated village	Limited	Limited	Industrial
Blue Island Land & Building Co.	Morgan Park	13	Incorporated village	Limited	Limited	Commuter services
Norwood Park Land & Building Association	Norwood Park	5	Incorporated township/ Village	Limited	Major	Commuter services
Pullman Land Co.	Pullman	-13	Incorporated township (Hyde Park)	Major	—	Industrial
Ravenswood Land Co.	Ravenswood	-4	Incorporated township (Lakeview)	Limited	Major	Commuter services

Developer	Settlement	Number of years between Plat and Incorporation	Kind of Government	Improvements		Economic Base
				Before Incorp.	After Incorp. by Govt.	
Sayles and Walker	River Park	20	Incorporated village	Limited	Limited	Agricultural processing/Industry
Riverside Improvement Co.	Riverside	6	Incorporated township/Village	Major	—	Agricultural processing/Industry
Rogers Park Land Co.	Rogers Park	8	Incorporated village	Limited	Major	Commuter services
Calumet and Chicago Canal & Dock Co.	South Chicago	-2	Incorporated township (Hyde Park)	Limited	Major	Agricultural processing/Industry
Warren, Keeney and Co.	South Evanston	5	Incorporated village	Limited	Major	Commuter services
Union Stock Yards Co.	Union Stock Yards	0	Incorporated township (Lake)	Limited	Major	Agricultural processing/Industry
Blue Island Land & Building Co.	Washington Heights	5	Incorporated village	Limited	Major	Agricultural processing/Industry
Brighton Company	West Roseland	11	Incorporated village	Limited	Limited	Not identifiable
M. M. Towle	West Hammond	17	Incorporated village	Limited	Limited	Industrial
Western Springs Association	Western Springs	15	Incorporated village	Limited	Limited	Market
Dingee/Wesler/Blodgett/Kline	Wilmette	3	Incorporated village	Limited	Major	Commuter services

Sources: Primary among the sources used to construct this table were Everett Chamberlin, *Chicago and Its Suburbs* (Chicago: T. A. Hungerford, 1874); James B. Runnion, *Out of Town* (Chicago: The Western News Company, 1866); and A. T. Andreas, *History of Chicago* (Chicago: A. T. Andreas, 1884).

*See Note on Tables for an explanation of settlement universe and categories.

†Categories of improvement: no improvements, limited improvements (grading and paving street, sidewalks, railroad depot, trees); major improvements (water, sewers, gas, electricity). Assignments based on known existence of at least one in a category by 1884.

TABLE 19

COMPARISON OF DEVELOPED SETTLEMENTS
TO ALL OUTLYING SETTLEMENTS, 1861–80*

	Total Settlements Founded 1861–80	*Total Settlements by Developer/ Development Company*	*(As a Percentage of Total 1861–80 Settlements)*	*Developer Suburbs with Major Improvements by 1880*
Market	6	3	(50%)	1
Commuter services	13	9	(69.2%)	7
Agricultural processing/ Related Industry	11	5†	(45.4%)	4
Industrial	3	3	(100%)	1
Not identifiable	4	1	(25%)	—
Total	37	21	(56.8%)	13

*See Note on Tables for an explanation of settlment universe and categories.

†It is worth noting that although these settlements fall in this category two of them are strongly industrial (Union Stock Yards and South Chicago), and are involved in industry that uses agricultural products, but does *not* serve as an agricultural center. The other settlements were both intended as commuter suburbs but were not initially successful, so the population survived by servicing its agricultural hinterland until commuters arrived later in the last century.

TABLE 20

COOK COUNTY POPULATION GROWTH BY AREA, 1860–80

	1860		1870		1880	
	Population	*% County Population*	*Population*	*% County Population*	*Population*	*% County Population*
Chicago	109,260	75	298,977	85	503,185	83
Contiguous townships	7,921	6	12,203	4	50,284	8
Lake View	(587)		(1,841)		(6,565)	
Jefferson	(1,395)		(1,813)		(4,876)	
Cicero	(1,272)		(1,545)		(5,182)	
Lake	(1,755)		(3,360)		(18,380)	
Hyde Park	(——)		(3,644)		(15,716)	
South Chicago	(2,053)		(——)		(——)	
West Chicago	(859)		(——)		(——)	
Remainder of County	27,773	19	38,780	11	53,620	9
Total	144,954	100	349,960	100	607,524	100

Source: A. T. Andreas, *History of Cook County* (Chicago: A. T. Andreas, 1884), pp. 341–42.

T A B L E   2 1

ORGANIZATION OF LOCAL GOVERNMENT IN COOK COUNTY, 1840

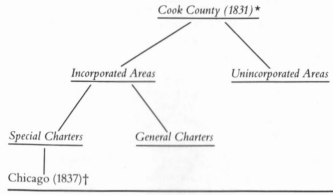

Cook County (1831)★

Incorporated Areas   Unincorporated Areas

Special Charters   General Charters

Chicago (1837)†

★Dates in parentheses are government foundation dates.

†Chicago originally incorporated under the General Town Charter Act of Illinois in 1833 and reincorporated as a city in 1837.

TABLE 22

ORGANIZATION OF LOCAL GOVERNMENT IN COOK COUNTY, 1860

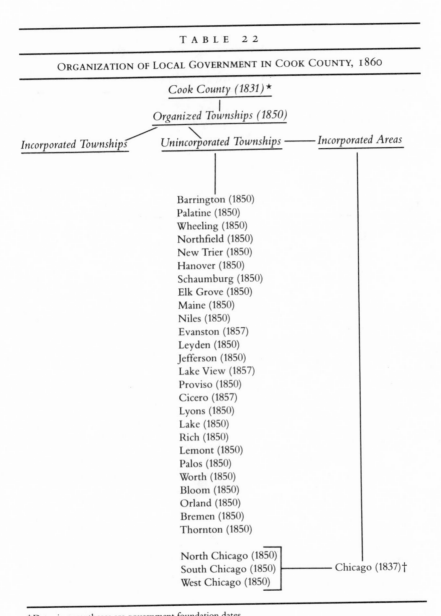

Cook County (1831) ★

Organized Townships (1850)

Incorporated Townships   *Unincorporated Townships* ——— *Incorporated Areas*

Barrington (1850)
Palatine (1850)
Wheeling (1850)
Northfield (1850)
New Trier (1850)
Hanover (1850)
Schaumburg (1850)
Elk Grove (1850)
Maine (1850)
Niles (1850)
Evanston (1857)
Leyden (1850)
Jefferson (1850)
Lake View (1857)
Proviso (1850)
Cicero (1857)
Lyons (1850)
Lake (1850)
Rich (1850)
Lemont (1850)
Palos (1850)
Worth (1850)
Bloom (1850)
Orland (1850)
Bremen (1850)
Thornton (1850)

North Chicago (1850)
South Chicago (1850) ——— Chicago (1837)†
West Chicago (1850)

★ Dates in parentheses are government foundation dates.

† Chicago originally incorporated in 1833 and reincorporated in 1837 as a city. It was composed of three unincorporated townships in 1860.

TABLE 23

BREAKDOWN OF ECONOMIC BASES OF SETTLEMENTS
IN COLLAR TOWNSHIPS, 1880*

| Township | Number of Settlements to 1880 | Economic Base (Percent Total) | | | | |
		Market	Commuter Services	Agricultural Processing	Industrial	Not Identifiable
Lake View	3 (100)	—	2 (66.7)	—	1 (33.3)	—
Jefferson	4 (100)	1 (25)	1 (25)	2 (50)	—	—
Cicero	4 (100)	1 (25)	1 (25)	1 (25)	—	1 (25)
Lake	4 (100)	1 (25)	—	3 (75)	—	—
Hyde Park	8 (100)	1 (12.5)	3 (37.5)	2 (25)	2 (25)	—

*See Note on Tables for an explanation of the universe of communities and various categories.

ORGANIZATION OF LOCAL GOVERNMENT IN COOK COUNTY, 1880

Cook County (1831)*
  Organized Townships (1850)

Incorporated Townships

Special
Cicero (1867)
Lakeview (1865)
Lake (1867)

General
Norwood Park (1874)
Jefferson (1872)†
Hyde Park (1872)†
Riverside (1875)

Unincorporated Townships

Barrington (1850)
Palatine (1850)
Wheeling (1850)
Northfield (1850)
New Trier (1850)
Hanover (1850)
Schaumburg (1850)
Elk Grove (1850)
Maine (1850)
Niles (1850)
Evanston (1857)
Leyden (1850)
Proviso (1850)
Lyons (1850)
Rich (1850)
Lemont (1850)
Palos, Worth, Bloom, Orland, Bremen, Thornton (1850)
Calumet (1867)

  North Chicago
  South Chicago — Chicago (1875)‡
  West Chicago

Incorporated Areas

Special
Palatine (1866)
Winnetka (1869)
Glencoe (1869)

General
Barrington (1872)†

Wilmette (1872)
Gross Point (1874)

DesPlaines (1874)†
Park Ridge (1873)
Evanston (1873)†
South Evanston (1873)
Rogers Park (1878)
River Forest (1880)
LaGrange (1879)
Lemont (1873)

Washington Heights (1874)
Blue Island (1872)

*Dates in parentheses are government foundation dates.

†Reincorporation dates.

‡Chicago was composed of three unincorporated townships.

TABLE 25

SUMMARY OF GOVERNMENTS OF SETTLEMENTS
IN OUTLYING COOK COUNTY, 1880*

| Generation of Foundation | Kind of Government | | | Total |
	Incorporated Village	Incorporated Township	Unincorporated	
1831–40	2 (20%)	1 (10%)	7 (70%)	10 (100%)
1841–60	6 (27.3%)	10 (45.4%)	6 (27.3%)	22 (100%)
1861–80	10 (27.1%)	13 (35.1%)	14 (37.8%)	37 (100%)
Total	18 (26.1%)	24 (34.8%)	27 (39.1%)	69 (100%)

*See Note on Tables for an explanation of settlement universe and categories.

TABLE 26

SELECTED POPULATION ESTIMATES IN COOK COUNTY, 1880–90

Year	Chicago	Hyde Park	Evanston
1880	503,298	15,716	4,400
1881	530,000		4,737
1882	560,693		5,100
1883	590,000	35,000	5,490
1884	629,985	40,000	5,911
1885	700,000	50,000	6,394
1886	825,880	60,000	6,852
1887	850,000	70,000	7,377
1888	875,000	80,000	7,942
1889	900,000	85,000	8,550
1890	1,099,850		9,205

Sources: Louis P. Cain, "To Annex or Not? A Tale of Two Towns: Evanston and Hyde Park," *Explorations in Economic History* 20 (1983): 70; and Helen Jeter, *Trends of Population in the Region of Chicago* (Chicago: University of Chicago Press, 1927), p. 52.

TABLE 27

INCORPORATED VILLAGES ANNEXED TO CHICAGO, 1890–1930

Municipality	Year of Annexation
Washington Heights	1890
West Roseland	1890
Fernwood	1891
Rogers Park	1893
West Ridge	1893
Norwood Park	1893
Edison Park	1910
Morgan Park	1914
Cleering	1915
Greenwood	1927
Beverly	1930

Source: Steven Owen Sargent, "Merger and Consolidation of Illinois Municipalities," (M.A. thesis, University of Illinois at Urbana, 1967), p. 18.

TABLE 28

MILES OF SELECTED IMPROVEMENTS IN CHICAGO, 1896–98

	Special Assessments *	Miles/ Sewers	Miles/ Streets	Miles/ Sidewalks
1896	$4,037,214.44	57.4	86.1	
1897	$2,102,951.45		58.6	232.3
1898	$2,122,757.35	48.0	36.7	252.8
Total/1898		1,388.4	1,248.0	5,101.6

Sources: Chicago, Department of Public Works, *Annual Reports,* 1896, 1897, 1898; Homer Hoyt, *One Hundred Years of Land Values in Chicago* (Chicago: University of Chicago Press, 1933), p. 492.

*Including pavements, sewers, sidewalks, water pipes, and street openings.

TABLE 29

ORGANIZATION OF LOCAL GOVERNMENT IN COOK COUNTY, 1900

Cook County (1831)★

Incorporated Areas Whose Townships Have Been Abolished (1905)	Organized Townships — Incorporated Townships	Organized Townships — Unincorporated Townships	Incorporated Areas
Chicago (1875)†	Riverside (1875)	Barrington (1850)	Barrington† (1872)
	Cicero (1868)	Palatine (1850)	Palatine (1866)
	Oak Park (1901)	Wheeling (1850)	Arlington Heights (1887); Wheeling (1894)
	Berwyn (1901)	Northfield (1850)	Winnetka (1869); Glencoe (1869); Wilmette (1872);
		New Trier (1850)	Grosspoint (1874); Kenilworth (1896)
		Hanover (1850)	Bartlett (1891)
		Schaumburg (1850)	
		Elk Grove (1850)	Glenview (1899); Morton Grove (1895); Edison Park (1892);
		Maine (1850)	DesPlaines† (1874); Park Ridge (1873); Riverview (1890s);
		Niles (1850)	Niles (1899); Niles Center (1888)
		Evanston (1857)	Evanston† (1873)
		Ridgeville (1898)	
		Leyden (1850)	River Park (1892); River Grove (1888)
		Proviso (1850)	River Forest (1880); Grossdale (1893); La Grange Park (1892); Harlem (1884); Maywood (1881); Melrose Park (1882)
		Lyons (1850)	La Grange (1879); Hodgkins (1896); Western Springs (1886); Summit (1890); Willow Springs (1892)
		Rich (1850)	
		Lemont (1850)	Lemont (1873)
		Palos (1850)	

TABLE 29, continued

Incorporated
Townships

Cook County (1831) *

Organized Townships

Incorporated
Townships

Unincorporated Townships

Incorporated Areas

Worth (1850) — — — — — — Evergreen Park (1893)

Bloom (1850) — — — — — — Chicago Heights (1891)

Orland (1850) — — — — — — Orland Park (1892)

Bremen (1850) — — — — — — Tinley Park (1892)

Thornton (1850) — — — — — Harvey (1891); Dolton (1892); South Holland (1894);
Thornton (1900); Homewood (1892); Lansing (1893)

Calumet (1867) - — — — — — Blue Island (1872); Riverdale (1892)

* Dates in parentheses are government foundation dates.

† Reincorporation dates.

TABLE 30

SUMMARY OF SETTLEMENTS ANNEXED TO CHICAGO BY 1900*

	Kinds of Government		
Generation of Foundation	*Settlements Comprising Incorporated Villages*	*Settlements in Incorporated Townships*	*Total*
1831–40	—	2	2
1841–60	—	9	9
1861–80	7	11	18
1881–1900	—	—	—
Total	7 (24.1%)	22 (75.9%)	29 (100%)

*See Note on Tables for an explanation of settlement universe and categories.

Appendix B

Maps

M A P   I

Major Settlements in Cook County, 1840

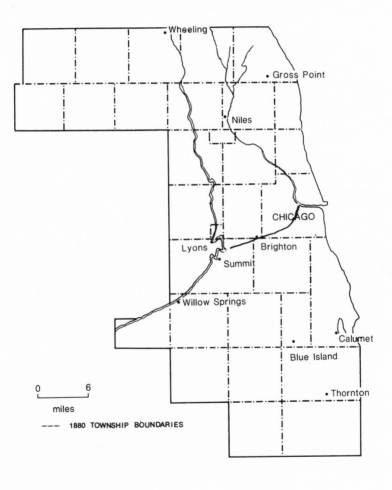

Wheeling

Gross Point

Niles

CHICAGO

Lyons   Brighton

Summit

Willow Springs

Calumet

Blue Island

Thornton

0   6

miles

———— 1880 TOWNSHIP BOUNDARIES

M A P 2

Outlying Settlement in Cook County, 1841–60

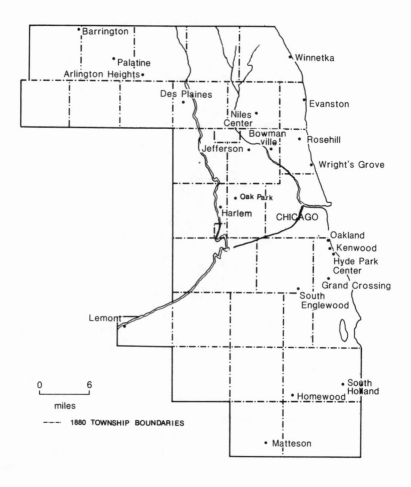

Barrington

Palatine

Arlington Heights

Winnetka

Des Plaines

Evanston

Niles Center

Bowmanville

Jefferson

Rosehill

Wright's Grove

Oak Park

Harlem

CHICAGO

Oakland

Kenwood

Hyde Park Center

Grand Crossing

South Englewood

Lemont

South Holland

Homewood

Matteson

0   6

miles

––·–– 1880 TOWNSHIP BOUNDARIES

M A P 3

New Settlements in Cook County, 1861–80

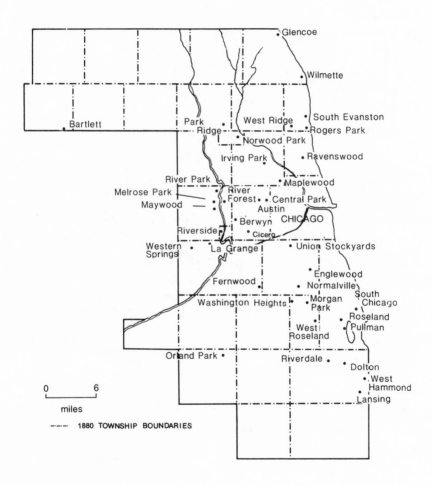

Glencoe

Wilmette

Bartlett

Park
Ridge

West Ridge

South Evanston

Rogers Park

Norwood Park

Irving Park

Ravenswood

River Park

Maplewood

Melrose Park

River
Forest

Central Park

Maywood

Austin

Berwyn

CHICAGO

Riverside

Cicero

Western
Springs

La Grange

Union Stockyards

Englewood

Fernwood

Normalville

Washington Heights

Morgan
Park

South
Chicago

Roseland

West
Roseland

Pullman

Orland Park

Riverdale

Dolton

West
Hammond

Lansing

0   6

miles

–·–· 1880 TOWNSHIP BOUNDARIES

M A P 4

New Settlements in Cook County, 1881–1900

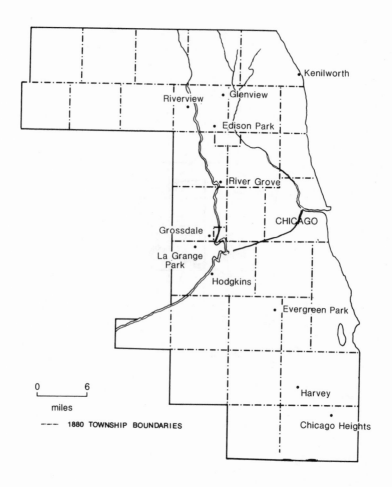

Kenilworth

Riverview · Glenview

Edison Park

River Grove

CHICAGO

Grossdale

La Grange
Park

Hodgkins

Evergreen Park

0   6

miles

----- 1880 TOWNSHIP BOUNDARIES

Harvey

Chicago Heights

M AP 5

WATER AND SEWERAGE DISTRICTS IN CHICAGO, 1857

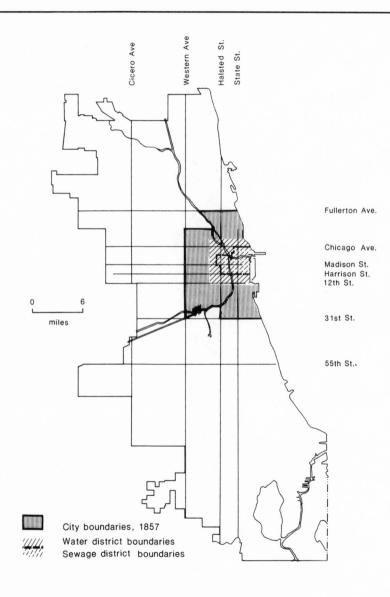

Cicero Ave

Western Ave

Halsted St.

State St.

Fullerton Ave.

Chicago Ave.

Madison St.
Harrison St.
12th St.

31st St.

55th St.

0   6

miles

City boundaries, 1857
Water district boundaries
Sewage district boundaries

MAP 6

EXTENSION OF CHICAGO WATER SYSTEM, 1878–90

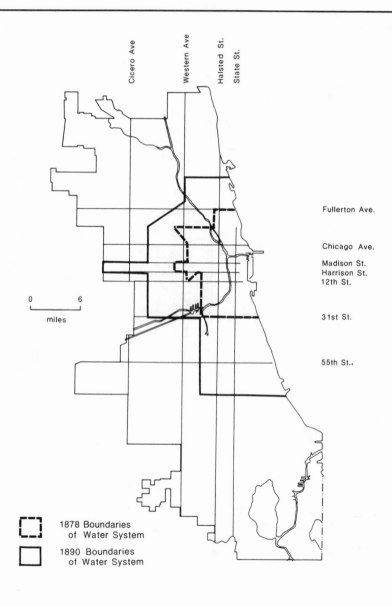

1878 Boundaries
of Water System

1890 Boundaries
of Water System

M A P 7

EXTENSION OF CHICAGO SEWERAGE SYSTEM, 1857–78

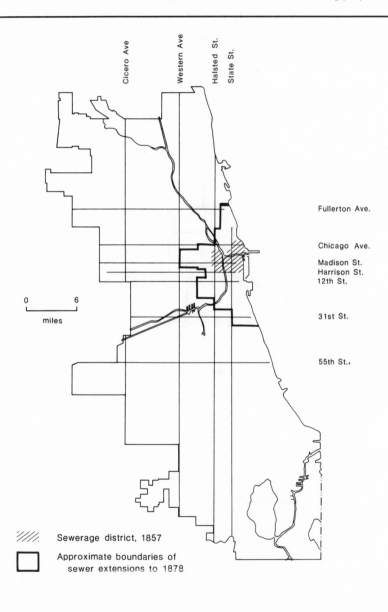

Fullerton Ave.

Chicago Ave.

Madison St.
Harrison St.
12th St.

31st St.

55th St.

0   6

miles

/////. Sewerage district, 1857

☐ Approximate boundaries of
    sewer extensions to 1878

M A P 8

SETTLEMENTS FOUNDED BY A DEVELOPER/DEVELOPMENT COMPANY IN COOK COUNTY, 1861–80

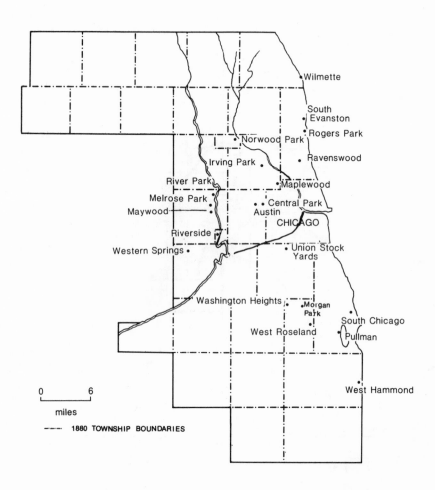

0 ___ 6

miles

----- 1880 TOWNSHIP BOUNDARIES

MAP 9

CHICAGO AREA PARKS AND BOULEVARDS, 1892

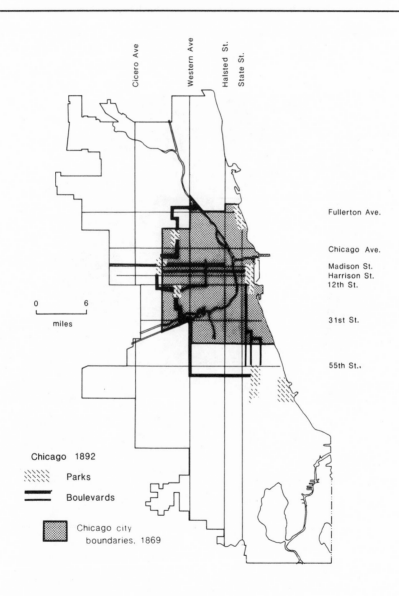

Cicero Ave

Western Ave

Halsted St.

State St.

Fullerton Ave.

Chicago Ave.

Madison St.
Harrison St.
12th St.

31st St.

55th St.

0   6

miles

Chicago 1892

Parks

Boulevards

Chicago city
boundaries, 1869

M A P 10

COOK COUNTY 1850, SHOWING TOWNSHIPS
AND THEIR POPULATION DENSITIES

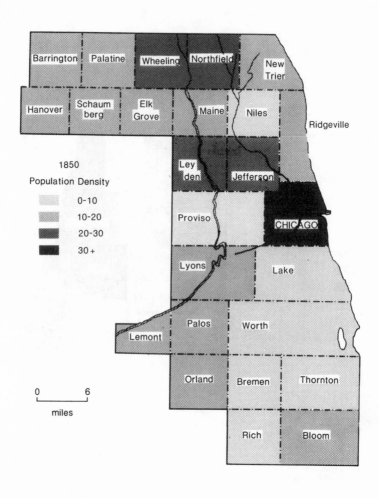

MAP II

COOK COUNTY 1880, SHOWING TOWNSHIPS
AND THEIR POPULATION DENSITIES

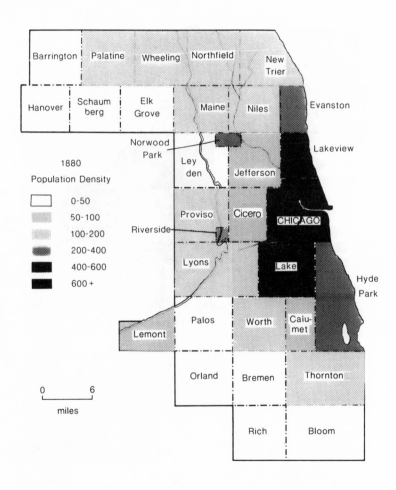

1880
Population Density

0-50
50-100
100-200
200-400
400-600
600 +

0   6
miles

M A P   12

MAP OF CHICAGO SHOWING EXTENT OF SETTLED AREA
BY 1899

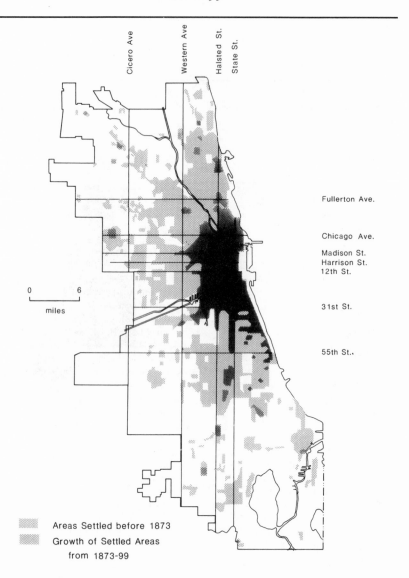

Cicero Ave

Western Ave

Halsted St.

State St.

Fullerton Ave.

Chicago Ave.

Madison St.
Harrison St.
12th St.

31st St.

55th St..

0   6

miles

Areas Settled before 1873

Growth of Settled Areas
from 1873-99

INDEX